The Discovered Self

Identity in the Therapeutic Age

Also by Albert Norton from New English Review Press:

Dangerous God: A Defense of Transcendent Truth (2021)

The Mountain and the River: Genesis, Postmodernism, and the Machine (2023)

The Discovered Self

Identity in the Therapeutic Age

Albert Norton, Jr.

Published by New English Review Press
a subsidiary of World Encounter Institute
PO Box 158397
Nashville, Tennessee 37215
&
27 Old Gloucester Street
London, England, WC1N 3AX

Cover art and design by Kendra Mallock

ISBN: 978-1-943003-99-0
Library of Congress Control Number: 2025931320

First Edition

NEW ENGLISH REVIEW PRESS
newenglishreview.org

This is the excellent foppery of the world, that, when we are sick in fortune, often the surfeit of our own behavior, we make guilty of our disasters the sun, the moon, and the stars . . .
—William Shakespeare

There are only two kinds of men: the righteous who think they are sinners and the sinners who think they are righteous.
—Blaise Pascal

We owe incomparably more to improved sewers than to psychology.
—Theodore Dalrymple

CONTENTS

INTRODUCTION

This book is about the worldview shift from morality to psychology. Therapeutic thinking means evaluating things and events and people according to how they make us feel. Moral thinking means deference to standards of virtue and vice that are hard-wired into the universe. Therapeutic thinking is fast eclipsing moral thinking.

This has happened over the course of the postmodern era: roughly the twentieth century to the present day in the twenty-first. The worldview of logos and of faith requires explanation precisely because we now evaluate it from another worldview altogether. We'll find that the therapeutic worldview is profoundly different not only from Christianity, but theism of any kind, and even Platonism and the logos, the divine reason and form and order implicit in the cosmos, as contemplated among the ancient Greeks at least as early as Heraclitus.

Before the advent of psychological man, the dominant world-view was that of the transcendent. Not necessarily that everyone believed in a Presence up there beyond the clouds, transcending this temporal plane, but certainly some something that explains the givenness of things, ontological categories and the unchanging nature of virtues and a common morality in human nature, even as lesser political and cultural changes ebbed and flowed in our experience. The transcendent worldview holds that moral values are objective, not subjectively invented in the inner being. They are universal, in that they apply the same to all. And they are unchanging, though from season to season our apprehension of them may evolve with innovations in propositional philosophy and shifts in cultural and moral hermeneutics. This was a Platonic vision of eternal ideals existing untouched by the foibles of people going about their daily business here below. What that worldview implied was variation in human beings, but eternality of morality and truth.

The universality of moral creeds are pointless, however, if not backed by supernatural authority. Social customs alone cannot hold a society together. When authority rooted in a sacred order is cancelled, it is replaced by human concentration of power, and power is an unstable and oppressive foundation on which to try to sustain a civilization. Before the therapeutic turn of Western postmodernism, it was taken for granted that the social order, regardless of its form of political and economic organization, had necessarily to be underwritten by a sacred order. That is, no society operated successfully for long on a purely naturalistic understanding of reality. This was true even among the pagans, for whom myths provided a super-structure. In the later monotheisms that super-structure consisted of transcendent principles reduced to creeds necessary to civilizing self-restraint.

The therapeutic worldview is imagined to be free of religious creedal constraints. This is not to say religion is entirely dead nor that it can't be confusedly intermixed with the therapeutic. There wasn't a sudden event, a flip of the switch, upon which we all became neurotic atheists. Rather, there has been a long slow glide from the heavens to the earth. Some continue to hold to the worldview of faith, in which religious creeds still hold authority. But for most, religious practice is nonexistent or limited to rituals and fellowship, without real substance. Influence of the therapeutic has mostly crowded out deference to the interdicts of creeds rooted in a sacred order. It is replaced by "psychological man," a conception traceable to Sigmund Freud, of warring inner impulses that drive us to place authority in the inner emerging self rather than externally in a looming God.

If religion is valid, its precepts cannot be reconciled with those of the therapeutic worldview. So what does that mean for religious practice in pluralistic societies? How does a person with the worldview of faith navigate the Brave New World of the therapeutic? We're experiencing, in the post-modern era, a slow-motion clash of visions. We need some sense of hope that psychological man does not extinguish what is best about us. To find hope, we must begin with understanding.

1

THE THERAPEUTIC
WORLDVIEW

Philosophy

In recent years there's been much commentary on the consequences of the loss of faith, and on the rise of a cult of victimhood, and "snowflake" emotional vulnerability to opposing points of view, and on discovered "identity," the newfound locus of personal "authenticity," the real self to be discovered. Such commentary hits all around the strange developments in our way of interacting with the world, but each typically generates understanding only in part, like with the proverbial blind men trying to understand an elephant. The shift to the therapeutic is a key to understanding how these puzzling developments are symptoms of the same disease.

During the postmodern era, defined here as roughly the century-plus since the turn of the twentieth century, there has been a profound shift in thinking. Objective, propositional truth as the basis for rationality had previously predominated, as a legacy of Enlightenment thinking. This way of thinking is held up, we might say, by the transcendent. If there is a God who created all that we know, then the logos[1] that permeates our reality is authored by Him.

---

1 *Logos*: word, associated with logic and mental rationality that produces it, and with the observed rational order in the universe.

Modern thinkers before the postmodern era were concerned with the consequences of rejection of God in an increasingly secularizing culture. Once transcendence is rejected, what holds up an objective and universal moral order? If there is no God we're at a loss to explain the rationality of the human mind and of the natural world. We struggle to explain the hierarchy of values that inhere in the conscience and that are reflected in the culture. Where does mankind's knowledge of good and evil come from, if not from that first Edenic rebellion against God's decrees?

Postmodern thinkers have tried to place production of truth, falsity, good, and evil in processes of humanistic thinking rather than transcendent Source. We can think of this as a shift from the vertical to the horizontal. Mountain and river were used in a similar way in this author's *The Mountain and the River/Genesis, Postmodernism, and the Machine*.[2] The purpose was to describe the horizontal perspective in postmodern "process philosophy," in order to contrast the vertical objectivity of values and truth which preceded it.

This was primarily an undertaking of propositions, however. That is, in the evolution of ideas through history, certain propositions replace others, and we can say larger abstractions like "postmodernism" rest on identifiable and more specific propositions like those comprising atheism, existentialism, pragmatism, and a dubious form of "democracy." This propositional thinking brings into focus the ideas we absorb from our cultural environment. As propositions they can be evaluated entirely in a rationalistic way.

Psychology

But there is another dimension, one that is not strictly propositional in nature. It may be expressed in thinking that is deeply subjective, and drawn from impulse and emotion, distinct from

---

2 New English Review Press, 2023.

purely rational mental process. It is allied with a religious impulse—
not its doctrines, but its call to our inner yearning. We might call this
the emotional dimension, the realm of pure feeling. It is the agitation in the human breast that stirs passion, anger, fear, sadness, and
the lightness of heart we call happiness. This dimension of thought
proceeds from the inner self without rigidly algorithmic rationality.
It is the source of the therapeutic worldview.

The worldview we set out to understand is sometimes called
simply "the therapeutic," a phrase that came into common use after
Philip Rieff's 1966 book *The Triumph of the Therapeutic*.[3] There are
other handles we could attach to this way of thinking. Rieff also
wrote of "psychological man," to mean someone in the grip of this
way of seeing the world. These phrases correctly imply that the
mindset has become pervasive, and constitutes a totalizing worldview like religion, or the rigid materialism of the New Atheists, or
the postmodern impulse toward an oceanic feeling of collectivism.
Carl Trueman, in his 2021 *The Rise and Triumph of the Modern Self*,[4]
similarly used the phrase "expressive individualism," which he borrowed from Charles Taylor's 2007 *A Secular Age*.[5]

In trying to understand the therapeutic worldview we must be
careful to recognize that emotions are ineluctable from ideas; and
ideas from facts. Before the advent of psychological man, we placed
feelings in service to ideas. This is the premise of the virtue of
self-control, for example. We're to control our impulses, and impulses are driven by emotion. We learn not to reflexively lash out in
anger, for example, but instead control that emotion and use our
intellect to reason through how best to handle the angering situation. And the criteria we employ to determine "how best" are ideals;
the hierarchy of values we absorb in our training-up as human be-

---

3 Subtitled *Uses of Faith After Freud*, ISI Books 2007 (first published 1966).
4 Subtitled *Cultural Amnesia, Expressive Individualism, and the Road to Sexual Revolution* (Wheaton, IL: Crossway, 2020).
5 Cambridge, MA: Belknap, 2007.

ings. Those ideals are higher principles of virtue. Universals, in that they apply to all of us and are the same for all of us. This is the external moral framework to which we learn to aspire.

Self-control is necessary to any exercise of empathy. Empathy is the ability to imagine one's self in another's shoes. That requires considering their feelings, not just one's own. This is a result of subordinating feelings to rational thought. Without that rational control of one's own feelings, empathy for another's cannot be formed. Psychological man's filtering of reality through his own feelings means his ability to empathize is impaired. This is the reason a person so driven by his own feelings can feel innocent while committing egregious, immoral wrongs against another, like cutting off a family member over political disagreement. Their feelings don't matter. The care and nurture of feelings is a one-sided affair.

Although feelings are connected to facts, feelings as feelings alone can be cherished and nourished and protected and defended and prioritized in a way that subordinates facts and reason. Thoughts are then formed by the feelings. This yields a debilitating way of encountering the world, in which the subjective and irrational interfere with the objective and rational. Emotions are not invalid, of course. We need to acknowledge them in ourselves and others to fully empathize with them. It's possible to lose the thread of self-control, however, and consider all our own emotions to be valid whether they are or not. We can fail to subordinate them to our propositional, rational thinking. This gives emotion priority over rationality; subjectivity over objectivity. This distorts our apprehension of what is true and good; false and evil.

Prioritizing emotions means reason takes a back seat, but rationality on subjects other than that which stirred up the emotions may remain untouched. One can be impulse-driven in some ways yet be quite effective at one's job, for example. Or quite intelligent in matters that don't touch on one's emotional susceptibilities. We are complex beings. We can be selective in our emotional immaturity.

A consequence to giving priority to the emotions is that they must be dealt with before the events that stirred them up. One's emotional well-being must be kept safe and secure before circumstances are rationally engaged. The primary concern is with one's psychological well-being, therefore. This is "psychological man." You don't want psychological man at the helm in an emergency, because upsetting emotions will divide the mind, or even require a time-out to process. He should not be seated in an exit row.

The therapeutic involves a subjective conviction that processing of feelings comes ahead of correct application of principle. This can be characterized as the triumph of the horizontal over the vertical; internal subjectivism over external hierarchical ideal. What matters to psychological man is the here and now of his own embodied being, not what he sees as an antiquated hierarchy of principles superior to humanity itself. One's sense of psychological well-being is the measure of success, rather than "doing the right thing." The "right thing" of yesteryear is outmoded, a misguided product of bloodless abstract principle. The thinking of psychological man is directed to (and formed by) the subjective sense of well-being in the embodied self, not disembodied principle residing in a discredited idealized objectivity.

We can readily imagine the result. A person who elevates emotional well-being ahead of values formed in an objective moral hierarchy subordinates reason to emotion. This is not just a matter of elevating internally-derived values ahead of rationally discerned ones. The process by which values are adopted is itself in play. The lens through which one views reality controls the perception of reality. The world looks different to psychological man, compared to the person whose outlook is rooted in the logos conception of objectivity bequeathed to us by Western civilization. The logos, absorbed into the Judeo-Christian tradition, is in process of being abandoned in the postmodern era.

We can approach this by opposing substance and process. Substance is the conclusion one draws. Process is the means by which the conclusion is reached. Psychological man places process ahead of substance, just as in the world of ideas the river inclination is put ahead of the mountain;[6] the horizontal ahead of the vertical; the immanent ahead of the transcendent. Emotional evaluation is the process, and so the substance is whatever feels subjectively most satisfying. This is how rational thinking is distorted and subverted by the therapeutic.

For this reason we should not be surprised to encounter the kind of self-absorbed negative character traits we find in psychological man. Here is a valid summary:

> a solipsistic focus on self-expression, self-empowerment, and pride; a radical emphasis of unabridged individual autonomy and liberation from all customs, taboos, and constraints, including all duties and relational ties; an extreme aversion to boundaries and limits on desire, and the self-creation not only of all aspects of personal identity, but of the body, nature, and reality itself; and ultimately an undiluted worship of the self and the will to power, hidden behind a mask of empathy, tolerance, and the language of the therapeutic.[7]

Brian Rosner suggests certain tenets for the "looking inward" way of thinking:

> The best way to find yourself is to look inward
>
> The highest goal in life is happiness
>
> All moral judgments are merely expressions of feeling or personal preference
>
> Forms of external authority are to be rejected

---

6 The conceit employed in *The Mountain and the River.*

7 N.S. Lyons, "Dark Enchantment," *First Things*, May 2024, a review of John Daniel Davidson's *Pagan America: The Decline of Christianity and the Dark Age to Come*, Regnery 2024.

The world will improve dramatically as the scope of individual freedom grows

Everyone's quest for self-expression should be celebrated.[8]

These read like a photographic negative of Christian confessions of faith. James Nolan Jr. summarized various thinkers on the subject, to arrive at the following components of the worldview:

— A sense of emancipation from external restraint, what Nolan called "the emancipated self," not so much a legacy of Freud, but of Carl Rogers (1902-1987), who Nolan described as a modern Rousseau: "Where Freudian psychoanalysis is essentially a therapy of adaptation, Rogerian client-centered therapy is one of liberation;"[9]

— The emotivist ethic, citing Alisdair MacIntyre, noting that "truth" is derived through sentiment or feeling rather than rational judgment or abstract reasoning;

— A new priestly class, that being the army of therapists available to assist and who thereby reinforce the therapeutic way of looking at the world;

— The reflexive pathologization of human behavior, with the effect of shifting away from individual moral responsibility for that behavior;

— A resulting sense of victimization;

— An overriding therapeutic ethos derived from various elements of modernization, which provides a sense of unity in the face of modern pluralism, on a quasi-religious basis; and

— Society-wide, a hyper-rationalization that culminates in a machine feeling, what Max Weber referred to as (translated) the "iron cage."[10]

---

8 Rosner, Brian, *How to Find Yourself: Why Looking Inward is Not the Answer,* (Wheaton, IL: Crossway, 2022).

9 Nolan, James L Jr., *The Therapeutic State* (New York: New York University Press, 1998), p. 3.

10 Ibid., pp. 1-21. The phrase is from Weber's *The Protestant Ethic and the Spirit of Capitalism*, 1904.

Emotivism

Emotivism is foundational to the therapeutic worldview. In his *After Virtue*, Alisdair MacIntyre defined it as:

> the doctrine that all evaluative judgments and more specifically all moral judgments are *nothing but* expressions of preference, expressions of attitude or feeling . . . .[11]

It would be easy to gloss over this description and miss its real significance. An emotivist can express what sounds like a moral judgment, but it's not, nor is it intended to be. It's an expression of feeling, only, so the listener must decode as he goes along. If the emotivist says it's wrong to discriminate on the basis of race, he expresses a feeling which happens to coincide with a valid moral judgment. But he can just as sincerely say the earth is flat. What's true is not his statement, but the genuineness of his *feeling* about it. You could dismiss the emotivist as immoral or incompetent, but he or she seems sincere, and besides there are too many who think this way, to assume they're all just habitual liars. What's going on? A way to explain the language use of the emotivist outlook, included in a review of *After Virtue*,[12] is provided by David Gross:

> Our moral arguments today are interminable because the values they express are incommensurable. Though the claims of the emotivists are not necessarily true, they happen to be true for contemporary moral philosophy: when people make moral arguments today they really are just making exclamations of (dis)approval while disguising these as rational arguments about facts.

Language use reflects the mental activity of the worldview: emotivist argument initiates in subjective emotional reaction, but then pro-

---

11 MacIntyre, Alisdair, *After Virtue, 2nd ed.* (South Bend, IN: University of Notre Dame Press, 1984), pp. 11-12.

12 https://www.goodreads.com/review/show/16106951

ceeds on the form of objective rationality.

Let's come at this with a hypothetical. You have to make a choice. Don't fight the hypothetical, make the choice. Choice #1: You kill someone, but immediately after the event you forget it, and go through your life with no memory of it. Choice #2: You don't kill anyone, but acquire a memory of having done so, and so must live with the guilt. Now choose. Seriously. Do it before you continue reading.

If you make the first choice, you will not suffer psychologically. This is the perspective of the emotivist because it satisfies the therapeutic priority of self-care. If you make the second choice, you bear the moral weight, though innocent. This is the perspective of someone who understands they live in a moral universe. It's not about you, there's a life at stake, and preserving that life is morally more significant than you having to carry unfounded guilt.

Emotivism isn't to be dismissed out of hand as emotional hysteria. It is based on the idea that all our actions, including those that seem to be altruistic, are actually only expressions of self-interest. Mother Teresa seemed to live a life of devotion to others, but maybe that just appealed to a misguided desire for ultimate significance, or she sought moral gravitas, or she wanted to be admired. So she acted from self-interest, says the emotivist, and her actions deserve no more praise or rebuke than anyone else's. The motivation of pleasing God is off the table, for the emotivist, because rejection of ultimate moral authority outside the self is what enables emotivist thinking in the first place.

If everyone acts on self-interest in everything they do, then it simply isn't true that we make moral decisions on the basis of abstract moral principle. In fact the hierarchy of moral values we say we subscribe to would have to be a fiction, and we're deluded. It would mean that when we think we're invoking moral absolutes of any kind, we're really just describing a matter of personal choice. Abstract moral principles are not really divorced from self-interest, in this way of thinking, so they can be dispensed with altogether, and we can cut to the chase: It's right (or wrong) because I *feel* it's right (or wrong). For the emotivist, the only arbiter of moral judgment is the self, and the self's judgment turns on psychological self-care.

The real significance of emotivism can be overlooked: it is the assumption that one's entire purpose is satisfaction of self-interest. In politics, all are assumed to vote and otherwise engage politically on the basis of self-interest rather than principle. Individually, self-interest means using others instrumentally, in unceasing manipulation, and an expectation of being manipulated in return. Applied at the political level, it means all-against-all power struggle; the absence of common principles to invoke in our discourse; only personal or group interests. This bleak vision results in never being released from the vicious cycle of instrumental interactions with others and with society. And it is reinforced in therapy, because moral right and wrong are eschewed in this environment in favor of psychological affirmation. Principle can never overcome self-interest, and therapy begets therapy, a self-reinforcing, imprisoning cycle.

Note that in his definition of emotivism, MacIntyre was in a sense doing some translating, just as we are here. That is, we are putting into propositional, objective terms a way of thinking that is neither. *Experience* of emotivism is not doctrinal. Just by describing it we attenuate ourselves from experience of it. To grasp its significance, we have to imagine our way of looking at the world does not involve thinking through a network of values, but rather is the product of the inner, emotion-driven impulses and desires. Resulting thought is directed toward gratification of those impulses and desires. Not purely, of course. For psychological man, the hermeneutical outlook on the world is a complex of emotivism and objectivity, but the latter in service to the former.

The therapeutic rests on the same subjectivity as MacIntyre's "emotivism." It is a platform for evaluating reality that is paradigmatically distinct from observation-based ratiocination according to externally-derived objective principle. As MacIntyre observed (and as Carl Trueman pointed out[13]) emotivism is therefore not a theory of meaning, but of *use*, so moral language and concepts are not employed for their objective meaning, but rather for purposes of stating subjective preferences. For the emotivist, imbued with the therapeutic worldview, subjective preferences supplant transcendent, objective authority. Feelings *are* truth, so they are expressed as such, as if they had objective authority.

This is deeply confusing for the moral thinker. It isn't even analogous to speaking a different language. It's more like speaking in code, with the same vocabulary and syntax, but with all the important words having a substituted and often contrary meaning. Psychological man doesn't lose the ability to string words together in a convincing way. But he does lose the ability to attach consistent objective meaning to the words. The objective thinker will necessarily be frustrated, or simply regard the therapeutic thinker a liar; or, perhaps, will learn to decode, substituting the therapeutic thinker's emotional preferences for the ostensible truth claims he makes.

There is a deeper, more disturbing effect of the language games, however. As the therapeutic mentality has become more prevalent, the confusion of psychological man becomes general. It is increasingly possible to make bold, self-evidently false assertions and have them accepted as true, because they fit emotivist-driven Narrative.[14] Example. "Trans women are women." It means a male who "identifies" as a female is a female. So it's based on one's feeling that self-autonomy controls external reality, even to the point of defying the objective reality of his sex. It imports a subjective ideo-

---

13 *The Rise of and Triumph of the Modern Self,* p. 85.

14 A story to support a metanarrative, more or less faithfully based on underlying facts relevant to politics or culture in society. In contentious political usage, parties propose and defend narratives, while attacking opposing narratives, because the respective narratives are devised to support metanarratives, the distilled principles behind activism in politics or culture. See also, *The Mountain and the River,* chapter 23.

logical point of view in place of fact. On top of that, it is incoherent, because an ontological male/female dichotomy is simultaneously invoked and repudiated. Desire to transcend the binary categories is possible only by first acknowledging the categories. Another example. "Love is love." Taken literally it is a pointless tautology, but it means one's feelings control over any claim to objective morality on the subject of sexual practice. To be clear, emotivist language confusion is not limited to controversy over gender ideology or homosexuality. It is a breakdown in rationality itself, impairing our ability to even express differences, much less reconcile them as necessary to live together in a civilized way.

It's important that we understand emotivism's origins. Postmodernism meant dethroning God and therefore abandoning objectivity in truth and values. That in turn produced crucial misunderstanding about the very scope of reality. We know physical things are real, and perhaps consciousness and thought as emergent from the physical, but this still leaves a vast territory of human experience that we're to imagine isn't real. Example. Are mathematics real? Certainly they describe real physical things, but are numerical relationships themselves real? We don't see numbers embedded in the hillside, after all, and numbers are only symbols anyway. How about aspirational ideals like honor, compassion, and humility? Are virtues like honesty and courage real? Vices? Is the boundary between them real? Or the ubiquitous taxonomical boundaries of this-not-that in our world? Most pertinently, is there a moral structure that is real and extant in the cosmos, or do we merely call some acts or omissions "good" and some "evil" to advance our interests and desires ahead of others'?

Before the postmodern era it was generally understood that moral good and evil are real, and form the moral structure that governs our world independently of our feelings about it. This was re-evaluated in certain philosophical circles in the early twentieth century, when theories evolved to separate morality from an abso-

lute moral structure. Emotivism is one such theory of ethical relativism, generated by A.J. Ayer and others, who argued that all value
judgments are *nothing but* expressions of feeling.[15]

Ayer was among the logical positivists who, for all their preten-
sions to analytic rigor, simply stated as if axiomatic a condition of
empirical verifiability to our apprehension of the world. The effect
is to exclude from the real anything that is not physical, a bit of circular reasoning that seems to validate materialist atheism. To say, as
the logical positivists did, that reality consists only in that which is
empirically verifiable is to say physically observable matter is real,
but not truth, falsity, justice, injustice, beauty, ugliness, good, or evil.
Because good and evil are not empirically verifiable, the reasoning
went, a statement that something is good or bad (e.g., "murder is
wrong") is not a statement of fact, but a statement of one's feeling
only (that he finds murder emotionally upsetting). Evaluative statements tell you something true about the speaker, in other words, but
not about the subject matter on which he speaks. Statements concerning morality, according to emotivism, can therefore never be
true-as-such.

Logical positivism is rife with inconsistencies, and has little
traction today, especially on questions of moral philosophy. Still, the
emotivist error persists, because the presumption of atheist materialism persists. If there is no sacred order, there is no foundation on
which to ground an understanding of moral structure. The natural
order considered separately from its Creator is insufficient by itself
because it is not authoritative and therefore cannot generate moral
values. It is a brute fact of existence only, inexplicably rational.

Therefore, if there is a moral structure to the world at all, it is
only the shifting and malleable structure imposed from time to time
in evolving social norms. That means it is not an independent and
objective feature of existence, but rather a set of conventions generated socially and temporally, always subject to change. Good and

---

15 *Language, Truth, and Logic* (1936).

evil are whatever I say it is, or whatever our society collectively says it is, and so it seems to follow that "good" and "bad" are defined only by how an act or omission makes us feel; that there is otherwise no real moral authority. We look inward, therefore, to subjectively answer questions of right and wrong.

As with questions of good and evil, so with questions of truth and falsity. In the postmodern era we don't say truth is hard-wired into the universe but morality isn't. It's all up for grabs, and so it seems valid to say something patently false is nonetheless "true" because of how strongly the speaker is committed to it.

Most people don't appreciate such sharp distinctions, however, between what is real and what is not. We tend to confusedly weigh moral questions, sometimes as if absolute, sometimes as if purely relative, depending on variables like how personal the matter is, how strong the ick factor is, and how a particular question is affected by our ideological predispositions. As a society we have not made the shift completely. Those on the postmodern cutting edge, however, are more likely to be given over to atheist materialism, ethical relativism, radical politics, and commitment to a project of ongoing self-therapy. They are more completely absorbed into the therapeutic worldview.

The spread of the therapeutic means we're losing the neutrality of fact-based language. The point of postmodern language games is to deceitfully eliminate differences, not to live together in mutual tolerance of them. Perhaps today we can continue to simultaneously speak in the two languages of fact and feelings. But tomorrow we'll forget fact-based language, and if there is any interaction at all it will only be shouting our personal desires and emotions, hearing nothing. The emotivist doesn't attempt to persuade on the premise of rational thought rooted in objective moral principle. His language—and therefore his thought—is centered on manipulation of others' feelings. MacIntyre writes that the key to the social content of emotivism is not mutual understanding, but "obliteration of any genuine distinction between manipulative and non-manipulative social relations."[16] When the pre-eminent values are self-care and self-actualization, radical self-absorption necessarily follows.

Presentism

Emotivism is a foundational disposition toward the therapeutic worldview, and so is presentism. Let's come at this with a kernel of understanding of Eastern mysticism. Eternal return is a variation on the reincarnation of certain Eastern religions. Friedrich Nietzsche employed it as a thought experiment to test one's determination to existentially self-actualize. Is this moment lived with the kind of significance it would have if repeated through all eternity? Milan Kundera employed it similarly in his novel *The Unbearable Lightness of Being*, unbearable because "*einmal ist keinmal*," once is never, by the test of eternal recurrence, so nothing we do matters.

In the dualist[17] Western vision, the body dies but the spirit continues to live, and the spirit is individuated; that is, it's still you. In the monist religions also the body clearly dies; we can see that plainly enough, but whence the spirit, if it is ineluctable from the body? It is envisioned as being released into a general undifferentiated spirit; a world-soul of some kind, or else is reconstituted in another body, possibly an animal body, if we imagine no transcendent God-breathed element differentiating mankind from other animals.

The concept of eternal return is distinguishable from (though influenced by) traditional Eastern reincarnation in that we're to imagine the events of a lifetime being repeated in an endless loop, and the idea, apparently, is that this endless repetition is what gives gravitas to what we do as human beings. Nothing is important if it's a one-off event (*einmal ist keinmal*) but our lives have meaning be-

---

16 *After Virtue*, p. 23.

17 Duality of material and spirit, in contrast to the Eastern or Spinozan one-substance conception.

cause we're living out a predetermined and repeated pattern, and the repetition is what lends significance. What you do in the next minute matters because you'll do it again in a succession of lifetimes for all eternity.

You might recognize in this way of thinking a variant of existentialism. Think of Sisyphus rolling the rock up the hill, again and again. This is an ancient myth but Albert Camus revived it in an essay in 1942 to express an element of post-war existentialism emphasizing ultimate individuality and what might be called "presentism." Camus didn't present his vision as one of pointless despair but rather as a means of saying all that matters is this present moment. We have no problem rolling a stone uphill, if the task is mentally separated from all that came before or follows after. It's just how we're spending this particular moment. Just like when you exercise, it's not oppressive because you have no intention of doing it in every moment for the rest of eternity. It's just a brief sacrifice of effort to enrich your life.

The point is, Sisyphus need not live in conscious despair of unending tedious repetition. He can live in eternal *present*. In reading these words you're not thinking about whether you will or won't re-read these words forever and ever into eternity. You're not thinking about it because you're concentrating on—and therefore lost in—the moment. It's possible to limit one's thinking only to the moment, all the time, and thereby avoid altogether large questions about eternity and purpose.

This is what is meant by "presentism," except that existentialism would place awareness of the present moment not merely in the willful concentration on the task at hand, but in an inability to see before or after. The problem with that, however, is that we have conscious self-awareness not just in the moment, but across time. It's why we consciously sacrifice today for a better tomorrow, for example. Squirrels collect nuts for the winter, but the foresight of human beings goes far beyond that kind of rote unselfconscious

instinct. Human beings who actually live in the moment, like animals, are yet human enough to be conscious of the pointlessness of
what they do. This is an element of our tragic sense, a concept to
which we will return.

Acute presentism leads to a loss of the felt sense of significance; to "disenchantment." This is evident in the people around
you struggling with life though they suffer from no obvious handi-
cap. Presentism is a symptom of malaise because it means putting
on blinders, so to speak, to the significance of what we do as against
the totality of our lives. Moreover, it is a symptom of despair particular to the totalitarian-leaning postmodern world, which has abandoned God, which means it has broken from sacred order[18] to underwrite the system of interdicts imposed through law and social
norms, which means power alone rules, not our voluntary seeking
of virtue, in love.

Here is an illustration of the evil of presentism, from Theodore Dalrymple's *Life at the Bottom: The Worldview That Makes the
Underclass.*[19] He wrote that many are in the underclass because of
dysfunctional values reinforced by elites, and as a result are "condemned to live in the eternal present," unable to see outside the
bubble of time and place in which they find themselves. Self-absorption takes the place of self-autonomy, and life becomes boring
except as momentarily enlivened in lawless release. Hapless floating
through a world made by others results in a delimited imagined
time-horizon:

> They never awoke to the fact that a life is a biography, not
> a series of disconnected moments, more or less pleasur-
> able but increasingly tedious and unsatisfying unless one
> imposes a purposive pattern upon them.

---

18 "Sacred order" as used here means recognition that a fixed morality in mankind's
experience is underwritten by spiritual authority over mankind, rather than merely
socially-imposed power.
19 Chicago: Ivan R. Dee, 2003.

The other major point to draw from Camus's use of the Sisyphus myth is the subjectivist perspective of Sisyphus. Just as time is chopped up into discrete moments with all our attention focused on one moment, so individuals are discrete from the mass of humanity and each is a severed unit of it, conscious only of self. All of reality is quantized. Severed units of time demark Sisyphus's range of attention, and he himself is a severed unit of humanity. We may feel we live in a digitized unreality. Meaning is not derived from society or a putative God. It must therefore emerge from within.

But meaning has to come from outside ourselves. If it's all self-generated we become a black hole of self-absorption consuming ourselves from the inside. We become small feral beasts like the morally-stricken future Pope Gregory in Thomas Mann's *The Holy Sinner*. Or reduced to a hard nut of lifeless matter rolling around pointlessly on the littered floor of the world. Nothing matters. And we see this in postmodern ideology. Even as we move to socialist orientation in our thinking vis-à-vis the *polis*, we paradoxically become atomized and alone.[20] In this way we are ready grist for the totalitarian mill, because in looking outside ourselves we see no God nor even objectivity of value. And so we look instead to the closest authority we can find, the self as Identity, though it unwittingly absorbs the dictates of collectivist dialectic, the febrile horizontal processing of social norms supplanting the logos.

Presentism precludes sacrifice, obviously, because if you're living in the moment all the time you're not squirreling away nuts for the winter. Sacrifice means giving up something now to create something better later, just as you study in school now for a richer tomorrow, or discipline your kids for their richer tomorrow—essentially training them to sacrifice, also. Sacrifice is a product of the tragic sense. It is the engine of creativity in the world, both in the daily actions of human beings and in the progress of societies.

The impulse to sacrifice is super-human in origin, exemplified

---

20 This was a significant point in Hannah Arendt's *The Origins of Totalitarianism*, 1951.

in religious truth imparted to us here below. Sacrifice happens because you believe in something outside yourself, and greater than yourself. This is important because the postmodern trope is that there *is* nothing greater than yourself, and so sacrifice becomes meaningless, and all is permitted except as interdicted by social mandate. The something greater for which you sacrifice is your own tomorrow, but also your children's tomorrow when you're gone, and the world's tomorrow because you've made it a little better rather than a little worse. Sacrifice is deeply creative in this fundamental way. When God created the world, He formed it out of Himself, and made it distinct from Himself. When we sacrifice for tomorrow we form the better future out of ourselves, a reality distinct from our present self. This is the source of creativity, and it starts with recognizing that there is something more important out there than the self. It's not all about me.

Worldview

A central thesis of this book is that the therapeutic worldview is destroying us. So let's be sure we understand what it is, and what it displaces. We'll start with the concept of "worldview" in the abstract.

Your worldview is defined by the combination of axiomatic presuppositions you have in place as you look out on the world to try to understand it. We don't all perceive it the same way. Growing out of infancy means grasping that others may see the world differently. Understanding another's point of view is a difficult but necessary undertaking. The ability to see the world through another's eyes is an essential element of our humanity, and necessary for any hope of living in harmony. It is, moreover, necessary to holding in good faith any presumption about the nature of reality, including human nature. We should make it our business all day every day to test our own perspective, and adjust when it's called for. It's important that we apprehend the reality that is there, instead of unquestioned fantasies of our own making.

In one sense, we could say there are as many ways of seeing the world as there are people. But that doesn't delineate worldviews, it merely reiterates our individual uniqueness. Some elements of reality are more significant than others, in explaining for example what a person is. You might hold the same worldview as someone who grew up on the other side of the world, though obviously your differing experiences in life will make you very different people. Likewise your next-door neighbor may hold very different ground-level assumptions about what is true and real, despite having experienced the world in much the same way you have.

It is possible to delineate certain worldviews according to how fundamental the differences are. If we could line up fundamental assumptions about reality—those we regard as axiomatic—we would find they cohere with other assumptions we hold, and the combination of them constitutes a worldview that differs from others in significant and consequential ways. Suppose you believe there is a supernatural reality beyond your physical and time-bound surroundings. That axiomatic belief will dispose you to embrace religion, and this will be an important element of your worldview. Suppose you believe all of reality is comprised of matter in motion. That axiomatic belief will dispose you to materialism.

Worldviews are not premised solely on metaphysics. Suppose you believe that our kinship within society calls for egalitarian sharing of resources, however generated. If you believe we are primarily social creatures, and that ego boundaries are or should be thin, your worldview is essentially socialist—not necessarily in an ideological or political sense, but in the simpler sense that the basic unit of humanity is society rather than the individual. That starting point will color all the opinions you hold and relationships you form and pursuits you undertake. In matters of the *polis*, you may find individualists cantankerous and puzzling, always insisting on the right to peremptorily withdraw from the body of which they are a part.

By contrast, if you conceive the person as essentially self-sovereign, joined to his fellow man only in the most fundamental natural associations of family or kinship, with all other social ties voluntarily joined and voluntarily sundered, then you'll find those of the more social disposition officious or even tyrannical in their insistence on asserting claims upon your energies, attentions, resources, and allegiance.

Suppose you believe social systems are prone to systematic injustice. That axiomatic belief will dispose you to critiques for identifying unjust social systems to be dismantled. A Marxist develops a suspicion concerning social systems believed to benefit the powerful at the expense of the weak. This essential skepticism then drives how he sees the world, seeking a vision of justice in reforms to dismantle those systems to the end of a more equitable society. A Fascist will reject this necessarily universalist vision in favor of a unified tribe, but both the Marxist and Fascist worldviews are socialist. Both tend to a totalitarian worldview, a social expression of humanity in place of individual idiosyncrasy.

These examples are intended to illustrate an incommensurability of competing worldviews. It can be difficult for the secularist to comprehend the religious, or the (classical) liberal to comprehend the illiberal "woke" left. The significance of worldview is that one cannot typically see outside the one they hold, without thoughtfully questioning their own most basic, and typically unexamined, axioms, or presuppositions, about the nature of reality.

The word "worldview" is normally intended to correspond to the German *Weltanschauung*, which is sometimes employed in philosophy to mean not merely an interpretive lens, but rather a person's comprehensive understanding of reality. We might use instead "comprehensive worldview," or "paradigm," or we might continue to use just "worldview," so long as we take it to mean a set of concepts or thought patterns that govern how we comprehend reality;

one's operating assumptions about how things work. It builds on a combination of principles taken to be axiomatic.

At the same time, however, we may be unaware of what those axiomatic principles are because they are so fundamental to our understanding. By definition, they are generative of all that follows, in the mind. They are a combination of seemingly uncaused causes in our ratiocination. They may seem so unalterable that we may not be entirely conscious of them. This is among the reasons one's worldview can be so intractable to change, and why the worldviews of others may seem so incomprehensible.

2
WORLDVIEW CONTRASTS

Physics or Meta-Physics

To understand one's own worldview, it is necessary first to imagine you held a different set of foundational assumptions about reality. It means mentally stepping into another worldview to examine one's own. And likewise, to understand another's worldview, one must first comprehend one's own foundational assumptions about reality, in order to contrast those of the worldview you try to imagine. Returning to the example of a materialist worldview, we can understand it better in contradistinction to an orthodox Christian worldview, which holds that the physical world of matter in motion is only part of reality; there is an unseen spiritual "world," too, which we might conceive as another dimension which includes but is not limited to those of physical space-time. The materialist and theist worldviews are mutually exclusive. If you believe there is no God nor immaterial spiritual reality at all—that is, if you're a materialist—that belief will have a large impact on your over-all vision of reality, and it will align you with other materialists though you may differ with them on lesser questions. Your answer to this important question about the existence or non-existence of spirit will inform many other convictions downstream from it.

In contrast to the strictly materialist worldview are views differentiated on metaphysics. Here are three, each a stepped-up increase in scope. First, the straightforward acknowledgement of immaterial concepts, virtues, and ideals, and moral good and evil, without supposing a source apart from the individuals and societies to which they attach.

Second, in addition to the first, a *logos* that may or may not be divine, but which is acknowledged as the source of order in the universe, and of rationality in the human mind. We should not take these as a given without pausing to consider why it should be so. *Why* is there a natural order to the universe rather than chaos? Why are we enabled to perceive it as such? What makes our thinking orderly and not random? The logos presupposes that truth and falsity are real in the cosmos, not mere human constructs imposed on what we perceive. The same could be said for moral values, the idea being that good and evil are real and not merely categories we somehow impose on our experience. Truth/falsity and good/evil are objective, meaning out there rather than just inside my subjective consciousness. They are universal, meaning they are the same for all of us. Their objectivity renders them universal; their universality proves them to be objective.

Third, and in addition to the foregoing, a supernatural, or spiritual reality, which could include the active God of the monotheisms, including the three-person Trinity of Christianity, wherein a transcendent and almighty God created the universe and imbued mankind with a spirit nature as well as material, and continues to superintend the workings of the material universe immanently, intervening as and when He chooses, as with the advent of the Christ. The logos of truth and moral good are authored by God, who informs the individual conscience.

These three have in common the perception that reality encompasses something beyond the material. There is yet another metaphysical view we should grasp because it begins to explain the formation of identity in the therapeutic age. It is the felt sense of self that is not merely my physical body, and nor is it a soul or spirit. What it is, therefore, is not at all understood nor explained. It mysteriously emerges from within, and so it is in that sense "meta" to the conscious workings of the mind. With this worldview one thinks rationally, because that is inescapable, but with an axiomatic starting point seated in the emotions and a felt sense of selfhood distinct from the logos perceived in the "I" of conscious self-awareness. It may be theorized (as with neo-Freudians) as originating in the subconscious, but such theorizing omits any explanation of how or why the subconscious creates the sense of self.

Logos or Therapeutic

Before the rise of the therapeutic and the postmodern rejection of transcendence, the foundational worldview to Western civilization was the religious, which in turn incorporated the logos metaphysical perspective. Even among those indifferent to God and to religion, it held cultural sway because it embraced the logos principle of order in the universe and in the rational mind discerning it. That logos principle is the necessary fundament to science. The religious and logos metaphysical worldviews give rise to moral forms and structures, a hierarchy of universal values understood as real and extant in the universe. This moral hierarchy was understood to be expressed in the interdicts imposed not only by religious creed, but through law and social norms. Some commentators in recent years who are not necessarily Christian themselves have observed that more of our current culture than we probably realize is the legacy of the Christian era in the West.[1] One can adhere to an un-

---

1 Two that spring to mind are Tom Holland, in his *Dominion*, (Little, Brown, 2019), and Jordan Peterson, in his public Genesis lectures of 2018. As of this writing, even arch-atheist Richard Dawkins has come around to understanding the significance of Christianity to the culture.

derstanding of ultimate truth and moral values as objective and unchanging and universally applicable, without adopting the specific metaphysics of Christianity.

The word "interdict" will be used here in its ordinary sense, applying it to society's restricting rules. We live under the rule of law, for example, and the laws are certainly "interdicts." But it also applies to social norms, some of which become social norms because they are—or at one time were—grounded in religious belief. For an obvious example, sex outside of marriage is considered immoral, in a society that subscribes to traditional Jewish or Christian interdicts. It is transgression of a moral interdict that was, until recently, also a social interdict. In opposition to interdict is "release" and "remission," both used in slightly different ways in the works of Philip Rieff, and so adopted here. The idea is that there is a release of the interdicts in certain situations. Sex *within* marriage, for example, is a remissive principle rendering certain sexual conduct licit. In this way sex is channeled constructively.

Just as a fish is presumably unaware of water, we may be unaware of our own worldview until we begin to perceive the outlines of another that deviates significantly from it. Here we undertake to understand the therapeutic worldview, but that's going to be difficult for someone already immersed in it. The rendering of the therapeutic worldview which will follow is written in the language of the objective, logos perspective. A religious/logos/objective thinker will have to think outside that box to understand the therapeutic. To do that, however, we need contrast, and perhaps in considering the contrast even the therapeutic thinker will come to understand the water he swims in.

Understanding a worldview by contrasting it with its opposite is what we undertook in our materialist/Christian example above. The therapeutic worldview is a subjective turn, and so can be contrasted with a worldview of objectivity. Indeed there are several oppositions in play, between the therapeutic worldview and the worldview that preceded it, and so we can examine them to begin to understand how marked is the shift from one to the other.

Objective or Subjective

We know the word "subjective" as a reference to interior thoughts or feelings. In saying for example that "beauty is in the eye of the beholder," we mean that beauty is not a characteristic of the thing (or concept) beheld, but is rather imputed to it, or not, by the beholder. It's equivalent to saying beauty is subjective. But if, on the other hand, we believe beauty inheres in the thing (or concept) be-held, that is the equivalent of saying beauty is an objective feature of that which is beheld. The mountainscape at sunset is beautiful re-gardless what I think about it. If a tree falls in the forest and no one is around, it still makes a sound. Thus, "objective" refers to that which is out there and not just in here: I consult the outside world rather than the interiority of my consciousness, to discern or reason to the scope of reality.

This may be a more significant distinction than we realize. All of our perceptions, whether originating internally or externally, are perceived over the medium of our consciousness. Consciousness is a curious thing—philosophers have puzzled over it since the dawn of time. It is a buzz of awareness that is informed by sensory per-ceptions, but it is obviously more than a sense-receiving phenome-non. It is the locus of thought and the source of self-awareness. And not only our individual self-awareness, but also of our partici-pation in a society, because our self-awareness includes awareness of others' self-awareness, so that the mutual playback of self- and oth-er-awareness creates not just conscious subjectivity, but conscious *inter*subjectivity,[2] the basis of social awareness.

_____

2 A person is a <u>subject</u> rather than an object. Self-perception is not simply self-aware-ness, but awareness of another's self-awareness. And, awareness of the other's oth-er-awareness. Such mutual self-awareness according to some thinkers (like Emile

Within that consciousness also is our rational thought process. Our thoughts proceed in a linear, "logical" way because of the logos; because they are oriented toward truth objectively existing in the world. Likewise our moral intuitions, if not corrupted by the therapeutic worldview, are oriented to the structure of moral values extant in the cosmos. The *logos* of rationality and morality in the natural order of the world enables us to reason in concordance with others. This is a reasonable working definition of *rationality*.

For all of that extra-physical activity of the consciousness, it is somehow mysteriously connected to the physical body, as a cloud of thought and perception and intentionality that moves with the body. Imagine you're walking along your favorite path through the woods. There's your body, walking along with your peculiar gait. But where is your *consciousness* of body and surroundings? Not inside the skull, that bowl of tissue and electricity, complex and awesome as it may be. Consciousness twines sensory perceptions of the external world in some way mysteriously to the workings of your physical body. The *where* of your consciousness seems to be a few feet above the path, moving along with your body. Intersubjectivity means it intersects, in a manner of speaking, with the cloud surrounding other bodies, and with the narratives that form the cloud surrounding an entire society.

There is no explanation for how the aware cloud of thoughtful agency[3] can be produced in biology. How could a physical system of cognitive functioning give rise to conscious experience? Why does it act on its own volition? What gives conscious awareness *agency*, making the consciously-aware entity a decision-maker in what it does

---

Durkheim) creates a social awareness distinct from the subjective awareness of its members, but accessible by them. If so that does not create consensus, however, it only creates individual awareness of the social narrative. This is an important distinction because "intersubjectivity" is sometimes confusingly used as a synonym for group consensus. It is used in this work as shorthand for the phenomenon of social awareness.

3 We will have much occasion to further discuss agency, one's exercise of conscious volition, which includes moral agency, choosing good or evil knowing them to be such.

next and what it thinks next?

It is inside that mysterious consciousness that we apprehend features both of the objective, exterior world, and of the subjective, interior world. The world out there presents itself to me. The self-awareness in here presents itself to the outside world. The resulting collision of tides rolling in and out dynamically enlivens our consciousness. Our conscious awareness is the forum for rational thought and moral awareness but also for emotion and internal introspection. We are, or can be, aware when the "eye" of our consciousness is directed inward or outward. We are able to distinguish subjective and objective.

But we are also capable of muddling them. That's what we do when we confuse emotional thought with rationality, for example. In a complex way, we can apply rational thought to irrational subjective premises. Or irrational conclusions from objective observation and rational thought concerning them. This is in essence what happens with the emotivist, one who processes rational thought through the prism of emotional reaction.

The therapeutic worldview derives from this muddling, for example when we grant to emotional responses authority over objective values. It's not that a person with the therapeutic worldview is incapable of discerning truth, or the hierarchy of values we describe as "virtues" and "vice." It's that he supplants such objectivity with a subjectively perceived state of emotion. The therapeutic worldview prioritizes an inward, subjective turn in the way we think, in which emotion, self-care, and psychological equanimity are replacement values, undermining pursuit of virtue. Perception of virtue (and vice) can be clouded by emotion, though they are real and extant features of the world.

The therapeutic worldview emphasizes subjectivity and self-care, but is not limited specifically to involvement of psychological therapy, as when we turn to a therapist to intervene in our patterns of thought. We should understand it to mean one's self-care therapeutic approach to everything: self as therapist of self. It's meant to describe maintenance of personal psychological equanimity, achieved through external affirmation, as a priority that comes ahead of individual striving for universal, objective, and impersonal virtues.

Vertical or Horizontal

We contrasted internal/external, and subjective/objective, to begin to get an understanding of the therapeutic worldview, from the perspective of the logos worldview. Here's another dichotomy by which we might come to approach the same point: a move from vertical to horizontal.

The vertical is unchanging and eternal. In religious terms, it is associated with God as Creator, the ground of all being. It can be associated with the vertical beam of the Christian cross. The vertical corresponds to transcendence of the material world. In philosophical terms, the vertical is associated with Being, in contrast to Becoming. We think of truth and moral values in vertical terms if we understand them to be objectively existing, unchanging with time, hierarchical, and authoritative.

The horizontal is changing and temporal. It can be analogized to the horizontal beam in the Christian cross. In religious terms, it is associated with God active in the world, His immanence, and a telos to history. "Telos" refers to an ultimate action or aim, so in Christianity, for example, it is the eschatological vision. But a quite distinct understanding of telos is presumed in Marxist historicism, to mean the dialectically-produced evolution of ideas toward utopian society; replacement of ends with means. We think of truth and moral values in horizontal terms if we understand them to be subjectively experienced, relative to time and circumstance, undifferentiated in importance, and personal. Historicism amounts to a replacement of ultimate goal with intermediate, human, activity. While the religious version of telos is oriented to ultimate ends and to ultimate meaning, the neo-Marxist version of telos is process oriented, making history itself a god-substitute. Both imply a purposed direction within the gradient of time. But one is pulled along by God; the other is pushed along by evolving society.

Before the postmodern era, truth was thought of on a vertical axis—vertical because we think of truth as "up" and falsity as "down." Likewise moral values—vertical because we think of virtue as "up" and vice as "down." If we understand the objectivity of truth and moral values, we understand also that they transcend our horizontal, moment-to-moment quotidian concerns. They are unchanging, and they are universal—applicable to everyone. Truth is truth for everyone, as is falsity. Virtues and vices are not self-created bespoke intellectual vestments, but constant standards for all people. We may encounter moral quandaries in a particular set of facts, but the moral values that give rise to those quandaries are fixed, not relative.

Honesty, for example, is a virtue and is the same virtue for everyone, it is not crafted for individual application. Indeed, the very word "virtue" in common usage implies a trait that is aspirational for all of us alike—we could not attach meaning to the word if it did not apply to something objective and unchanging and universal. A person may prioritize a moral value differently from another person, but the values themselves are unchanging. The priorities of value engaged by the individual are judged by universal standards. One can do a poor job of weighing competing values in making a particular judgment, precisely because values are universal. Were values relative and individual, there would be no basis for saying they are well or poorly weighed in the first place.

In the postmodern era, the vertical gives way to the horizontal. Postmodern philosophy is a series of propositions representing this shift. As the philosophical ideas have become generalized and ap-

plied, they have sickened Western culture.[4] Upon rejection of God
in the postmodern era, morality and truth were theorized to be generated in the flow of social process rather than fixed, transcendent
Source, and as a result were understood as relative to time and place,
and from individual to individual. As Charles Taylor noted, "the
entire ethical stance of moderns supposes and follows on from the
death of God (and of course, of the meaningful cosmos)."[5] Truth
and moral values could therefore be conceived on a horizontal
axis—moving and changing as society "progresses."[6]

A similar shift from vertical to horizontal takes place psychologically. This shift is sometimes referred to as a shift from moral
absolutism to "moral relativism," and decried as such by conservatives. But it's actually worse than they think. As we've seen in recent
years, the morality paradigm is replaced altogether by a self-care psychological paradigm. For those fully given over to it, morality has
not become "relative" at all. It remains quite absolute, but with socially-derived values in place of eternal moral ones. The problem
with "moral relativism" is not so much the relativism part, but the
moral part. Morality is supplanted by psychology.

Let's pause and consider what "morality" even means. It implies an objective standard by which we measure our acts and omissions, but that's not the source of the self-righteous dudgeon we
observe in psychological man. It would be better to employ a different vocabulary to discuss right and wrong from the therapeutic
worldview, but as occurs pervasively in the postmodern era, language is employed ambiguously, to enable shifting meanings for
fraudulent ends. Moral absolutism in the emotivist therapeutic worldview does not mean reference to eternal and unchanging values. It

---

4 This was a key theme in the author's *The Mountain and the River,* and also *Dangerous
God/A Defense of Transcendent Truth* (New English Review Press, 2023 and 2021).

5 *A Secular Age,* (Cambridge, MA: Belknap, 2007).

6 Hence the title of *The Mountain and the River*: the vertical unchanging mountain
gives way to the horizontal flowing river. Progress is a function of social dialectic
producing a historicist telos that supplants religious forms of telos.

means only the strength of subjectively-felt conviction. That conviction feels as if it is internally wrought, but (as we will see) is actually absorbed from the social dialectic.[7] The psychological disposition is warmed and affirmed by embracing the social dialectic as one's own. In this way it becomes possible to confuse indignant self-righteousness with morality.

With the worldview of objectivity, we measure ourselves as well as the outside world according to the vertical orientation of truth and of values. With the advent of the therapeutic worldview, the vertical measure to which we compare ourselves becomes watered-down or misshapen. We employ instead mostly horizontally-developed criteria. Instead of the postmodern roil of social process to tell us propositionally how we should think, there is an internal roil of emotion to tell us how we should feel. Our feelings then govern our thoughts and actions.

The internal shift from vertical to horizontal cannot be complete, however, because emotions cannot change reality. The mind still works rationally, when it works from therapeutic premises. In adopting the therapeutic worldview, we *rationally* substitute psychological well-being for objective virtue and truth. A corrupted vertical conception remains, so that even as changeable emotivism governs thought processes, it is confusedly articulated in the language of the vertical and rational. As Alisdair MacIntyre pointed out, psychological man does not use moral language for its objective meaning, but rather for purposes of stating subjective preferences, and those preferences are given as truth claims. To say this in a different way, psychological man is rational but not all the way down. The therapeutic worldview means a change of foundational premises, not an entire abandonment of rationality. We can build rational thoughts on the shifting sand of changing emotional states.

---

7 "Dialectic" refers to evolution of ideas over time, theorizing them as sourced in social process. The idea is attributed to Friedrich Hegel (1770-1831) and is central to Marxist theory. See *The Mountain and the River*, chapter 12.

It bears emphasis that the collapse to horizontal is similar for society and for individuals. For society, the horizontal means social process generates truth and value. For individuals, the horizontal means emotivism prescribes truth and value. There is a cross-pollination, so to speak, in narrative-producing intersubjectivity.[8] Individual emotivism entails absorption of the horizontal perspective from society. Society's horizontal perspective entails absorption of the therapeutic from individuals. Radical politics feed emotivism; emotivism feeds radical politics. There is thus a coincidence of woke and therapeutic.[9]

Captivity or Agency

We've so far made occasional reference to the concept of agency: the exercise of conscious volition toward a self-determined goal; the conscious *intentionality* in how we live our lives. To understand the therapeutic worldview and its effect on us, we should understand agency, and its source. We can approach this by viewing it from its opposite, and the antonym proposed is *captivity*. The principle behind captivity is that upon relinquishing individual agency in whole or in part, we become vulnerable to *ideological* capture, the embrace of a flawed and totalizing system of ideas that depart from reality.

Agency is an individual's volition and capacity to act. It can be understood in the language of causation. A person's behavior is *caused* by his intention and execution. To say that people have agency is to say they are beings with the ability to form intent to act, and to act. It is something more than material cause and effect. It contem-

---

8 "Narrative" is a story developed socially, a vision we collectively share, and there can be competing narratives. "Intersubjectivity" is the buzz of mutual self- and other-awareness, a social consciousness.

9 It seems well-established that there is a gap in well-being as between liberals and conservatives. E.g., Ian Leslie, "Why Does Being Left-Wing Make You Unhappy?" *The Ruffian* (Substack), April 13, 2024.

plates a being with ability to form the intent, rather than behavior being predetermined or inexplicable. This is evident in the exercise of moral agency. Human beings choose evil or good, knowing them to be such.

In coming to terms with the therapeutic worldview, we're really asking what a person is. The therapeutic contemplates one kind of being. The opposing worldview we've described variously as religious, or logos, or objective, contemplates another. Obviously people make decisions and act on them all day every day, as they go about making a living, managing relationships, and so on. But we're concerned here particularly with *moral* agency. People make good and bad moral decisions all day every day, as well. Indeed, our dignity as human beings rests on the exercise of moral agency. Agency and dignity are not merely coincident—each is a function of the other. Human dignity rests on the exercise of positive moral agency; it is diminished in the exercise of negative moral agency. Seeking virtue and avoiding vice is acting with dignity. Therefore, ceding any agency to others—as we do with collectives of government and other power centers—diminishes our range of personal moral agency, and therefore diminishes, concomitantly, individual dignity.

Even within the range of moral decision-making left to us, we can fritter away dignity. If we come to think of our decisions as essentially amoral,[10] then we're simply getting through life like animals, living in the moment with no larger over-arching purpose. The exercise of individual moral agency presupposes a larger purpose or meaning to what we are as human beings, as is discerned in religious belief.[11] If we allow a shift in our worldview from logos to therapeutic, we're also allowing for a shift from moral to amoral. The amoral therapeutic outlook means diminution in agency and therefore in personal dignity.

---

10 Not to be confused with "immoral," an amoral outlook presupposes our acts and omissions have no moral nor immoral component; that we have no moral agency.

11 This point is well made in Marilyn Simon's "In Praise of Sin," *Submission* (Substack) May 15, 2024.

The reason to be particularly concerned with moral agency is that this is the point of contrast with psychological man. Not that the therapeutic entirely erases moral agency, but that the quality of moral decision-making is altered. In adopting the therapeutic worldview, individuals adopt a self-care paradigm over a responsibility paradigm. Psychological self-care means a comfortable sense of belonging, what Freud referred to as the "oceanic feeling" of infantile oneness with the mother, wherein we lose ourselves in community. This impulse is indeed infantile, in that it is avoidance of individual moral agency in favor of social identification. Therapeutic rather than moral thinking is likewise an avoidance of moral agency, and therefore erodes dignity.

3

THE DISCOVERED SELF

The Negotiated Self

Allusion to the self as "discovered" relates to the concept of agency. In the therapeutic worldview, the conception of self occurs passively; discovered rather than formed in the active exercise of agency. In the logos worldview, by contrast, the conception of self might be called the "negotiated self," or the "integrated self."

Let's approach this by first describing the former way of thinking about how the "self" is formed, what we are calling here the "negotiated self." Out there is God's moral universe. In here is the weird and startling "I" of my own metacognition; my self-aware consciousness. It is in this personal consciousness that I look out on the world and engage with it. This is active and intentional participation, the self not just passively receiving and processing world-facts, but interacting with people, places, and things in a way that informs the conception of self. This is a "negotiated" sense of self because it is formed dynamically in my agentic participation with the exterior world. I push against the world and it pushes against me, and I form a conception of my place in that world through participatory interaction with it. The resulting sense of self is in this sense "negotiated." I am porous to the exterior world in my openness to the world's opinion of me. My parents in a sense tell me who I am, along with siblings, friends, mentors, teachers, and the wider world. But all of these influences don't simply land on me and stick, forming a pastiche of one-dimensional me. Rather, I participate, in the exercise of agency, in embracing or rejecting principles or persons or propositions that swim toward me from that exterior world.

The self, in this understanding, is formed in a "place" that represents the point of my interaction with the world outside my head. That place of interaction with the exterior world is the living edge of my formation of self, like the cambium of a tree alive to the tree's interactions with its environment. The focus of the negotiated self is the world out there. Introspection concerning the self is subsidiary, to use the language of Michael Polanyi.[1] The conception of selfhood is tacit knowledge, building a self-confident but outward-directed sense of self, instead of excessive introspection about the person within that is presumed morally pure, resulting in a vulnerable, victimize-able sense of self. The negotiated self is just me in here interacting with the world out there.

The negotiation with the world entails putting oneself on the line, so to speak, morally. It means accepting responsibility for what one does and doesn't do. To fully grasp this, we must first grasp the reality of a moral structure to the world. We must leave behind a materialist understanding. Returning to our consideration of metaphysics, "materialism" is the philosophical premise that all of reality consists in matter in motion, plus certain immaterial realities like thought and morality that we take to be merely emergent from the material—in this case the workings of the brain. Our concept of moral good, for example, would be taken by the materialist as merely an evolved mental preference, perhaps because sociability makes us more fit for survival. Materialism resurfaces from time to time in the history of ideas. Most recently it was the absurd New Atheist[2]

---

1 *Personal Knowledge*, (University of Chicago Press, 1959).

2 Largely overtaken now in the public conversation, but New Atheist thinking is

presumption that one can declare God a fiction, subtracting Him entirely from reality, without reckoning with nor defending the resulting reductionist materialism. In the materialist and emotivist view, good and evil have no independent existence; they are religious terms applied to what are really just preferences or social norms, some of which may be codified into law. Implicit in the materialist worldview is a deterministic presumption that we move through the world mechanistically, reacting to stimuli, like the little ball in a pinball machine. People may have complex interior mental lives, but ultimately there's no real agency. And therefore no moral responsibility. We're just animals.

Moral good and moral evil are real and extant in the world, however, just as are love, and spirit, and mathematical realism,[3] and Platonic ideals, and the categorical ontological differentiations unfolding into the complex physical and idealistic structure of the world.[4] A recognition of the reality of moral structure; of the existence of good and evil, underpins religious worldviews.

Agency corresponds to the reality of the moral structure; the moral structure corresponds to agency. We decide to act, and act, on our own volition *because* we live inside a moral structure. Every act or omission undertaken by us in that intersection between the interior consciousness and the exterior world is a moral act. Of course, the structure is hierarchical, so not every act (or omission) is of equal weight. But merely stepping outside our door is a moral act, as is leaving the door closed. The moral structure governs that intersection between interior consciousness and world-facts outside our metaphorical door. There is no opt-out to the moral structure of the world.

---

represented in early 21st-century works by thinkers like Richard Dawkins, Daniel Dennett, Sam Harris, and Christopher Hitchens, and a host of others who considered themselves updated versions of Enlightenment lumiéres.

3 See discussion at *Dangerous God*, chapter 2.

4 A central theme of *The Mountain and the River*.

The Divided Self

But suppose I desire to avoid moral responsibility for what I do and don't do? This desire becomes acute, if I have rejected God, because there is then a felt need to disregard also His moral structure to reality, because that moral structure inheres in the conscience, and so continues to indict; it creates a dissonance in my simplistic atheism. This dissonance uncomfortably supervenes upon the negotiated self.

The self alive to moral implications of agency must turn inward to escape it, to re-examine selfhood without the searing indictment that evil resides even in me. The turn inward is a way to resolve the dissonance; to cease looking outward to harsh moral reality, and turn instead, to a comfortable interior terrain I think I can control. My exercise of consciousness is then turned away from the imperatives of agentic decision-making in a morally charged world. It is turned inward to negotiate a different kind of landscape, one imagined to be amoral, consisting of subjectively-felt instincts and emotions.

When one looks outwardly at the world from this perspective, it is not to exercise one's own agency to interact with it on its own (moral) terms. Rather, it is to assess world-facts in relation to their impact on preferred interior psychological well-being. A bit like losing oneself in a video game.[5] The self being formed is not the result of a negotiation with the exterior world. It is instead formed in the interior being. Instead of having an integrated, single point of consciousness of self, a *me* formed in thinking and interacting agentically with the external world, I process world-facts on dimensions of host and identity, no longer integrated, resulting in the internal dissonance of a divided self.

Before further explanation, let's pause and consider how this

---

5 An interesting speculation is whether porn or over-indulgence in video games might habituate the user to alternate-reality existence, thus easing the transition from the logos to the psychological worldview.

double perspective is possible and even inevitable. We're considering "the discovered self," but then what self is doing the discovering? How can there be a discovering self that is distinct from the discovered self? The idea of a divided self is not so strange as it might seem at first glance. Whenever we turn inward to plan or self-recriminate or resolve to do or not do something, we necessarily adopt a two-dimension conception of self. We do so for example if we undertake any form of self-improvement. There's the self that determines to improve, and simultaneously the self being improved. If you decide you need to eat better and start exercising, that's you as subject making the decision, and another you as object charged with carrying it out. You make the New Year's Resolution; another "you" keeps it or fails to keep it.[6]

Perhaps you're tired of being late so you set your watch forward five minutes. Who are you fooling? Your self-as-resolution-maker orders your self-as-resolution-adopter to obey the falsified timepiece, and it's possible for that other self to go along with it. There's conflict, of sorts, but it's resolved in purposeful self-delusion. It is a tactic by which the agentic goal-oriented self attempts to overcome the resistant pleasure-oriented self; a purposeful self-division.

There is likewise a two-dimension of self-conception as a result of our intersubjectivity. That is, you have a purely subjective self-conception in your solitude, but then when you interact with others (or even just one other) socially, you adopt simultaneously another self-conception: how you imagine the Other conceives of you. This means recognizing their subjectivity, and then seeing yourself anew through the Other's eyes; through their subjectivity. You carry both of these subjective conceptions of self in your social interactions, and this double-conception is what enables not only a

---

6 For this insight, see Kathryn Schulz, "The Self in Self-Help," *New York Magazine*, Jan. 4, 2013, cited by Elisabeth Lasch-Quinn in her introduction to *Ars Vitae*, University of Notre Dame Press, 2020.

"we" perspective in addition to the "I," but social narratives more generally, the ability to imagine oneself a part of a family or tribe or nation or even humanity. It reifies concepts of what "we" are about. In this way we perceive not just material facts of our environment but "social facts" owing to our being social creatures.

The dissonance in selfhood can become even more attenuated than that. The "discovered self" presents passively. It is "discovered" rather than created like the negotiated, integrated self. As a passive discovered thing, it may feel like the answer to an extreme of alienation or anger at the way the world is, an escape from anxiety over irreconcilable and even hostile worldviews. Ideology may present itself as a way of smoothing the differences; as therapeutic. Psychological well-being seems to reside in finding the flow and going with it, and that in turn seems to mean declining to resist the ideological turns presented by zeitgeist narrative. And so we can willingly divide the mind, in self-delusion imagining the ideologically compliant discovered self to emerge unbidden and uncreated.

The divided self is recognized sometimes in psychology, though perhaps with inadequate understanding, or encrusted with materialist theory. J.D. Laing, for example, in a book actually titled *The Divided Self,*[7] agreed with Freud that society is repressive, and in this way at least joined the New Left neo-Marxists in perceiving the self as formed in social oppression, and accordingly fueling the therapeutic presumption of self afloat in a sea of buffeting storms. Despite this point of agreement with Freud, he critiqued Freudian psychology as taking the person in isolation, a set piece of id, ego, and superego, rather than as relational entity. In this respect Laing can be seen as a postmodernist, taking his cues from social process and flow. He was not wrong about there being a social dimension to a person's make-up, but took social oppression as the source of "ontological insecurity" manifesting in a schizoid tendency to a divided self. In this way he (with many others, of course) was midwife

---

7 Penguin Books, 1990 (first published 1959).

to today's trauma industry.

One of Laing's key theses was that the schizoid[8] response to neglect or what we might now call psychological trauma can be a sense of having a separate self more true than what presents to the outside world. Laing was an ardent existentialist in his psychiatry, so in his view, neglect or instances of what we might now call trauma threaten the schizoid's very sense of existence, resulting in "ontological insecurity." A feature of the schizoid personality is that the inner person (what we might now call "Identity") is not withdrawn from the world and its harshness, but to the contrary is touchily vulnerable; more sensitive, not less, to pressures against his "ontological insecurity," his very sense of existence: "the ordinary circumstances of everyday life constitute a continual and deadly threat."[9] Ontological insecurity, according to Laing, results in a schizoid "divided self."

Resilience

The therapeutic mindset creates the divided self. The project of seeking therapeutic wholeness *presupposes* an internal self distinct from that which presents to the external world. This is in part a legacy of Freud's concept of the internal interaction of id and superego. After Freud we're all alert to warring inner drives and consequent need for care of the inner being. This sensitivity impairs resilience, making one actually more vulnerable to disappointments in close relationships; more likely to consider them traumatic, and more likely to ascribe psychological harm to them. "Ontological insecurity" results not from heightened trauma, but from heightened sensitivity.

It is psychological harm either way, however. As with so much

---

8 Laing used "schizoid" to means an inclination toward neurotic self-division that stops short of psychotic.

9 *The Divided Self*, p. 42.

else in life, the answer is not to attempt to eliminate the stressors, but to strengthen oneself against their impact. The therapeutic mentality reverses this understanding, so the vulnerable are "traumatized" by ever less traumatizing circumstances. The response of the vulnerable is schizoid, to use Laing's language: a division of self. The true self is seen as the vulnerable inner being protected by the combative attention-directing self fending off threats from the world. The therapeutic mindset reinforces perception of trauma, which debilitates resilience, which makes one vulnerable to mistaking any upsetting environment as traumatic, which reinforces the victimhood mentality of the mindset, all in a vicious spiraling-down. We become more subject to traumatization or "ontological insecurity" because the therapeutic imperative itself debilitates that resilience. Therapy begets therapy. It was not true that we are all vulnerable all the time to serious psychological harm, but it is becoming true as we increasingly buy into the ideology of fragile victimhood. Hence the ubiquity of therapeutic identification of a vulnerable, to-be-protected inner self, manifesting as discovered Identity, in a mental health pandemic exacerbated rather than ameliorated by therapy.

Without stronger resilience, internal dissonance seems easier to manage than dissonance with the outside world. The therapeutically sensitive person can develop a departure from integrated selfhood. The dissonant, divided self manifests in a discovering self and a discovered self. The attentive self on tenterhooks against stirrings of psychological trauma discovers an emerging self that is timorous and vulnerable to victimhood to the point of seeking therapeutic wholeness at the expense of an objective moral sense.

The Discovered Self

Rather than assuming a single integrated point of consciousness, a me formed in thinking and interacting agentically with the external world, I may process world-facts on two dimensions of self-hood, which we can call host and identity. I passively receive and internally process the (presumed amoral) facts of the external world, but in doing so I become host to another manifestation of self, my *Identity*. Both host and identity are imagined passively formed rather than the product of moral agency. Host processes psychologically; Identity is the passive result. This is an outsourcing of the agency of the "I" of consciousness, leaving self-as-host the passive spectator of what the esoterically[10] charged inner being does in the exercise of *its* conscious agency. Denial of personal agency means denial of moral responsibility. Self-as-host receives Identity mystically and esoterically. It seems to well up unbidden from the depths of the subconscious. Identity is the self discovered.

Identity-formation is a rejection of abstractions of universal moral value, in favor of embodied, subjective reactions to the world. This seems to be felt, not chosen. The self-as-host is the passive recipient of world-facts. Then the processing of those world-facts internally leads to another sense of self, this being self-as-identity. We don't choose our Identity, as that would be an act of moral agency, part of a reality we wish to avoid. Rather, self-as-host messianically discerns a stirring in the inner being which produces Identity. Self-as-identity seems to emerge from the interior unbidden, a self that is manifested rather than chosen.

This separation of self in dimensions of host and identity is a mechanism for unimagining one's own agency, to the end of avoiding moral responsibility associated with the exercise of agency. Self-as-host is reduced to passive vessel observing emergence of the self-as-identity. Identity is thus the discovered, rather than negotiated, self.

---

10 "Esoteric" refers to specialized knowledge accessible to only a few. The meaning implied here is such knowledge received internally from mystical source. For the Gnostics, spirit imparted gnosis to the inner subconscious self. For those captured in the ideology of the therapeutic, the social *geist* is the esoteric but unacknowledged source of the inner knowing.

But in reality, identity only *seems* to emerge. The dynamic of choosing—agency—is veiled in the dissonant two-dimension host/ identity formation of self. The affirmative moral choices of the negotiated self are replaced with passive and amoral recognition of emerging identity. This is a roundabout form of self-deluded moral evasion. To admit to oneself that this is actually a purposeful activity kept just under the surface of the active consciousness would be to cancel the magic; to expose the affirmative choosing rather than continue the illusion of passive reception. This form of moral evasion requires hiding from self the agentic element of one's being through irrational mental circumlocution. It is an elaborate way of attempting to avoid moral fault.

There isn't really a passive recognition of emerging identity. Nor is Identity derived esoterically, to emerge from the inner being. It is chosen. We bring this about on our own. As in all things, we act, and we act as the immortal beings that we are. It is necessary to maintain the mystique of esotericism, however, to hide from self the agentic choosing, and thus the reality of the moral universe in which we participate, by choosing. And thus responsibility for our moral choices. Identity seems to emerge from the subconscious unbidden, but it is in fact chosen.

We are quite capable of hiding this process from ourselves, and that's what we do when we speak of "Identity," and when we conceive of self-as-identity; a being passively formed rather than chosen. We don't actually receive identity passively, so as to "identify as" gay or trans or dysphoric or asexual or traumatized or dissocial. We choose those things, and our choosing is, as with all our acts of agency, a moral choice. Undertaken in a moral universe. There is no escape from the world God created, into a cramped little interior space safe from His omniscience. Try as we might, we can't hide from God in a psychological turtle-shell of our own making.

4

THE THERAPEUTIC CULTURE

Individualism and Agency

We've thus far approached the therapeutic worldview primarily from an individual standpoint. We'll continue to consider the worldview and its effects on individuals caught up in it, but will turn now also to its effects on society. As the therapeutic worldview has developed and spread, the entire culture comes under its sway. The therapeutic worldview of individuals becomes the therapeutic *culture* of society. This doesn't just mean lots of people now hold the therapeutic worldview. It means our social awareness itself becomes increasingly given over to the therapeutic, accelerating its engulfing of individuals. Of you.

Before proceeding, we should again pause to be careful of our terms. There is increasingly confusion about the individual "I" of self-conscious awareness. Who or what am I, in contrast to the collective, or to humanity down through the ages? What do we mean when we contrast "individualism" with "the collective" or "society?" Some of the language used in discussion of the therapeutic worldview makes this question more difficult. Charles Taylor for example writes of "expressive individualism" as a descriptor of the therapeutic worldview. Likewise Carl Trueman, who writes that "expressive individualism"[1] results in the phenomenon of psychological man. Mary Harrington in a 2021 essay[2] close to these topics wrote that "untrammeled individualism" results in *de facto* Satanism. They're all quite right, but this kind of phrasing is confusing. What writers using this expression mean is that people adopt an attitude of lawlessness, and follow their desires wherever they lead. As with the occultist Aleister Crowley: "Do what thou wilt shall be the whole of the Law."

But this is a superficial reading of what's going on. Yes, there's an orientation to lawlessness, but for most entrapped by the therapeutic this is quite gradual and presents as self-evidently proper. It doesn't come on suddenly as full-on satanic possession. It is first felt as a necessary release of interdicts to allow for the emergence of true inner Identity. Freedom is understood not as maximum expression of individual agency, in contradistinction to collectivism; but to the contrary as small-s socialism, the ecstatic sense of community and uncritical support of *its* agency. The collective one may desire to bring about—by supporting radical politics as against troglodyte conservatives—returns esoterically as revealer of inner Identity. Such a person is not expressing his individualism vis-à-vis the collective. He's defending the Identity buried in his psyche against repressive verticals in authority[3] which deny it.

This version of "individualism" is the opposite of self-responsibility and independence vis-à-vis the state, the kind of virtuous self-reliance formerly associated with the word, as when we used the phrase "rugged individualism." In this way different and conflicting meanings are crowded onto this word "individualism," so we must

1 In fact, the phrase is in the subtitle to his *The Rise and Triumph of the Modern Self: Cultural Amnesia, Expressive Individualism, and the Road to Sexual Revolution.*
2 Unherd.com, "How Satanism Conquered America/Untramelled Individualism Is No Longer a Sin," Sept. 15, 2021.
3 A Rieffian term, converging the "vertical" as discussed in the last chapter with "authority" understood as sacred authority rather than mere politically-imposed authority.

be conscious of which meaning is actually in play. "Individualism" properly understood is an incident of freedom, and freedom is only possible if we accept the objectivity and universality of hierarchical values; the givenness of them extant in the world: the logos, and moral realism.

The therapeutic culture actively swims away from freedom and individualism. "Individualism" as the word is used now is a morally withered thing when it is taken to mean only licentiousness. In a maximally free society, individual agency is not relinquished to the collective. If it is, the collective imposes *its* interdicts of law and social disapproval. We certainly do not live in maximally free societies, in Western democracies. We live under ever-increasing and onerous interdicts, the opposite of what we should expect in a maximally free society of individualists informed by conscience. This corresponds to the drift to socialism, which in turn corresponds to the rise of the therapeutic culture.

It is important to understand that the orientation to therapeutic self-care does not mean simply self-focus, to the exclusion of all else. It's not mere selfishness, but something more insidious: a negative adjustment in conception of what the self is. Under the baleful influence of the therapeutic we picture ourselves passive in self-formation and defensive in emotional self-protection. This conception pushes out its opposite: the agentic, individualistic independence that befits children of God.

This is what makes psychological man radically small-s socialist, though he paradoxically projects "expressive individualism." Rather than interacting willfully with the external world in the exercise of moral agency, he imagines he passively observes himself emerging from the interior of his mysteriously charged being. That emergent being, Identity, is vulnerable, and so the protective instinct is turned inward to protection of that Identity. The desire is to step out into the world protected in its therapeutic needs, especially the need for acceptance and blissful fellow-feeling.

Realism and Relativism

Psychological man is thus eager to give himself over to society, but not as it is in its present state. Society must be re-calibrated to impose no boundaries that would interfere with his Identity formation. That is not to say he wants a society in which anything goes. To the contrary, he wants a society in which very particular social rules of engagement obtain, rules very different from those inherited from the logos worldview.

Here we must make an important distinction. On the one hand, "morality," implying that standards of right and wrong are unchanging and objective and universally applicable and extant in the universe; and this synonymous with *moral realism*, the understanding that moral structure is a reality in the cosmos, in the same way other intangibles like mathematics and beauty and ontological dualities are real.

On the other hand, there are "ethics," sometimes used in contrast to "morals" to imply that standards of right and wrong are merely prescribed by social norms. Ethics refers to values assigned in a paradigm of *moral relativism*, meaning we might regard as "ethical" those values that are socially-generated, process-generated, situational, contextual, and mutable.

To reiterate, the therapeutic worldview doesn't mean an absence of ethical standards. But the paramount desire is for inclusion and acceptance, and that colors how one thinks about applicable standards. It seems to require moral relativism rather than moral realism, because moral relativism rests on an ethic of mutual acceptance; a social consensus concerning "tolerance" as the you-do-you ethos of "tolerance of everything except intolerance."

Moral realism, by contrast, means adherence to standards beyond society itself. Consequently, it may portend judgment and disapproval. It may mean trying to adhere to moral standards impossible to meet, so one must live with the tragic sense of not living up to one's potential, and of that unmet potential pointing to an unattainable ideal. It means accepting the reality of sin in everyone, and consequently of one's own sin. This environment feels contrary to one's therapeutic interests because it impedes dissolving oneself into a oneness of humanity, in which all values are formed and re-formed collectively in the horizontal flow of time and circumstance, in which we can align ourselves without dissonance or discomfort.

Adherents of the realist view that there is a moral structure above society itself create angst for psychological man because they interfere with the all-welcoming embrace he wants. His political distress is sourced in the continuing divide. A comfortable accepting society requires all-in participation in the ethos of moral relativism. There is no room for moral realism because one drop spoils the whole batch. Lingering allegiance to moral realism presents as a brooding menace, preventing one from relaxing into a Oneness of therapeutic mutual care. The striving for virtue and against vice presents a continuing uncomfortable tension with the therapeutic. From the perspective of psychological man, moral realists create boundaries that serve only to divide, perpetuating unending strife and division, the opposite of mutual acceptance. Universal embrace of a relativist and self-care ethos is therefore an essential political aim of those infected with the therapeutic worldview.

This conflict of visions has riven society. Logos thinkers puzzled by the sudden questioning of moral realism try to make sense of how so many of their neighbors, so fast, have sunk below the surface of the therapeutic flood. It happened because the language of therapeutic self-care has crept up on us, abetted by God-questioning prosperity. Strategically ambiguous language is the primary means of advance, and a secondary is disinclination to grapple hard questions of principle. Kindness is a virtue, who could argue with it? But kindness is not the only virtue, and in any event kindness is not synonymous with uncritical acceptance. Kindness may require acknowledging rather than suppressing the reality of moral virtue and vice. If the moral structure of the universe is real, kindness dictates reinforcing rather than denying that reality. Maybe there is a God who judges.

Ideology

The desire for oneness with society manifests as support for ever-expanding collectivism, comprising government but also non-government power centers and mechanisms of social consensus-seeking. The ideology of the therapeutic advances this collectivism, and is advanced by it.

The power of ideologies is derived from rejection of God. When we un-imagine God we conceive ourselves loosed from that comprehensive and greater-than-human power. This is untenable for human beings, so we immediately turn to replace Him with some other greater-than-human power, and this invariably takes the form of a collective, a Babel-tower formed to replace the now-missing God.[4] The mechanism by which we make this turn is *ideology*. "It is the tendency of ideological politics to turn human beings into instruments, not only through compulsion and intimidation, but through their own choice to behave and think according to its dictates."[5] Ideologies by their nature are deceitful, and their deceit is employed to gather up and exploit the agency of individuals ceded to the collective. An ideology is a totalizing, comprehensive, but fraudulent set of ideas resting on unsound principles concerning human nature. The therapeutic worldview is such an ideology. It is a cult of resurgent Gnosticism.

The therapeutic worldview contributes to the dissipation of individual agency. The concern is with psychological self-care, not

---

4 The Tower of Babel story of Genesis, chapter 11 is archetypal, pointing to the repeating pattern of man-made controlling systems to supplant devotion to God and the moral universe He created.
5 Mark Schiffman, *What Is Ideology?* (Wiseblood Books, 2023).

with maximum individual freedom. As the therapeutic worldview spreads, societies respond with social mores devised to enhance psychological well-being. Social mores result in legal and social interdicts imposed for purposes of mental health, rather than freedom. Mental health, in turn, is presumed served best in a socialist world-state from which distressing disagreement and dissent have been eradicated.

What is the most important thing to psychological man? He is driven by his emotions, so it is that which is most satisfying emotionally. Socially, that means acceptance. He desires acceptance of other people above all, and especially above commitment to seemingly bloodless abstract principles like those represented in what was formerly called "virtue." The more universal the principle, the less it resonates. The you-do-you ethos is not so much an assertion of the value of tolerance, as it is a means of fostering mutual acceptance. Psychological man is not driven so much by what is best for others, in his relationships, as by what is best for his own desire for a satisfying (to self) feeling of community. Charity (in its general sense) toward others is not directly a motivator for psychological man, because emotivism impairs his ability to empathize. Acceptance of others serves his own feelings, so long as he can perceive it returned. His indifference masquerades as virtuous tolerance.

According to the therapeutic mentality, the worst sin is to prioritize hierarchical moral standards above mutual acceptance. This means, paradoxically, that there can be no mutual acceptance in the case of those who hold to a logos or objective point of view, because logos man is ruining it for those who want, as in John Lennon's *Imagine*, no religion and a brotherhood of man in which "the world will be as one." Psychological self-care means a comfortable sense of belonging without dissent from hold-outs; a Freudian "oceanic feeling" as of infantile oneness with the mother, wherein the person is unaware of boundary between self and Other. Desire for acceptance dovetails with the desire to avoid individual moral agency. Each reinforces the other.

Psychological man first conceives himself part of society, and of society as the locus of exercise of agency. He's not alone responsible to God; his god is society, and he desires to be at one with the agency-exercising society. There is no loss of righteous indignation, to be sure, but the indignation is against those who insist on moral realism at the expense of elastic moral relativism. Transfer of agency to society means: It's not up to me to help my fellow man, I outsource that to the collective (the government); it's not up to me to exercise sexual restraint, that's a matter of emerging Identity; it's not up to me to act justly, there's only "social justice."

The supreme value is oneness with mankind, and that is understood to require the extirpation of alterity[6] wherever it is found. The highest moral value is openness to others. That means moral judgment regarding others' personal conduct is forbidden, as it would reinforce or revive a feeling of other-ness. The trouble is that such an open-ended notion of tolerance also means form-inducing moral interdicts are erased, as every person goes his own way unguided by moral structures of religion or any replacement for religion. When the moral scaffolding is removed—from the individual or from the *polis*—the structure collapses. And the effect on the individual, psychological man, is that anything goes, personally, except disloyalty to the zeitgeist, because that is society's substitute for moral expression. Deviation from Narrative is separation from one's fellow man. That isn't moral agency, it's captivity, because the individual's agency is absorbed by the collective. He is no longer free, but he *feels* comfortable.

The individual consciousness is irreducible, but society is re-

6 Alterity is otherness. It means in particular the ability to see another's point of view; to place oneself in the other's shoes, so to speak. This is essential to social engagement because it is the basis for empathy, and for moral values formation, and it is the feature of a person-to person relationship in which awareness of the other contributes to one's self-identification. It is also the basis for intersubjectivity.

ducible fractally in free associations of people. We are moral agents, and we lose that God-given agency to the extent we cede any portion of it to the collective. Your consciousness is experienced by you alone, and by it you can say "I am"—not with the omniscience and omnipresence of God,[7] of course, but with a knowing not shared with any other person. This is a necessary incident of God-given agency. To the extent we exist as a collective, the collective has agency *and not us individually*. Reciprocally, to the extent we have agency, we are *not* a collective. Having agency means we are responsible for what we do and don't do, because we individually have the moral law and it is real.

Authority and Power

In Jewish and Christian traditions, "transcendence" is that property of God that is ordinarily above and beyond direct human experience, evidenced to us only indirectly. All that physically exists is not self-created, therefore it had to have a transcendent Source. The mystery of there being anything at all—"Being" in the abstract—appears to require transcendence.

Materialism is the stance that all of reality consists in physical matter in motion. Taken too literally it is clearly belied by obviously immaterial but real "things" like thoughts, concepts, values, and so on. These can be regarded as "meta-physical." Such meta-physical realities obviously transcend the physical but also themselves are necessarily transcended. There is a "meta-meta-physical," we might say, a transcendent source of all Being, including both the material and the immaterial realities like thoughts. Similarly, there is clearly a moral hierarchy in play, and it is the same hierarchy for all of us. Truth is the same truth for all of us. These facts demand a transcendent Source as explanation.

---

7 Exodus 3:14; John 8:58.

"Immanence" is that property of God that is active in the world. This means looking not at static existence for significance, but also life events, and history. Things move and change. The world is dynamic. Its movements are accounted for in different ways, as with Aristotle's theory of causation: God as necessary "prime mover" to all that follows. This idea is understood religiously to be not just a far-off uncaring pure actualization, but rather One who generates a telos to history, adopting a people-group for His own and bringing about a reconciliation with mankind in the Christ. Prayer makes sense because of God's immanence.

The significance of the religious grounding for these words—transcendence and immanence—is *authority*. They're not just two different ways of thinking about the divine, represented in the vertical and horizontal beams, respectively, of the Christian cross. They are the basis for the religious authority behind interdicts on conduct. It means the interdicts of a religious society are backed by sacred order.

In *The Triumph of the Therapeutic*, Philip Rieff didn't say much about religion *per se*. Rather, he wrote of "sacred order" necessary to underwrite society's interdicts; to maintain the "vertical in authority." If there is no *sacred* order to underwrite the *social* order, the interdicts lack the necessary authority, and then all authority evanesces, and value verticals collapse. In this way authority is replaced with power. Positivist[8] edicts of society supplant natural edicts of supernatural authority. This is not sustainable, in the long run, because people subject to the positivist edicts come to see them for what they are: arbitrary exercises of power by some against others. Why should I obey the next nonsensical IRS regulation I encounter?

---

8 "Positivism" here means that which is man-created, rather than that which is divinely-ordained. Positivist law, for example, means political regulation not rooted in interdicts of conscience. Licensing laws, for example, are positivist, while the criminal law is an instance of natural law, that which is "written on the heart." "Positivist" or "positivism" refers to interdicts socially generated, and not presumptively backed by sacred authority. Such social norms are developed through Narrative, the social conversation, without being backed by authority higher than society itself.

There could be jail or fines, of course, but that's coercive threat, not *authority* for its edicts.

It's important to understand the difference between authority and power. In fact, it would be accurate to say the failure to understand the difference is both cause and effect of our drift toward totalitarianism. When raw power alone drives interdicts, we may chafe at first, but eventually come to think it normal that we follow the rules set by those in power for the sake of continuation of that power, rather than ourselves willingly internalizing the interdicts of sacred authority. The social order comes to rest on forced compliance rather than willing deference to authority beyond human power. Nietzschean "will to power" supplants the sacred order.

"Virtue is its own reward," we like to say, but what we really mean is that it has divine reward even if not earthly reward. And likewise, divine punishment is a consequence of vice, even if society around us takes no notice. Now there are earthly consequences to virtue and vice, as well, but these carry only social and temporal rewards and punishment. Shame or approbation by society, rather than internal guilt or moral confidence. The thought is that if you cheat on your taxes and the government doesn't find out, it doesn't count. The rules lack divine authority. What's left, then, is only human exercises of power, in the forms of civil codes and social approval or disapproval.

With divine authority imagined out of existence, the words "transcendence" and "immanence" lose their original meaning. We continue to use them, however, in our public discourse, so obviously they carry new meanings. "Transcendence" still means exceeding normal limits, but those limits are not those of the material world, past which we reach the divine. Instead they're limits of traditional society or individual effort or some other limit suggested by context. "Immanence" still means activity within temporally-defined limits, but that activity is no longer divine. Instead it is social- or idea-driven, invisible yet originating entirely within humanity. "Spirit" or "spiritual" is similarly desacralized, to mean something like the immaterial animating force behind social movements, or philosophies like Marxism which presuppose a materialist telos in Hegelian dialectic.[9]

Those driven by their desires insist on a secular orthodoxy which explicitly rejects moral realism backed by the authority of sacred order. It was formerly understood that truth and morality were a given in the cosmos, and they are not self-generated, they were Authored, and the Author's establishment of interdicts of morality constitute the sacred order. This is what we should understand in the word "authority." Its etymology, like that of the word "author," suggests creative origin, including the ultimate creativity of the Divine. We misuse the word when we conflate it with human power, such as that exercised by people in government or at high levels of media, the professions, NGO's, and massive international corporations, collectively a Babel-tower of man-made Machine power.

In pre-therapeutic times, morality was understood to be built into the law. For example the criminal law was a floor on acceptable conduct in society, and all were presumed to know that law because we all were presumed to have it "written on the heart," found in God-imbued conscience. And thus it was authoritative. The natural law is an expression of love, because it is a system of minimal interdicts against transgression, given us by God to allow us to live together in peace. Increasingly, however, positivist law is imposed upon us. All law is coercive, by definition, and so positive law is purely an exercise of coercive power by the collective. It does not lack power, in our collective systems, but it lacks *authority*, properly understood.

Because therapeutic ideology eschews an objective moral code, all law and all social norms can be considered positivist, and we begin to lose track of the distinction between natural law and positive law. All law is taken to be an expression of collective power. That

9 See, *The Mountain and the River*, chapter 12.

means the law is made up by collectivist power concentrations and we're all expected to live by it. Like the law, social norms are a positivist form of interdict. Social norms are no longer interrogated for the source of their authority. In the therapeutic culture, society, not natural law, is expected to form bases of social approval and disapproval, and those not according to morality, but according to the collective's prescriptions for therapeutic mental wellness.

There are thus two sources of interdict. One is the objective, eternal, conscience-imbued moral interdicts which the sacred order underwrites, in cultures that acknowledge a sacred order. Another is the system of social norms we arrive at as a matter of social negotiation. Augusto Del Noce distinguished these as "tradition" and "traditionalism." The social rules not rooted in sacred order are interdicts that come into being through postmodern process philosophies, the through-line of which is that the personal is political. In postmodern thinking, everything is political, including cultural developments, which is why we live in unceasing *kulturkampf*. Erasure of the distinction between private and political enables not only the therapeutic worldview, but the reflexive radicalism that accompanies it.

Interdicts in the current culture include the normalization of sexual deviance, in direct contravention to the interdicts based on sacred order. It would be correct to put licentiousness down to "expressive" or "untrammelled" individualism if the only source of interdicts were moral, backed by sacred order. But the other kind of interdicts, those imposed socially by the push-and-pull of Narrative, are not individualistic. Quite to the contrary, they are formed by society, and a person who treats them as solely authoritative is perforce radically conformist. Society, for him, has replaced God. Society on this thinking collectively dictates what we think and how we behave, and psychological man willingly conforms. That's totalitarianism, not individualism. Individuality is crucial to living in freedom. A slide into collectivism, as with our creeping economic socialism and the redefinition of "democracy," means a slide into lawlessness, meaninglessness, anomie, emotional instability, and, ironically enough, isolation. This slide is ineluctably intertwined with the rise of the therapeutic.

We have been using Philip Rieff's linguistic dichotomies of interdict vs. remission, and renunciation vs. release. Similar attempts to portray these pervasive dualities exist in ancient philosophy, and more recently in René Guénon's quality and quantity; in Friedrich Schiller's form impulse and sensuous impulse, and in Iain McGilchrist's thesis of master and emissary brain hemispheres. Or mountain and river, as in this author's work adopting this duality in the title.[10] In the second verse of Genesis the duality is expressed in the spirit of God in contrast to formless void. The impulses represented by these dichotomies are in opposition, which means there is a continuous tension between them. This suggests the possibility that one might overrun the other. The interdictory impulse might lead to a cultural rigidity so controlling as to become authoritarian. The remissive impulse is to remove interdicts so that we are free to feel and be whatever we wish. Unchecked this leads to a lack of self-discipline, a thinning of boundaries on conduct, an inability to plan for tomorrow, and vulnerability to totalitarian ideological control.

This matters because we can recognize in it also the ongoing tension between love and power, as the touchstones for human motivation. There is always and ever a desire for political power. The remissive impulse is not itself authoritarian, by definition, but has that effect by opening itself to interdicts from those who acquire power through our (remissive) lack of vigilance against it. Inattention can thus lead to authoritarianism through the back door, so to speak.

But also through the front door, if we learn from what is going

---

10 *The Mountain and the River/Genesis, Postmodernism, and the Machine*, (New English Review Press, 2023).

on in prosperous Western democracies now. The remissive impulse means pushing for constraint and control against others—those who have the temerity to impose or maintain interdicts. The result is to place all in the political realm, both the interdictory and the remissive, reinforcing power in the corporatist machine that super-intends the social conflict. Government and allied private power centers stand in for parental authority, holding back the squabbling children.

It would be tempting to equate the interdictory impulse with the political right, and the remissive with the political left. But it's necessary to broaden the discussion. There's no old-school political left/right spectrum anymore. Political disagreements are no longer limited to public vs. private perspectives on resources. Instead the chief divide is anthropological: what is a human being? One who is guided by rational perception of universal values? Or one driven from within by the inner id, haunting a palimpsest landscape of subtraction and erasure, of a glory that once was?

Coercion by Narrative

What are the highest moral standards in society now? Not honesty, selflessness, humility, service, or gratitude, the opposites of psychological man's character traits. Those would be moral aspira-tions of an individual aspiring, alone within the conscience, to ob-jective virtue. Not aspirations of psychological man. The therapeu-tic mentality means emotional well-being is the highest goal, and what serves that goal is acceptance socially, above all else. As we've seen, however, there can be no mutual acceptance between the worl-dviews of transcendence and the therapeutic. So there is unending enmity between the two camps.

The way through for psychological man is to bring all into con-formity to his vision. His ultimate value is communitarianism, to be experienced as an oceanic feeling of community. It is an inversion of the religious impulse, re-directing it from the vertical to the horizontal; to humanity itself. This value is served, in turn, by open borders, metaphorically and literally. Therefore the ultimate virtue is acceptance; the ultimate sin is bigotry. Social virtues, that is, rather than personal ones.

The therapeutic worldview therefore tends to coincide with a socialist worldview. Material wealth is important to psychological man, but not as important as the desire for oneness with one's fellows. Religion is out, in the therapeutic worldview, but not the religious impulse. The religious impulse becomes manifested in communitarianism, the utopian warm bath of fellow-feeling; of ecstatic community. Inequality interferes with that emotion-based vision. Because the therapeutic is based in emotion more than rationality, failures of political socialism—always and everywhere—fail to resonate. Next time will be different. Human nature must bend to psychological man's priority of emotional fellow-feeling.

The implications of the therapeutic mindset for traditional liberalism should be obvious. No longer is there to be a balance between individual freedom vis-à-vis social power centers like government and monopolistic institutions of commerce and information and technology. That balancing would require ongoing political tension that does not serve the therapeutic mindset. Instead the power must be imagined relinquished in favor of a consensus of self-care standards. Power centers are to wither away in the resulting socialism much like the state was imagined to wither away under communism, in classical Marxism.

What are the effects? What are we living through now? There is a growing sense of confinement and restraint, imposed socially first and legally next. It's about control, and it has a machine-like inexorable feel. The pace of control we intuit is accelerating. The version of socialism we devolve to as a result of abandonment of the transcendence worldview (and rise of the therapeutic) means that deference to social norms has itself become a social norm. This is the basis for social credit scoring. We no longer question the malleability of social norms—why yesterday's norm is not today's. Indeed, this is a purposed goal in modern totalitarian surveillance states, like China is now and like the prosperous Western societies are rapidly becoming.[11] We learn to cease questioning why society's say-so makes something "normal" as we accept the inevitability of its value fluidity. Positivism vanquishes rationalism and the instinct of moral order in the cosmos. We don't pause to consider that all manipulation of Narrative is just a form of lying.

What makes a person "dysfunctional" is psychological limitation, a falling out from social norms. The word "dysfunctional," like the word "disorder," further reinforces the idea that people are machine-like. We operate like we're supposed to, but if we break down we need to go into the shop for therapeutic repair. And the criteria for repair; that is, what we're to be repaired-to, is the set of attitudes and behaviors that society decrees. The machine self-conception feeds the therapeutic, and vice versa. To the extent we adopt the therapeutic approach to well-being, we compromise individual selfhood, willingly placing our moral sense in service to society, a larger machine of which the individual machine is but a part. This entails throwing over the competing vision of selfhood as governed by natural moral law.

Social norms may, for a time, coincide with those previously established by the religious worldview, but that changes. As we've seen in the last century, social mores evolve away from unchanging standards toward positivist social norms[12] which by their nature mutate over time; sometimes quite rapidly. Ask the survivors in Eastern Europe of both the Nazis and Stalinists. Or observe the overnight sexual revolution of the twentieth century. It's not just that society has adopted positivist social norms; it's that adherence to social

---

11 See, N.S. Lyons, "The China Convergence," *The Upheaval* (Substack), August 3, 2023.

12 Social norms developed through Narrative, the social conversation, without being backed by authority higher than society itself.

norms is itself a new norm. The transition from vertical values to horizontal is thereby accelerated.

Another consequence of the therapeutic vision and its accompanying machine self-conception is that we regard the self as primarily good except as corrupted by society, rather than the reverse: our inclination to evil except as reinforced to the good. What is good is deemed governed not by conscience informed by unchanging objective value, but rather by therapeutic transmission of social norms. Those norms are malleable in response to political and cultural influences. The driver for those influences is power, but power exercised (in this instance) to advance therapeutic well-being. Humanitarian impulse is thus co-opted into service of what amounts to totalitarianism.

The implications of the therapeutic mindset for traditional liberalism should be obvious. No longer is there to be a balance between individual freedom vis-à-vis social power centers like government and monopolistic institutions of commerce and information and technology. Such balancing would require ongoing political tension by which political power is constrained. This does not serve the therapeutic mindset. Instead the power must be relinquished in favor of a consensus of self-care standards. And this means bullying to conform.

5
VICTIMHOOD

Religious Impulse

How does the therapeutic mindset lead to bullying others to conform? It happens through the cult of victimhood. The strange but factual existence of this cult is puzzling to those outside the therapeutic mindset. Much is said and written about it, but most is descriptive rather than explanatory, such being the limitation of speaking from inside one worldview, about another. Let's attempt to understand and explain the *experience* of felt victimhood as best we can from the logos perspective. That felt sense of victimhood doesn't build on a logical progression, so we must approach it from different angles until the whole emerges.

As we will see in the historical rise of the therapeutic (chapter 8) Christianity has had a profound impact on the way people think of victims and victimization. In the postmodern, post-Christian era the supernatural elements of Christianity have been abandoned by most, but the concern for victims remains. In fact it is the one Christian virtue that is valorized ahead of all others. With regard to concern for victims and victimization, psychological man wants to out-Christian Christians.

Why, though? Religion is a "place" of mystery wedded to dogma, and though pertaining to Spirit, must be parsed in rational theology and in creeds, liturgical practice, community, and a striving for understanding the whole of a person. When the dogma of interdictory creeds is removed along with external trappings of religious practice, what's left is mystery, and a felt pull toward it, that we call religious impulse. The religious impulse persists in psychological man in a confused way because he draws also on other impulses easily confused with or overlapping the religious, especially the desire for community, and acceptance, and psychological well-being, and commitment to a socially-reinforced structure of right and wrong. The religious impulse drives deference by psychological man to certain elements of religion even as he dismisses its creeds. Charisma still draws him even if he regards organized religion a man-made bastion of hidebound superstition.

Because the lingering religious impulse may not be recognized as such, by psychological man, the origin of his sympathy for victims is likely taken as an unexamined and axiomatic first principle. But if so, why? The articulable principles of the therapeutic worldview, such as they are, provide no real answer. We must go deeper into the mystery of the religious impulse, beginning at the beginning.

"In the beginning, God created the heavens and the earth." The primordial division of this-not-that is creative, yet in creating, it destroys. Oppositional conflict in material things, and ideas, and supernatural presence whereby Nothing becomes something requires the collisions that destroy potential to create actual. All of reality is the result of these cascading and intersecting collisions of this-not-that, beginning with emergence of the first Idea from the soup of potentiality.

We can understand the result of oppositional binary conflict in terms of sacrifice, beginning with formless potentiality sacrificed to the actual and formed. The differentiations proceed: heaven/earth; ideal/physical; virtue/vice; and on it goes, the ever-unfolding differ-

entiation that sacrifices potential, the not-yet-defined arena of possibility, in favor of actual.[1] The religious impulse to structure and
form, the mountain rather than the river, comes always at the expense of impulses to unwinding and dissolution, to a sub-rational
pool of aesthetics and intuition into which creativity is again possible. Each movement is a sacrifice of the other: actual for potential;
potential for actual. There is building and unbuilding, the unbuilding a sacrifice of actual for potential and so a new cycle can begin.
The impulse to deconstruction is also the impulse to creativity and
renewal.

Sacrifice is at the heart of religion. It is most clearly visible, in
the Judeo-Christian tradition, in the Abraham/Isaac story of substituted sacrifice, and in the crucifixion, but also in the herem[2] of the
Flood, and Jericho, and against the Canaanites. Sacrifice means victims. We may perceive ourselves to be victims, at various stages in
the ceaseless drama of sacrifice and renewal of Creation. Sacrifice,
and its attendant victims, are of the essence in renewal of creative
life, as with the death and resurrection of the Christ, and like in every application of justice (herem, conflict, opposition, revolution)
to produce something new, shaking off the old, the desiccated, the
useless, and the condemned, in favor of an anticipated glorious new
dawn. We sacrifice as a matter of course and by unexamined instinct, such as by saving money, disciplining children, and by holding
emotion in check when it would not serve higher moral principle.
All of our lives are circumscribed by sacrifice, and sacrifice means
victims. Sacrifice and victimhood are at the heart of religion and of

---

1 On this analysis we can think of the oppositional tension between the pagan and the
Christian worlds. The pagan a centering of "primacy of possibility," in Philip Rieff's
terminology, giving way to the Christian actuality of God transcendent and immanent.
This is abstract but relevant because as the Christian world elides into the postmodern,
we witness a reversion to pagan possibility—an arena of creativity, perhaps, but also
one of dissipation and dissolution. See discussion of three "worlds" in Rieff's *My Life
Among the Deathworks/Illustrations of the Aesthetics of Authority*, (Charlottesville,
VA: University of Virginia Press, 2006).

2 Or "cherem," or "kherem," in English pronunciation; a holocaust, or all-out destructive war to eradicate a people group.

the religious impulse.

The archetype of all sacrifice is that of the innocent victim who is yet powerful enough to turn that sacrifice into salvation: the Christ. Willing sacrifice for a better tomorrow requires victimhood: every sacrifice is sacrifice of a victim. This religiously-informed impulse to sacrifice, and therefore to victimhood, means self as self-sacrificing victim. Psychological man does not abandon this religious impulse to sacrifice and to concern for victims in the sacrificing. Quite to the contrary, he valorizes victimhood, and in his therapeutic fervor, valorizes it most strongly in himself.

Identification

In his victimhood, psychological man also "identifies" with the victimization of others. This is an element of his intersubjectivity; his desire for acceptance and melding into the communitarian collective, but it is also an element of the religious impulse, in which a central concern is for the victim. The victim is oppressed in his victimhood. Affirming the victim status of the oppressed is also affirmation of the oppression paradigm. And affirming the victim status is thought to require denouncing or rejecting or "canceling" those who don't accede to the oppression/victimhood paradigm of postmodern ideology. Affirming another's victimhood amounts to subjectively valorizing it: placing oneself in "allyship" with the ostensible victim class. One "identifies" with victims not just in the sense of sympathizing with the putative victim's plight, but in the sense of feeling with the victim the pain of their victimhood. This means, for psychological man, emphasizing his own victimhood. The need is strong. If he's not actually a victim, he will create his own sense of victimhood from whatever materials are at hand.

Postmodernism consists in horizontal process philosophies that attempt to generate meaning for human existence, upon the putative death of God, from the temporality of Hegelian historicism. Though the postmodernist is dismissive of old-time religion and the God it represents, he nonetheless has not converted entirely to dogmatic and sterile materialist atheism because the religious impulse remains, and because materialism does not explain the metaphysics obvious to all. The atheist lives with as much mystery as the theist. There is more to us than matter in motion. The religious impulse remains after we think we've eradicated religion.

The postmodern thought to which we are now heir, if we're not vigilant, attempts to displace religion, so it sublimates religious themes like mystery and sacrifice and communitarianism and worship of something greater than ourselves. Included prominently in postmodern thought is ongoing concern for victims, and this includes the impulse to overthrow victimhood itself. The concern for victims and against victimhood in the abstract is stronger than ever now that the salvific effect of Christ's sacrifice is mostly ignored in the prosperous post-Christian West. In the postmodern imagination we're back to the pagan world of power and fate, the primacies of possibility, but with the Christian promise still haunting us. The concern for victims and victimhood includes especially strongly the concern for self-as-victim, amenable upon the demise of Christianity to psychological self-care for its mitigation.

Counting oneself a victim is reflexive in the therapeutic mindset. Even a person who fits no political presumptive victim category, like a white heterosexual male, may "identify" as a victim by demonstrating allyship; by activism for ostensible victim groups. Or, by casting about for some personal basis for victimhood: an unhappy childhood; coercive religious practice; unfair employment treatment; or a nonspecific felt sense of oppression at the hands of "fascist" elements of society. A person given over to the entire subjectivity of psychological man is likely to feel especially aggrieved by presumptive oppression, further inducing him to self-identification as victim or ongoing stance of allyship with victims. Even aside from personal identification with victims, there is identification with political stances against putative victimhood in the abstract.

Agency

Once upon a time, society's deference to universal principle created a sense of community, because that universality of values meant they applied the same to everyone. We held moral points of reference in common even in disagreement about their application to specifics, mutual tolerance being among the shared values. That feeling of community has rapidly dissipated with the rise of the therapeutic because the universality of the logos was abandoned upon the turn inward to psychology. The unifying effect of the universality of virtue and vice is lost, in the postmodern dispensation, and its replacement becomes collectivist Narrative. Mutual tolerance is not a feature of this way of thinking. Instead the expectation is that a sense of community must arise from consensus. The consensus takes the form of allegiance to social Narrative. Narrative comprises a common story-line, the story of ourselves. Because it displaces virtue (including the virtue of tolerance) as primary guiding principle, it attempts community by coercion and bullying of would-be dissenters. This creates a community, of sorts, but certainly not a pluralist one. We can feel wholeheartedly a part of the common weal only by accepting the ideological metanarrative that the "consensus" Narrative produces, and by excluding those who cling to objectivity and immutability of truth and morality.

The shift from morality to the therapeutic therefore necessarily entails a ceding of individual agency to the collective. The collectivist tendency to cede personal agency isn't just a switch in perspective or adoption of another point of view. It's not throwing one's lot in with one political party over another. To do that requires agency. To say a person cedes agency is to say he no longer himself makes the decision to align with principle. He decides on a particular social vision, and his agency ends there. Society then decides for him in the form of approved Narrative, and he rates himself a "good" person by his Narrative-supporting collectivist bona fides. His last act of agency was to assign it to society.

Now where does this leave him? Put yourself in his shoes. He has invested his soul in the movements of society, and so also its Leftist vision of God-indifference, historicist telos, dialectical process, and a centering of psychological well-being. This is the flow of ideas and of feelings he's given himself over to. Anyone outside that flow, meaning anyone who retains moral agency and allegiance to moral realism, is necessarily a mortal enemy; a barbarian outside the gate. Psychological man is without defense against these barbarians. His society, of which he is now ineluctably a part, must bar them at the gates and pour boiling oil on their heads.

We considered agency several times already, but its significance cannot be emphasized enough if we are to understand the victimhood element of the therapeutic. It is conscious volition. If a person gives up his agency in some arena like the political and moral and religious, he is like the one who casts out an unclean spirit without then being filled by God:

> When the unclean spirit has gone out of a person, it passes through waterless places seeking rest, but finds none. Then it says, 'I will return to my house from which I came.' And when it comes, it finds the house empty, swept, and put in order. Then it goes and brings with it seven other spirits more evil than itself, and they enter and dwell there, and the last state of that person is worse than the first. So also will it be with this evil generation.[3]

Now consider what this means to victimhood for the individual, naked and alone, without recourse because he's given it up, dependent on society for succor. Society invariably disappoints, because it's really only a battleground, tumultuous and harsh, forming

---

3 Matthew 12:43-45.

and re-forming direction on the basis of power struggles fraudulently articulated in terms of morality. The individual puts all his hopes in the collective wisdom of society because his intuition of intersubjective consciousness tells him this is not just the social element of his being, it is who and what he is in totality. Hence "totalitarianism," as we will see in chapter 14.

The resulting wounds are self-inflicted but are perceived as further victimhood at the hand of oppressive barbarians at the gate, who in their wildness are unwilling to come into the gates unarmed, so as to bask in acceptance of flesh-and-blood community rather than remain with their gods of bloodless abstraction like universality of truth and morality. Most fearsome are those hoary deep-mystery Christians of yesteryear, out there in the darkness and rain, in their dripping raiment of animal skins.

Status

In the postmodern age, victimhood confers status, and where victimhood cannot plausibly be claimed, victim "allyship" is substituted. Let's consider the valorization of victimhood in light of René Girard's analysis of it, for example in his *I Saw Satan Fall Like Lightning*.[4] Scott Alexander summarizes from a non-religious standpoint Girard's main point about mimesis in understanding the substitutionary atonement of the Christ and the falling away of Christianity:

> This is kind of how Girard thinks about Christianity. The Son of God brought from Heaven to Earth a single Word of the ineffable Divine speech, and that word was "VICTIM". At first it was whispered only by a few disciples, so softly it could barely be heard at all. But as missionaries spread the faith, the word grew louder and louder until it became a roar, drowning out all merely-human metaphysics / psychology / ethics.

4 Maryknoll, NY: Orbis, 2001.

> At some point it no longer needed the Church as a carrier vehicle. Like Oedipus, it killed its parent. The Church, it might seem, is not maximally designed to help victims. It has all these extraneous pieces, like prayers and cathedrals and Popes. And isn't prayer offensive when we should be engaging in direct revolutionary action to free the oppressed? Aren't cathedrals [] a gaudy celebration of wealth, when that money should be used to feed the poor. Doesn't a celibate clergy create conditions rife for child sexual abuse? As the single divine Word grew louder and louder, Christianity started to seem morally indefensible, and began to wither away like the pagan faiths it supplanted.[5]

We should pause a moment before throwing another clod in the grave of Christianity, however. Throughout all of history until the day before yesterday, no one cared much about how the structure of society might oppress or victimize individuals, because stratification of worth among people groups seemed the natural order of things. But then along came Christianity with its concern for the poor, and over time this conviction that all people are equal before God morphed into the idea that all people are equal in intrinsic worth and dignity, and that morphed into the idea that all people are equal—period. The natural progression of thought then proceeds a step too far: to conclude that if people manifest differences in, for example, intelligence, diligence, affability, or good looks, that can only be the result of social structures that create the inequality.

Enter Marx. Militant atheism was a cornerstone of his whole system of belief, but so also was the Christian-enculturated idea that victimization and oppression should be eliminated where possible. These elements persisted in later permutations of Marx but also in postmodernism more generally. Even if you don't understand Marxism or the continuation of its transgressive instinct in other variants of postmodernism, you can still see the problem with making vic-

---

5 *Astral Codex Ten* (Substack), "Book Review: *I See Satan Fall Like Lightning*," November 17, 2023.

timization the greatest of concerns. The desire for equality, and hence against oppression and victimization, exceeds the boundary of reality, and like a river that over-runs its bank, brings destruction. The ineradicable fact of actual innate human inequality by every conceivable measure is a hard limit to achieving neo-Marxist ideals of equality.

We try anyway. The underlying assumption is that if we eliminate oppression, we eliminate victims, and if we eliminate victims, we achieve full equality. Hence the oppressor/oppressed paradigm and sensitivity to victimhood. Now this seems superficially unobjectionable, because no one would say victimization is a good thing, or that eliminating it is bad. The problem is that victimhood is thought to correspond to inequality. Because actual inequality is ineradicable, so is the new conception of victimhood. This may be perversely desired by transgressives because it self-validates the premise of systemic oppression. We know there are victims because there is systemic oppression; we know there is systemic oppression because there are victims.

Now with that hyper-concern for victims in mind, we can return to Girard and his idea of mimetic desire. Of the hundred toys in the playroom, you want the one toy the other kid is already playing with. It has value to you because *he* values it. This is the psychological dynamic addressed by the tenth of the Ten Commandments: "you shall not covet . . . anything that belongs to your neighbor." Girard called it "mimetic desire," and regarded it as a fundamental motivator of human beings.

More than that, mimetic desire feeds an escalating cycle of social tension, that may be relieved in scapegoating an innocent victim. Not a person who is innocent altogether, necessarily, but innocent of the immediate occasion for scapegoating. Maybe his only crime is being awkward and dorky in gym class. But he's "guilty" of something because we all are, and so all of us are potentially the scapegoat. Because none but Christ is wholly righteous, in better moments we see the pattern of injustice in dumping societal tensions onto an innocent victim.

Christ's sacrifice at the hands of the mob was the sacrifice to end the cycle of scandalous mimetic desire, because He was not another hapless Barnabas, but God the Son, and so bore "the sins of the world" away with His sacrifice. There's more to this foundation of Christianity, of course, but this much relates the significance of mimetic desire, and how it becomes a "social contagion" until relieved in violence, even violence against a mere scapegoat. If Girard's analysis is accurate, it means people can and do act irrationally on the basis of the irrational actions of others, and this can spread among a people group like a virus.

Sin to Syndrome

The therapeutic worldview entails a shift from morality to psychology; from sin to syndrome. What does that mean for our sense of identity? It goes a long way toward eliminating guilt for ways of being we'd prefer not to measure on a scale of ultimate right and wrong. It's easy to fail to count the cost of this shift. It means there is no moral guilt, but diagnosis of psychological disorder takes its place. The cost is a sense of helplessness, and therefore victimhood, because we are in the grip of psychological disorder. Or if not presently disordered, our frailty requires vigilance against external threats that might create it, reinforcing the therapeutic mentality even among those not yet "diagnosed."

The moral paradigm preserves your agency (and therefore your dignity). If you fail, you can do something about it. It's not you, it's the conduct. Go and sin no more. But if you have a psychological disorder, it *is* you, and you're marked thereafter as vulnerable to relapse into the symptoms of disorder, helpless against each buffeting tide. Such agency as you have is spent in erecting walls against challenges to the boundaries of the disorder. That means also erecting walls against challenges to the entire disorder worldview. You're not just protecting yourself against triggers of your specific disorder. You're protecting yourself against re-substitution of the morality paradigm for that of the therapeutic. In your specific disorder(s) and your therapeutic outlook, you walk through the world vulnerable and afraid, always in a state of presumptive victimhood.

Whatever bad thing you're undergoing is caused by diagnosed or undiagnosed psychological "dysfunction," which means it's not your fault, but neither can you do anything about it. If you drink too much you may decide it's a form of self-medication against some other psychological issue—perhaps you put it down to trauma or abuse or neglect or whatever else your therapist iatrogenically foists upon you. You don't feel the responsibility to do something about it because you can't help it. You're a victim.

The subjective feeling of helplessness incapacitates the individual, and it is contagious, spreading through society as ideological virus; a collective mental illness.[6] Things we would have considered "sin" in an earlier day are now considered psychological disorders, because the problem is thought to no longer be sin, but *consciousness of* sin, for those who see the world through the lens of their emotional well-being. The problem is not your bad behavior, it's your disorder, and so feelings of guilt are just misguided. Sin is an outmoded concept because you *choose* to sin, and you don't choose your disorder. Religion itself is indicted by this shift: religion is seen to produce consciousness of sin that is unnecessary and debilitating, and worse, obscures disorder that needs attention. The therapeutic worldview doesn't just compete with the religious, therefore. The worldviews as worldviews are actively hostile to each other.

If you think people in general have gone crazy during the last

---

6 A good summary of the particular maladies that derange people collectively is "The Cluster B Society," at *City Journal*, September, 2023. It's inescapable that one's mental health is profoundly affected by the ideas prevalent in the surrounding society. Poor mental health can be a matter of social contagion.

several years, you're right. They have. Some of us do ok and some barely have their heads above water, but uncountable millions wallow in mass delusion about what a human being is. Social contagion of what should count as mental illness is not unprecedented in the history of the world. In fact the postmodern era provides conclusive proofs of it. What is unprecedented is the shift from an objective foundation for truth, to a shifting flow of irrational emotion. It is a worldview shift, across society, and as we have noted in discussing "worldview," that means we can lose sight of objectivity of truth and of values altogether, adrift now in the ceaseless flow, with no land in sight.

Inequality

We can go behind victimhood status to find the aversion to inequality that seems to generate it. And we can go behind the aversion to inequality to find the self-care desire for social acceptance that prompts it.

The unavoidable reality of the world is inequality. There is significant variation in the physical, moral, and intellectual capabilities of people. More variation than we tend to appreciate. Consider intellectual prowess necessary to function in the working world independently. If we measure the statistical variation from mean in intellectual ability, we will find that a significant portion of the population is not really capable of working at an ability level that, quantized in money, would even feed themselves. At the other end of the scale is brilliance making profound contributions to the human condition but with remuneration nowhere near commensurate to that contribution. And even such wealth as is accumulated, at that end of the competence scale, is typically plowed back into social benefit through investment and charity.

The point is that people are unequal ontologically, *ab initio*, from the ground up. They are unequal in strength, stamina, intellect,

compassion, and perseverance; and in abilities to learn, to commu-
nicate, to address details, to scale conceptually, to be dependable, to
take care of their own affairs, to demonstrate general competence.
The variation in human competence is greater than we tend to think
because we settle out in normal life pathways among people in a
similar social hierarchy. The sharecropper doesn't know the finance
bro's world. Nor vice versa. The differences in people will necessarily manifest in social hierarchies. This is inevitable.

And yet we value equality as an ideal and as a social goal. What
do we mean by equality? Individuals differ in ability, but above them
all there is an unchanging set of values, applicable *equally* to all, in
Western democracies. This is what is meant when we say we are
equal before the law though we are manifestly not equal in the sense
of being the same on any measure of human ability. Those values
above are ideals; they *transcend* our quotidian transactions. We look
up to those common ideals; this is what is alluded to when referring
to them as "vertical." This is a foundational understanding within
the worldview of transcendence. Equality is among the transcendent values applicable to all, but it doesn't mean we're all the same.
It means only that we have the same human dignity, and that the
ideals apply equally to each of us.

This is troubling to some people. In part it is troubling because
of abuses: exploitation or oppression by the powerful, in transgression of the principle of equal application of transcendent ideals.
What should be the response? One would be affirmation of the
ideals, to the shame of transgressors. This is how chattel slavery was
overcome in the West, for one example. This would be the effect of
interdicts like standards of honesty and charity and avoidance of
covetousness. It would mean renunciation of impulses to exploit
one's advantages in ways that exploit another's disadvantages.

But another response is applied from time to time in history:
critique of the social structures that inevitably result from the fact
of innate inequality of human beings. This takes the form of at-

tempts to dismantle social hierarchies and spread individual burdens across society. These are movements like that which culminated in the French Revolution, and progressive taxation, and redistribution-ist programs, and social welfare initiatives. It is the impulse behind the variants of Marxism. These are moves toward socialism. Social-ism is a response to dissatisfaction with the reality of inequalities among people. It manifests a desire to mitigate inequalities by level-ling social engineering. A premise is that we do not achieve commu-nity so long as there are oppressors and oppressed; so long as some are victims of others. Inequality of any kind necessarily means vic-timhood, on this view. And the existence of victims is understood to mean the absence of cherished community.

The therapeutic worldview hastens the move to socialism be-cause psychological man identifies with victims, and that identifica-tion means more than simply expressing solidarity. Psychological man conceives himself as a victim in actuality, because of the con-tinuing oppression of the logos worldview, interfering with the vi-sion of utopian community. Transcendence, objectivity, and univer-sality together are taken as an oppressive leaden anchor to the world, fixing us immobile so that we can never achieve the golden shores of equality and acceptance. This anchor consists of antiquated be-lief in fixed categories, values, hierarchies. Inequality always and ever pushing out equality, the prerequisite to communal mankind.

In the therapeutic worldview, the victimization happens at the hand of God, because He made us this way. It is always about God, even in rejecting Him.

Ressentiment

Why does the victimhood mentality correspond to radical po-litical and cultural views? If you believe that minorities are system-atically oppressed, and you place yourself in (or "ally" with) one or more of the many minority classes, you are a victim, and that minority victim mentality is a key element of your Identity. Erasing the victimization feels like erasing the self. You feel like a victim because the belief in systemic oppression requires it. Systemic oppression creates victims; victimization forms identity; identity relies on systemic oppression. Circular reasoning from which there is no escape.

What is the source of systemic oppression? It will invariably be presented as some combination of racism, sexism, sex-category-based bigotry, colonialism, parochialism, ableism, religious exclusion, moralistic judgment, classism, elitism, and so on. Perhaps some or all of these are lumped together in a catch-all phrase like "capitalism" or "fascism." This non-exclusive list consists of ways a person can feel (or be made to feel) less-than in some way. It is understood as an oppressive system postmodern ideology seeks to overcome. It is the essence of deconstructive thinking, neo-Marxist "social critique," ongoing re-examination of why people are so different and so stubbornly unequal no matter what socialist efforts are undertaken to collapse the bases on which one person can be made to feel less worthy than another.

The feeling will not go away so long as there is inequality, but there always will be inequality. One way through, without ongoing resentment, is recognition that there is something greater and eternal outside ourselves, to which we can aspire, and for which we are not dependent on other people—something that transcends our petty differences. If we can draw near to God regardless of the station we find ourselves in, fairly or unfairly, and this-world differences are not all of our experience, then there is no reason to grind the teeth at feeling reduced in comparison to another through no fault of our own.

On the other hand, if this is all there is; if there is no life beyond this present moment, and the only minutes I get on this planet require me to live in subjugation by virtue of my group in contrast to other groups that deem themselves superior just by virtue of race or wealth or whatever—well then I may feel justified in raging

against the machine. The machine is not merely the increasing automation of society (a subject to which we return in later chapters) but
what we may come to perceive as systematic normalization of superior and inferior status among people groups. There being no source
of righteousness in pursuing (non-existent) objective virtues, one
can nonetheless feel righteous in ongoing effort to dismantle systems of oppression.

What drives all this is feeling: resentment at being cast into an
inferior status, and solidarity with others similarly oppressed. That
resentment is not merely protest of unequal treatment. It is a deeper identification. The buzz of resentment at perceived oppression
informs the inner Identity. The radicalized individual doesn't decide
on this Identity, nor negotiate it socially. Instead he discovers it as
the true self within. His Identity is formed and sustained in the
posture of negation and transgression against the vertical, objective,
and meritocratic value system of transcendence. Preserving Identity
is not a preference, for him; it is a matter of his very survival. Identity must be preserved, so resentment must be preserved, so the
sense of oppression must be preserved, so the ongoing continuous
posture of negation and transgression must be preserved, and so
the social turmoil that results must be a permanent state of affairs.

In Nietzschean terms, this is "ressentiment," a feeling of hostility against the oppressive structures which justify transgression
against the value system of transcendence believed to support it.
This creates a "morality" of indignation against the oppressive system, in place of the moral realism of objective and universal virtue/
vice. This replacement value system justifies the person in their
ressentiment and reinforces them in an ongoing state of negation
and transgression. In this way they can set aside self-responsibility
for their failures, and avoid moral fault for it. To sustain the self-justifying ressentiment, one must participate in the ongoing "progressivist" push, regardless where it goes. This is not the construction of
a new utopian vision. It is only resistance to the world as it is. The

fault is not in me, it is in the created world. It's God's fault.

This is unavoidably a consequence of the profound shift from moral realism, in which we think of ourselves as moral agents responsible for our acts and omissions, to supposing that everything we do is passively, amorally, reactive, and so we're not morally responsible for any of it. On this thinking it may seem to make sense to relax on the therapist's couch and have all the trespasses of others totted up to explain our feelings of inadequacy or anxiety or depression and then to harbor righteous indignation because our own failings were the cause of circumstances we did not choose.

6

CHARISMA

Charism and Transgression

In this section we use the word "charisma" in place of religion, to emphasize that it is a combination of both interdict and release, in balance, and arises from a religious impulse held in common among all people, including those in thrall to the cult of the therapeutic worldview. Charisma includes the creeds of religion derived from revelation, but it also includes mystery and intuitive attraction. The phrase is borrowed from Philip Rieff, and from his book by that name, *Charisma*.[1]

"Charisma" as used by Rieff doesn't mean personal magnetism. It means an otherwise difficult-to-define sense of deep mystery that attends openness to the divine. You might use "religious impulse" instead, so long as you attribute the phrase to something ominous and real, more real than that which is tangible; a reference to the ground of all being, roughly described in phrases like Tao,[2] Brahmin, and Almighty God, Maker of heaven and earth. David Bakan, in *The Duality of Human Existence*,[3] relevantly approved Sigmund Freud's conception of the unconscious *id* as a hedge against

---

1 Rieff, Philip, *Charisma*, (New York: Vintage, 2008).
2 C.S. Lewis' word for the ground of all being in his *The Abolition of Man*, 1943.
3 Bakan, David, *The Duality of Human Experience*, (Boston: Beacon, 1966).

the idolatry of pat dogmas in place of mystery: "One must always be filled with the sense of that which is not yet realized."[4] Ultimate concerns of religion, then, can be a subjective and psychological matter, rather than merely creedal theology.[5]

Religion provided a kind of mediation of opposing impulses. On one hand, the impulse to restraint and discipline and rule-making and rule-following, the impulse described as "interdictory," requiring "renunciation" of the transgressive impulses. On the other hand, the impulse for release or remission, an emotive desire for freedom from external restraint. Rieff's "charisma" encompasses both, in proper balance, a way of describing in non-doctrinal terms the entirety of the religious impulse.

A couple of key quotes from *Charisma* will summarize Rieff's concern. First, "The therapeutic is that terrible beast who has been slouching toward Bethlehem,"[6] referring to Yeats' poem *Second Coming*. The "terrible beast" phrasing gets interpreted and re-interpreted all the time. One interpretation might be anti-Christ. As the therapeutic impulse infects our culture, it replaces the faith impulse, and in this way can be understood as the destructive, rotting worm of our society. Second, "the therapeutic is the ideal anti-type and real successor of the charismatic."[7] The therapeutic is not just what comes after the worldview of faith, in other words: It is in binary opposition to it and entirely supplants it. The charismatic must be creedal, and as such introduces new "interdicts" in our lives. Instead of "interdicts," we might think of forms, boundaries, restrictions, scaffolding, constraints, and like terms. By contrast the therapeutic, Reiff writes, is "a releaser of the interdicts, a transgressive figure." It doesn't construct, it deconstructs.

Perception of charisma also means perception of guilt, our

---

4 Ibid., p. 7.
5 See also, Foster, Charles, *Being A Human*, (New York: Metropolitan, 2021), p. 126.
6 *Charisma*, p. 3.
7 Ibid., p. 5.

conscious awareness of sin. And that leads to what Reiff called a need for "renunciation." So we have a renunciatory instinct against the evil we produce. That results in creeds. Creeds are systems of interdicts; moral rules necessitated by consciousness of sin and the renunciatory instinct. You can think of the Apostles' Creed or the Ten Commandments as examples. Creeds are language descriptions of the moral structure, or forms, or systems of constraint on which a society is built. They are intended to codify the moral structure extant in the cosmos.

Failing to perceive charisma, or outright rejection of it, means rejection of guilt and the creeds and interdicts it produces. What takes its place is the therapeutic mindset. Sin is not the problem in that mindset; guilt is. Management of guilt in the inner psyche is the therapeutic project, not management of the sin. The therapeutic amounts to rejection of an ontology of mankind with endemic sin: reality imagined without the Fall.

The mindset is "therapeutic" because it means psychological self-care, which is required to protect the true self from the corrupting sense of sin. It's not sin that corrupts, on this thinking, but *consciousness* of sin. Consciousness of sin is not understood to construct character. It is understood only to induce guilt and shame. Psychological man, with the therapeutic worldview, assumes consciousness of sin to be formed from creedal interdicts, rather than the other way around: creedal interdicts from consciousness of sin.

One's Identity, the authentic, true inner being unsullied by consciousness of sin, must be allowed to emerge from the formless void of the subconscious, the Freudian roil of competing inner impulses. This requires both transgression of interdicts, and ongoing nurture of the emerging innocent inner being. No wonder, then, that the therapeutic worldview entails an acute suspicion of all normative institutions. Religion is a threat, but so also all tradition formed on a presumption of transcendence, or logos, or Platonic ideal, or universality of moral values.

The therapeutic disposition is transgressive, which means it's not a competing creed, but rather transgression of creeds formed in charisma. You might think of the therapeutic transgressive as creedal because after all it involves articulable tenets of belief, but those tenets are negations, not affirmative beliefs *sui generis*. It is more accurately an anti-creed. The creedal disposition builds through interdicts, while the therapeutic deconstructs through transgression. The therapeutic disposition presupposes that deconstruction is necessary because the interdicts produce authoritarian repression of the innocent inner-formed self, Identity, which the therapeutic disposition creates and then nurtures and protects.

Deconstruction means transgression. Transgression without something to transgress makes no sense. One cannot transgress the established order if there is no established order. There can be no charisma without creed, but neither can there be transgression without creed. Both religion (or charisma) and irreligion (or transgression) depend on creed. One constructs it; the other deconstructs it. This is why hard left activism, which is a reaction to norms founded on the religious impulse, nonetheless has a religious feel. This is why the secularist materialist perspective in the culture is an utter lie: it pretends to an absence of dogma, as it deconstructs its competing religious dogma. Therapy dissolves the dignity of the integrated self, because it transgresses moral creed while claiming neutrality as to moral creeds.

Transgression is, as the word suggests, contravention of an ordered system of thought rather than its own system of thought, which means that one transgresses interdicts without imposing interdicts, which explains why the impulse to political progressivism never involves disclosure of the endpoint of progress. There isn't one. The essence of postmodern thinking is process without disclosed purpose.

The impulse to transgression is seen in the addition of the "Q," for queer, to the acronym for contrived sub-categories of human based on sex attraction or self-conception or practice. "Queer" was at one time a term of derision, but is adopted with "pride" as a catch-all expression of transgression of heterosexual normativity.[8] What does "queer" denote? No particular category of sexual "identity;" it is by design a negation only, a stance of transgression. It expresses what Mary Harrington called "Normophobia,"[9] a reaction against any normative institutions because they imply constraints against otherwise untrammeled freedom of "free-floating individual desire." The concept of queerness purports to reject categorical givenness, yet it creates its own loose category in that it is not-that-thing: a category, but the one category purportedly not formed in constraint. It seeks the chaotic formless void, in opposition to created structure. This attitude of rebellion against any givenness of things, like traditional family patterns, is reflexive transgression.

For those with a lingering attachment to interdicts formed in charisma, this just looks like an unspooling of all values; a dismantling of the system of interdicts rooted in revelations of God. It means the collapse of civilization, when extrapolated to its logical conclusion. But for transgressives, God and the moral hierarchy descending from Him are a fiction, so it's ok to hate God and the system of the world constructed by belief in Him. And there is no perception of irony in decrying hate in the abstract while hating those who perceive charisma and actual sin and accept interdicts against it. It is a dishonest ideological war, not really racism or bigotry or colonialism or any other linguistic mallet barbarians employ to demolish the structures of civilization.

This idea of interdict and transgression explains how people are on this left and right political spectrum we think we understand. They aren't so much expressions of certain political opinions as they are expressions of how one evaluates the system of the world

---

8 According to James Lindsay, it is derived from David Halperin in his 1995 book *Saint Foucault* (p. 62), see *New Discourses*, "Queer Theory is the Doctrine of a Sex-based Cult."

9 Harrington, Mary, "Normophobia," *First Things*, April 2024.

he finds himself in. If you think it's authoritarian and oppressive and bounded by repression and hate, you'll want it loosened in a flow of social movement toward ever-increasing individual liberty. But you will be of a rightist disposition if you think the culture is so lacking in necessary interdicts of sinful man that we're unwinding to a chaos that tends to totalitarianism: political absorption of the individual, rather than his liberation.

The collective of government and allied power centers becomes "authoritarian" when it oppresses people, forcing manipulative interdicts against individual will. By contrast, it becomes "totalitarian" when the individual will is diminished from within, as happens when individuals relinquish agency to the collective. Authoritarianism means felt oppression. Totalitarianism means a hollowing-out of self, rendering it more easily absorbed into the totalitarian state.

The vehicle to totalitarianism is ideology. A totalizing ideology does not oppress individuals against the exercise of their agency, but rather seduces them into giving it up. This becomes possible when they are worn down on the margins with incremental little intrusions that in isolation seem defensible and so don't raise the alarm of totalitarian control. If in the culture the resisting individual will is diminished, then subjects of the collective more readily accept ever-expanding collective constraints without complaint. In fact they will resist the return of their agency, because the totalitarian ideology includes the element that individuals find their fullest expression in the collective. This is the very essence of fascism, as articulated by Benito Mussolini, who coined the term. It is also the essence of woke postmodern progressivism, moving us globally to a fascism with Western post-liberal democratic characteristics.

The references made here to totalitarianism are not fanciful or frivolous. Authoritarian regimes are oppressively coercive, but totalitarian regimes re-shape individuals so that coercion becomes unnecessary. This follows the politicization of everything. The personal is political; there are no private spaces. It's hard to imagine a more obvious invasion of private spaces than with sexual politics. Even sex-separated toilets are considered fair game for substitution of the will of the collective.

Sacred Order and Secular Disorder

Rieff makes clear at the outset of his seminal *The Triumph of the Therapeutic*[10] (1966) that the starting point for all of what follows is the death of God in the postmodern imagination. He cited thinkers like Matthew Arnold and Friedrich Nietzsche who, in the nineteenth century, presciently worried about what would come next upon the crumbling of the religious structure for how we understand ourselves as human beings. The question, he wrote, is no longer Dostoyevsky's: "Can civilized men believe?" but rather "whether unbelieving men can be civilized."[11] This point is even more central in his much later work *Charisma* (2008),[12] and he expanded on it in his posthumously published *My Life Among the Deathworks*.[13]

A "deathwork" is Rieff's word for markers of cultural decline that exemplify the vanishing of sacred order. He uses many examples from art, like the works of Picasso and Duchamp, but the idea is not limited to art. He writes that there are three "cultures," or "worlds." The first culture is based on the "primacy of possibility," and can be summed up in the word *fate*. You can think of it as corresponding to the mindset of the pagan, pre-Christian world. In the second culture, social order rests on sacred order. It is a culture of *faith*, corresponding to the religious disposition to humility and consciousness of the moral structure of the world. In the third culture

10 *The Triumph of the Therapeutic/Uses of Faith After Freud*, 2nd ed., (ISI Books: 2007), first published 1966.
11 Ibid., p. 4.
12 New York: Vintage, 2008.
13 Rieff, Philip, *My Life Among the Deathworks/Illustrations of the Aesthetics of Authority*, (Charlottesville, VA: University of Virginia Press, 2006).

the operative word is *fiction*. It jettisons sacred order and attempts to recall the mythic "primacies of possibility" of the first world, but produces only fictive simulacra to cover over naked exercises of power. These three cultures can coexist, but over time one or the other can come to predominate. Obviously the cultural transition is a gradual thing.

In a culture in which moral authority is backed by sacred order, there is a balance between interdict and remission. Rieff illustrates with the Michaelangelo painting on the ceiling of the Sistine Chapel. The most famous section is "The Creation of Adam" (or "Creation of Man"). The idea is that all of life is to be lived in that tiny space between God's hand and man's. This is the resolution of the tension between mankind's God-breathed and dust-formed selves. Interdict and remission are balanced here.

What happens in the third culture is that we come to think of this liminal space as constraining, such that we need to be liberated. Indeed, (and departing now from Rieff), Michaelangelo's master-work could be understood as setting up an ambiguity on this point. God is reaching for man, but the posture of the man's hand could be read as indifference. As in the Calvinist view, God does all the work, so to speak. The man is reclining on solid ground, but God is in motion. God reaches for man, and we infer man has not rebuffed God, but perhaps the opposite is true? That man withdraws from God? Instead of an imminent joining, there would then be an imminent sundering, wherein man has just become separated from the sacred order and is therefore in that snapshot of time before realization of the free-fall; to be followed by urgent and spontaneous lament: "Oh, my God!" The fall is the cancellation of authority, precipitating the imminent collapse of logos. As in our world today. It is mankind in that moment of realization, of what he has done to his progeny.

All liberationist impulses derive from this deathly rejection of sacred order. As in the French Revolution, the model for all post-Enlightenment liberation movements. They are all constituted of a buzz of suspicion and skepticism of verticals in authority, beginning with rejection of God. Freud is grouped with Marx and Nietzsche among figureheads driving a "hermeneutics of suspicion"[14] that in turn drives the liberation impulse. Of course it's not really liberation at all; it is imprisonment in a deathwork of meaninglessness. As in Matthew Arnold's poem *Dover Beach*, this third world:

> Hath really neither joy, nor love, nor light,
>
> Nor certitude, nor peace, nor help for pain;
>
> And we are here as on a darkling plain
>
> Swept with confused alarms of struggle and flight,
>
> Where ignorant armies clash by night.

The absence of sacred order behind society's interdicts is more consequential than we tend to realize. We retain a remnant of God-given conscience, but we are capable of attributing its source to the strictures of social norms, instead. That removes it from the

---

14 Paul Ricoeur's phrase, see discussion in *The Mountain and the River*, chapter 14.

transcendent to the immanent, and then immanence re-conceived without divine authority. There is then no authority at all behind the interdicts we live under, other than that of society. Society's strictures are not backed by a sacred order, so instead of authority for its interdicts there is only power to coerce.

For just one example of how this is so, consider critical theory,[15] such as critical race theory, a bankrupt ideology which becomes possible only when power pushes out authority:

> Without objective truth and moral judgments, the only thing to rest your philosophy on is power. Indeed, this is what critical theory has done. Critical theory, while denying the possibility of objective moral truths, focusses on power dynamics. That is a "tell." The entire philosophy focuses on elevating the "oppressed" in relation to the "oppressor." If we're to follow this argument to its logical conclusion, there's no limit to the kinds of resistance the oppressed should use against their oppressor. Power dynamics are necessary to interrogate, but without an objective moral standard to judge against, it results in an amoral war of all against all—where the only limit on your action is your self-interest. Simply, I can do what I want to become as powerful as I can.[16]

Power displaces authority, in the progression to an oppressive society. As the natural God-informed conscience is diminished, collectivist coercion to norms dissociated from religion increase. This is an obvious recipe for increasing authoritarianism, giving way to totalitarianism.

It can be argued that one can be ethical without belief in God, therefore reliance on sacred order is misplaced. It is true that one can reject God and behave in a way we might regard as consistent

15 As distinct from "critical thinking," the salutary practice of testing a proposition according to universal criteria beyond the subject matter, like consistency, coherence, relevance, factual accuracy, and so on.

16 Andrews, Jack (pseudonym), "Embracing Scylla and Charybdis," *Law and Liberty,* March 26, 2024.

with morals divinely decreed, but where then do the ethical standards come from? If they are not written into the universe in some way, they are merely decreed by society, and as we've seen, society's standards over time prove to be elastic to the point of providing no standard at all. What we regard as atheist ethicality is really just living in a society still partially informed by fading religious interdicts. "Morality" in this environment is parasitic. Those who express moral dudgeon, without reference to sacred order,

> are sheltered by convictions which belong, not to them, but to the society of which they form a part; it is nourished by processes in which they take no share. And when those convictions decay, and those processes come to an end, the alien life which they have maintained can scarce be expected to outlast them.[17]

Religiously-informed social norms may fade slowly, but they will in time vanish. There will still be social norms, of course, but they will be malleable norms in service of power, which the therapeutic serves. Society formed on natural law politically, and buttressed by religion morally, will become unrecognizable and even inconceivable, anomalous in our history books if remembered at all.

In a religious society, God is understood to inform the pre-social conscience. This phrase, "pre-social conscience," is meant to suggest the individual conscience is divinely informed, pre-existing internalized social norms. Religious interdicts result, and those in turn may inform social norms. In a Godless society, social norms diverge from the pre-social conscience, setting up a dissonance in the individual. Example: premarital sex feels wrong, but society says it's ok. Moral decline results when the dissonance is dissipated in the evolution from pre-social dictates of conscience, to the dictates of social norms. God-given conscience is diminished as purely social interdicts are internalized. Society becomes the god. Society itself

---

17 Arthur James Balfour, *The Foundations of Belief*, (London, 1895).

provides the immanentizing force. There is believed to be nothing outside the atheist "immanent frame."[18] The spirit of the age replaces the spirit of God. The divine authority of interdicts is removed and the naked coercive authority of the *polis* remains.

This is unsustainable. The significance of the loss of divine authority for society's interdicts is that its coercive power can no longer be mediated by mutual deference to higher, transcendent authority. There are two alternative and ever-polarizing ways people can respond. We might think of them as right and left, in today's oversimplified political duality. One, grudging compliance only as necessary to avoid punishment or to share in forcibly collectivized resources. Individual self-government is diminished to the vanishing point and the coercive rules of society are morally both floor and ceiling to conduct. This is what we would expect in a totalitarian state: all moral authority and therefore all agency in the state, and minimal agency retained by the individual. Two, obsequious compliance. The replacement to obeying the conscience is an exquisite sensitivity to the dictates of the collective; an acceptance of the collective's sole authority in its entirety; and a slavish desire to comply with its interdicts in letter and spirit to avoid the opprobrium of society consequent upon deviation from its Narrative.

The latter of these two responses is abetted by the therapeutic worldview of psychological man, because his first principle is psychological self-care. Other principles, like truth and justice and fairness and freedom, are in service to the first principle, which is to say they are denatured of any residual potency. Such abstractions are

---

18 A too-clever phrase used to mean, really, its opposite: the entire absence of divine presence in our lives. An example is Martin Hägglund's *This Life, Secular Faith and Spiritual Freedom*, (Anchor, 2020), as a way to subtly put brackets around this-world socialist political organization to avoid interference from any transcendent source of authority. A similarly confounding phrase, "immanent contentment," was used by Benjamin Storey and Jenna Silber Storey *Why We Are Restless*, (Princeton, NJ: Princeton University Press, 2021) beginning at p. 3 to mean happiness in the here and now, with the effect of willfully ignoring the possibility that this life in the body is not all there is.

easily mangled in the march to unanimity in how we go about discovering the interior self. The goal of discovering and rescuing the
self within, Identity, is not served by principled consideration of
what those abstractions actually mean, because of fear that doing so
might open a fissure between the emerging self and the society that
forms it.

The Tragic Sense

Agamemnon, the king of Argos, has been away for the whole
of a ten-year siege of Troy, and is now returning victorious, with a
captive Trojan princess, Cassandra. Waiting for him is his wife
Clytemnestra. Imagine her looking out to sea from the battlements
of Argos, watching for the beacon fires of his return. Her hands are
clenched before her, grasping and knotting her garment. She wears
a sorrowful expression and far-off gaze, combined with a resolute
aspect. Is she wondering what the lapse of years will mean? No, it's
worse than that. Before Agamemnon departed, he sacrificed their
daughter Iphigenia to the gods for fair winds to Troy and victory.
For ten years Clytemnestra has nursed a resolution to kill Agamemnon in retribution. She's anticipating that moment come at last.

This is the subject of a Greek tragedy by Aeschylus, c. 500 B.C.
Vengeance is not the way, but one can certainly put herself in
Clytemnestra's sandals. Agamemnon's murder has long been decid-
ed. She's not nervous about what she's about to do. She's sorrowful,
because of what she's suffered for the last decade, combined with
the tragic inevitability and necessity (in her mind) of Agamemnon's
death and her impending hand in it.

Martha Bayles writes in *The Hedgehog Review*[19] that the emotions
associated with dramatic tragedy were traditionally pity and fear, but
with the important distinction that the emotions in play are not

---

19 "The Character of Tragedy," Spring, 2024.

those of the characters in the drama, but yours as you watch. You're meant to feel what the characters do. In this example you feel pity for Clytemnestra but also, because of your mimetic appreciation of her plight, a kind of fear at what you yourself are capable of in like (tragic) circumstances.

In those pagan times a sense of fate ruled, it was the heavy sense of inevitability. The pagan sense of fate was among the subjects of Boethius's 523 A.D. *Consolation of Philosophy*, in which, among many other things, he's trying to shake loose the lingering pagan notion of *fate* in contrast to Christian *faith*.[20] We often think of the pagans' sense of fate as meaning they were bobbing along as playthings of the gods, with no say in events, but that's not exactly right. There was still a sense of personal responsibility, in fact the Greek tragedies typically turn on the moral failing of a prominent character, one for whom we nonetheless feel some sympathy.

In Theodore Dalrymple's *Admirable Evasions*,[21] on the subject of, as the subtitle reads, *How Psychology Undermines Morality*, the theme is that the "tragic sense" opposes the perspective of psychological man caught in the cult of the therapeutic worldview. He quotes portions of Samuel Johnson's *Rasselas*, in which Rasselas is forced to face the dichotomy of high-minded rational principle, on the one hand, and the just-as-real realm of intuition and emotion and irrationality, on the other. In this way Dalrymple takes us back to an aspect of "tragedy" as meant by the ancient Greeks: the understanding that rationality (Apollo) stands in juxtaposition to irrational or subconscious instincts of eros and death (Dionysius), including potentially destructive instincts to intoxication and even insanity—pertinent especially in the context of our current mental health crisis that is caused by therapy rather than cured by it.

---

20 These incidentally correspond to the first and second worlds described by Philip Rieff in *My Life Among the Deathworks*, presaging the third world he labelled *fiction*, the re-emergence of pagan "primacy of possibility" but degrading former structures of civilization.

21 New York: Encounter Books, 2015.

The religious point of view similarly takes the Dionysian disposition into view—not intoxication and insanity, but the emotional, instinctual, dream-like sense of something beyond rationality, like where music takes you. It is the source of the "numinous" religious impulse, charisma, the felt sense that there's more mystery than we suppose; indeed, God stands outside the beingness of all things, encompassing even the sense of irrationality and mystery and lyricism and a child's giddy sense of inexplicable glee. He is ineffable, a rational word to describe the irrational also within His remit.

A theme of this work is that self-absorption erases one's God-given moral agency. Dalrymple's is that the person lost in the cult of the therapeutic lacks a tragic sense. Are these the same thing? Another form of the word "fate" is "fatalism," meaning a sense of the inevitability even of dire events, as exemplified in the Greek tragedies. In pagan times there were thought to be gods pulling levers to direct this rainfall and that birth, but with no overarching telos to human life. People were expected to follow the social prescriptions of tradition, and that was what "honoring the gods" meant, as we can see in Plato's telling of the trial and death of Socrates.

The "tragic sense" means sensitivity to what can happen when we depart from what we understand as morality. In the "immanent frame" of both paganism and postmodernism, our understanding of morality is formed more from society than from the conscience. Social formation of what we regard as morality is therefore common to both paganism and postmodernism,[22] but there are at least a couple of important differences.

One, psychological man does not acknowledge the social mores absorbed selectively because he strongly desires acceptance and communitarianism. Instead he believes himself to be acting on the agency of his inner-formed Identity. He expresses his individualism by following the herd, ironically enough. The pagans were not bur-

---

22 First world and third, in Rieff's terminology.

dened with the faux-individualism of the postmodern. Their lives were circumscribed by social convention, reinforced by placation of the gods.

Two, in postmodernism, there is no sense of a moral authority above people or societies, God having been dismissed in the imagination, and the Machine collective having been given power formerly reserved to individuals. This is new in the history of the world. Even the pagans had some sense of an overarching non-human moral authority. Here for example is Antigone,[23] rebuking Creon the king who sentences her to death for violating his decree that no one bury her brother:

> CREON: Tell me, . . . Had you heard my proclamation touching this matter?
>
> ANTIGONE: It was public. Could I help hearing it?
>
> CREON: And yet you dared defy the law.
>
> ANTIGONE: I dared. It was not God's proclamation. That final justice that rules the world below makes no such laws. Your edict, King, was strong, but all your strength is weakness itself against the immortal unrecorded laws of God. They are not merely now: they were, and shall be, operative for ever, beyond man utterly.

She's saying the king's decrees do not trump the natural law. The gods did not hand down anything like the Ten Commandments, and they were more idiosyncratically goofy than people. And yet, there is somehow a logos in the universe occupied by them and by us, and the moral law cannot be traduced by anyone, even a king, without consequence. That isn't true for psychological man. He follows the dictates of imagined and felt Identity, and his sense of right and wrong lacks universality.

There is something that exposes in sharp relief all the petty

---

23 In Sophocles' eponymous tragedy *Antigone*, c. 441 B.C.

cruelties and inanities of the world. It's the reason we see evil for what it is. That something is perceptible in the tragic sense that has always been with us, but is lacking or denatured in postmodern ideology and its subjective counterpart in the therapeutic. Why do people still use the phrase "tragic sense" in contradistinction to whatever postmodernism leaves us with? How does the lingering tragic sense help us understand the feeling of being hollowed-out of meaning in the postmodern era, with its attendant turn inward to psychological self-care? Why now the rise of therapeutic Identity in place of external source of meaning?

Freud mostly made things up, but he wasn't wrong in placing instinct in the subconscious. Indeed, it might be said that the root-level axioms for our outlook originate there. That was the supposition for example of Miguel de Unamuno in his *Tragic Sense of Life*.[24] He observes that a person's subjective intuitions inform his outlook on life, which in turn informs his intellectual convictions. The subconscious in a sense authors the conscious. Our inner, axiom-forming subconscious is in turn formed in the Spirit of God. A relevant inference is that the alternative imagined source of axiom-setting is the "spirit" of self alone, and thus the latter is the source of the therapeutic worldview.

For de Unamuno, we don't "merely" exist, instead we have "a furious hunger of being that possese[s us], an appetite for divinity."[25] This marks him as a Christian existentialist, like Kierkegaard before him. The felt sense of "hunger" is sometimes described in other ways, such as the diffuse and dissonant "yearning" Alvin Plantinga identifies as being sourced in alienation from God.[26] This hunger or yearning we all have, whether we attribute it to separation from God or not, is the tragic sense. Or to say what amounts to the same thing

---

24 Translated by J.E. Crawford Flitch, (SophiaOmni Press, 2014), first published 1912.
25 Ibid., p. 30, citing San Juan de los Angeles.
26 *Knowledge and Christian Belief*, (Grand Rapids: Eerdman's, 2015), see, Norton, Albert, *Intuition of Significance*, (Eugene, OR: Resource Publications, 2019).

in reverse: the dissonance we experience, which we call the tragic sense, is the numinous felt presence of God, whether we acknowledge it as such or not.

De Unamuno writes that we wish never to die and this longing is our true essence. But we do die, and this is the tragedy. It's not tragedy for a lion or a dandelion, but it is to metacognitive mankind, bearer of the tragic "I" of consciousness:

> If consciousness is, as some inhuman thinker has said, nothing more than a flash of light between two eternities of darkness, then there is nothing more execrable than existence.[27]

Our consciousness is metacognitive: aware of our own mortality and of ultimate moral judgment. Sin means death but sin is unavoidable, and this produces the tragic sense. Metacognition also means social awareness, intersubjectivity producing our sense of society as a "being" unto itself in which we participate. That means awareness of collectivist "social facts" (in Emile Durkheim's phrasing) or what has been described here as social Narrative. The Fall is the event of metacognition in mankind, the introduction of the tragic sense. We allow social Narrative to become rival to God for our allegiance. We dismissively turn from God when we turn instead to society as adjudicator of moral right and wrong.

The tragic sense could be written as "the hunger of immortality." It arises from this phenomenon of fullness of conscious self-awareness particular to human animals: consciousness of the potential absence of consciousness. We cannot really conceive ourselves as not existing but we try anyway, and in the imagination balance on that bubble of existing/non-existing, and this contributes to the tragic sense. The tragic sense drives us to contemplate religion, but persists even if we remain irresolute concerning it. "The

---

27 *Tragic Sense of Life*, p. 33.

problem of the duration of my soul, of my own soul, tortures me."[28]

With consciousness of our mortality and of existence/non-existence, we go about devising immortality-alternatives: fame, or Nietzschean eternal return, or dissolution into world-soul and reincarnation. Or else we push past the inconceivability of non-existence, to pretend we conceive it anyway, a leap of faith to annihilation upon death, the photographic negative of religious faith. In Jewish or Christian terms, the tragic sense is explained in the primeval story: knowledge that all passes because we have not eaten of the tree of immortality, yet we are God-breathed, and so consciousness of our mortality presses upon us as the aberration that it is. The tragic sense is religious despair, the seed of faith.

The thirst for eternity drives love, in people. Love is the manifestation of our hunger for immortality, the sense that nothing is truly real unless it be eternal, and love is eternal, while indifference and hate are the hallmark of the temporal and fleeting and dying. Love drives sacrifice: giving today for a better tomorrow, and not just for ourselves, but for our progeny and even for the abstraction of society, that attenuated sense of fellow-feeling. Upon crossing over we desire that others, too, would open their eyes and see God, the reason for our hunger for immortality, the reason for our discomfort in our tragic sense.

The hunger for immortality fades as its prerequisite of spiritual truth fades. At mid-twentieth century, despite the partial victory of liberalism over dark forces of totalitarianism in the Second World War, and of ensuing prosperity and optimism in the West, there continued a decline in religious belief. Not religious practice, necessarily, or at least not immediately, but certainly genuine openness to a supernatural reality declined. It was replaced, as the century wore on, by a hard resignation that this is all there is; that there's no point nurturing hope in an afterlife that was after all deeply mysterious and seemingly ephemeral in the first place. And so the tragic sense

28 Ibid., p. 55.

faded, too, meaning there was no longer a higher cause to justify honor and dignity in any long-suffering element to our existence. As a society, it seemed ever more appropriate that we go to a palliative self-care mode, rather than holding out for a future that might be glorious but might be illusory.

Enter the existentialists. "Existentialism" is often treated as a distinct school of philosophy, but is it, really? How is the soul-hunger of Kierkegaard like the soul-deadness of Nietzsche, or the self-formation of Sartre? Existence precedes essence, in the new dispensation, and the essence-formation is an interior project of manufactured meaning. I am solely the author of me. Having killed God, the postmodern project is maintaining a cheerful nihilism. That mysterious gleam we pursued in the darkness of deep forest out there turns out to be a furtive glimmer in here, in my subconscious being, an emerging Identity that is all the mystery left to us. Mystery that calls to us resides within, not in the cosmos out there.

The therapeutic worldview is an avoidance of the questions of existence and mortality, because it is merely a maintenance program, process without purpose. It therefore means dissolution of the tragic sense, the necessary prompt to finding significance to life. Thus the demise of the tragic sense: self-love overcomes any hope of return to the Lover of our souls.

7
THE SUBRATIONAL MIND

Rational and Irrational

For psychological man, feelings govern action and thought. Instead of the rational process whereby logic impels the connection of linked thoughts in a direction of objective truth, emotion impels the connection of linked thoughts in a direction of psychological self-care.

Re-consider that so far this whole presentation is from the logos perspective of rationality; of verticality; of objectivity; of transcendence. It may therefore be difficult to access for someone imbued with the therapeutic worldview. But one has to start somewhere, and hopefully, the remnant of rationality left in psychological man will let him see this as a glimmer of light in an otherwise murky swamp. If not, perhaps psychological man will, despite his atrophied rationality muscle, perceive with emotionally-heightened acuity the descriptions here of the therapeutic way of perceiving the world, and that in contrast to the rationality underpinning the world to which he is heir.

Postmodern process philosophy governs what's left of rationality.[1] The therapeutic operates on irrationality. What makes it ir-

---

1 Again, a main point of *The Mountain and the River*, so not further explicated here.

rational is simply departure from rationality: the logic internally whereby one thought "causes" the next along a line oriented to objective truth, and the logic externally in the natural order of the world, which makes it amenable to our rational understanding. The irrational therapeutic operates in confused tandem with rationality applied to postmodern propositions. Postmodern philosophy and the therapeutic worldview coincide in the same individuals. The woke are also the emotionally vulnerable.

How might we describe the irrational, using the language—the logos—of the rational? We can do it through imagery, symbolism, consideration of the religious impulse, and, ironically, psychological theory.

Most of us are familiar with the opening words of Genesis: "In the beginning God created the heavens and the earth." This statement is packed with truths of ontology, the bursting forth into existence of all things. The mystery of the nothingness that birthed somethingness is rightly likened to the pre-rationality that births rationality. With that in mind, let's hurry on to the second verse: "The earth was without form and void, and darkness was over the face of the deep. And the Spirit of God was hovering over the face of the water." This imagery depicts a chaotic swirl of potentiality not yet formed into substance. Matterless form and formless matter. It is the earth and yet it is "void." There is water without form to contain it. Whatever else we may take from this mysterious language, we should see in it the moment of pre-creation potentiality. Not a nothing, but rationality inchoate; pre-rational irrationality.

More imagery. Consider the wanderlust we often feel, to explore the unknown. It may motivate us to move across country or keep walking to see what's around the next bend. There's something about being at the edge of frontier, itching to transgress it, because there is a sense that the unknown also means possibility. Exploration beyond a frontier is movement to the unknown, like the waves pushing ocean water onto the beach: an in-between zone, an area not this nor that, and therefore a gateway to the other, the unknown, the golden promise.

Among pagans there was a fascination with the time-between-times, dawn and dusk, because it was a merging of binary day and night, and therefore seemingly a stepping-off place to a new form of space-time altogether, which is neither day nor night, nor here nor there. Likewise with the dreamworld, and the half-wakefulness between sleeping and rising. Imagination told them that once the binary is broken, a new form of creativity is possible. As with the time-between-times, so with intermediate places: the beach, the riverbank, the tree line, the distant horizon. All suggestive of the capacity to lift off from here and land "there," whatever that may mean, over beyond the frontier.

These images represent a thinning barrier to our time- and space-bound existence. It also represents danger, because mythically the in-between times and spaces also represent the matterless form and formless matter of the chaotic pre-creation potentiality Genesis discloses. It is thus with any thinning of binary opposition, by which we make sense of anything. Rational thought rests on this-not-that thinking, and so dimension-defying in-between boundaries are mythically also a line between rational and irrational.

In deep history there was a strong stamp of binary order on existence because the material needs of space-time existence required it. But in human nature there is a desire also for the thinning of orderly restraints, hence the pagan fascination with the dissolution of binary order, pulling away at the human power dynamic impressed upon us by necessity. Emotional and creative needs can exist in a substrate of irrationality, and are met in this declension from order. The opposite is true, too: rationality is drawn up from irrationality by God, or if not God, then the logos of rationality the Greeks wondered at long ago.

The religious impulse is often observed to rest on something other than empirical observation and reason. It is not the testing of a scientific hypothesis. Rudolf Otto, for example, described experience of the "numinous," that can be consciously captured in spiritual sensitivity which is not rational, but felt more on an emotional or instinctive level.[2] Numerous writers and thinkers describe something similar, a yearning for the presence of God,[3] or intimations of the divine, for example in the poetry of William Wordsworth.[4]

It is noteworthy that not all subscribe to this subtle sensitivity to the divine, most notably for our subject Sigmund Freud, who was quite hostile to religion[5] and attributed religious feeling (perhaps with a sneer) to the desire to return to the safety and comfort and "oceanic feeling" of the womb. He wrote "I cannot discover this 'oceanic' feeling in myself."[6]

And, considering Freud again, we can look to the subconscious. By virtue of being subconscious, it's irrational, and further by virtue of being subconscious, we can't know its content. We can infer the existence of the subconscious, however, as when we feel something bothering us emotionally until its significance manifests in conscious thought. Freud based his whole developing theory of the psyche on the existence of this sub-rational sub-conscious realm, but never seemed to consider it the potential locus of emotional sensitivity to the numinous.

David Bakan much later attempted to do that for him,[7] sug-

---

2 E.g., *The Idea of the Holy*, translated (from German) by J.W. Harvey, 1923 (first published in 1917).

3 As with Alvin Plantinga's description of how belief in God can be basic in epistemology, see his *Knowledge and Christian Belief*, Grand Rapids, MI: Eerdmans 2015, and discussion at Norton, Albert, *Intuition of Significance* (Eugene, OR: Resource Publications, 2019).

4 E.g., "Ode: Intimations of Immortality from Recollections of Early Childhood," 1807

5 As he made plain in many of his writings, perhaps most notably his *The Future of an Illusion*, transl by W.D. Robson-Scott, (Mansfield Centre, CT: Martino Publishing, 2010), first published 1928; the "illusion" being religion.

6 Freud, Sigmund, *Civilization and Its Discontents*, translated by James Strachey, (New York: W.W. Norton, 1961), p. 24, first published 1930.

7 Bakan, David, *The Duality of Human Experience*, (Boston: Beacon Press 1966), pp. 9-16.

gesting that the mystery of subconsciousness is a valid concept because it gets at the opposite of idolatry. Idolatry means putting God in a box stamped "dogma," but a box cannot contain the ground of all Being. For Bakan, Freud's conception of the unconscious began to get at that ineffable open-endedness, making "ultimate concern" a subjective and psychological matter rather than only a theological one.

Remember the foregoing discussion is an attempt to rationally describe the irrational, through imagery, symbolism, consideration of the religious impulse, and psychological theory. The purpose is to contrast the rational, logos worldview to the irrational, therapeutic worldview. We spend our waking lives in the conscious rational world, if we are not psychological man, but we can imagine the unconscious as a seething roil of emotions and impulses and instincts.

The most basic motivation for those captured by the therapeutic worldview is care and protection of that inner subconscious, the locus of the irrational side of human existence. It is the primary locus of feelings and emotions, and for psychological man these have priority over putatively objective principles, bloodless and disembodied virtues and abstractions like good and evil and truth and falsehood. The subconscious pit can be likened to the earth formless and void, with darkness over the face of the deep; the primordial crucible of creation, and so felt to be (rather than reasoned to be) a fitting rival to the rational application of form and substance to the world.

As we will see in a later discussion of identity-formation and Gnosticism, the subconscious is not merely the intuitive side of humanity in contrast to the reasoning side, like the dark side of the moon in contrast to the illumined side. Prioritizing emotion, intuition, instincts, and impulses means also prioritizing the destructive over the constructive, and chaos over order. It is a capitulation to the transgressive Thanatos or death-driven aspect of our psychological make-up.

It is thus the antithesis of the religious worldview, as we can see just in the first verses of Genesis we've cited. The whole point of the early Gensis narrative is the ontological coming into being of the material world from the spiritual, and part-spiritual/part-material mankind in it. It is the ascendancy of ordered structure and form to the universe, including the hierarchy of moral values that draws us out of contemplation of our navels and toward the attainment of virtue; of loving God and loving mankind; all as over against a demonic scattering impulse to chaos, nihilism, and death.

Conscious and Subconscious

We've employed a series of dichotomies to attempt to explain the therapeutic worldview. These are ways of looking in on the original dichotomy between the logos and therapeutic, to emphasize their opposition. We've several times differentiated between conscious and subconscious, because the subconscious figures prominently in the therapeutic worldview.

Let's pause to be sure we have our terms straight. "Cognition" means conscious, rational thought. It is therefore in opposition to what could be described as mental process that is not actual thinking; that which responds to stimuli and affects rational thought, but is not rational thought itself. "Precognition" is sometimes used to mean awareness of future events, but here a more relevant definition would be pre-conscious awareness: sense impressions and instinctive or emotional responses preceding active cognition. In this use, it is equivalent to pre-consciousness.

"Consciousness" is the mind's active awareness of self and the external world. "Pre-conscious" therefore refers to activity of mind that precedes active consciousness. Cognition is rational thought occurring in the conscious mind as it actively and continuously sorts sensory experience. Consciousness includes self-awareness of active cognition. Preconsciousness is irrational or sub-rational mind activity not yet brought forward into active consideration of the rational, conscious mind.[8]

As previously noted, rationality relates to "logos:" active thought proceeding in a "logical" way because oriented toward truth objectively existing in the world. That logos extant in the natural order of the world enables us to reason together. We can refer to the opposite of "rational" as "irrational" or "subrational" because it precedes or is a departure from active logical reasoning, yet is a function of mind. This is the "location" of emotion, instinct, impulse, and intuition. Thus, a correspondence in oppositions:

Cognition	Precognition
Consciousness	Preconscious/subconscious/unconscious
Rational	Irrational/subrational

We might add to these corresponding oppositions as follows, to better understand the contrast in worldviews:

Thought	Emotion
Logic	Randomness
Waking	Dreaming
Agency	Receptivity
Inhibition	Disinhibition
Objective	Subjective
Philosophy	Psychology
External	Internal

8 Freud made a distinction that is not made here, between preconscious and unconscious states. He theorized the subconscious as the seat of emotion, impulse, and instinct, and the "location" for repression of them. Freud's "pre-conscious" just meant unrepressed latent thoughts, presumably in a sort of holding space to be called forth to consciousness.

Interdiction	Remission
Constraint	Release
Transcendence	Immanence
Sacred	Secular
Vertical	Horizontal
Logos	Therapeutic

Obviously these oppositions are not mutually exclusive; that is, one with the therapeutic worldview is not devoid of rationality; one with a logos or external worldview is not devoid of intuition. But they are suggestive of the different ways of looking at the world.

A useful way to consider how these two sets of oppositions interact is to consider the work of Iain McGilchrist, especially in his 2021 *The Matter With Things.*[9] An underlying thesis is that the brain's left hemisphere and right hemisphere have distinct functions, yet must integrate, to operate together, in a mentally healthy person.[10] The left hemisphere is invoked for hyper-rational, agentic, controlling brain function, the matters in the left column above, whereas the right hemisphere has a wider function of world-awareness, corresponding more to concepts in the right column. Importantly, the left hemisphere should be "emissary" to the "master" of the right hemisphere, but they must be properly integrated in a mentally healthy person.

It's not as simple, therefore, as saying the concepts in the left column are "good," and those on the right are "bad," any more than it is useful to describe all political disagreements in terms of left and right. Indeed, the difficulty with the therapeutic worldview is not that it's all inwardness and passivity. The difficulty is that it rep-

---

9 McGilchrist, Iain, *The Matter With Things*, (London: Perspectiva, 2021).

10 There are some indications that autism disorders represent a partial disconnect in the two hemisphere's proper joint functioning, which would help explain a correlation between autism and signifiers of the therapeutic worldview.

resents a distortion of proper balance, in which the left hemisphere overpowers its master in the right hemisphere, bringing focus and attention on psychological needs ahead of all else, with a loss of perspective about interests and concerns of others. From the outside this looks like depthless self-absorption, because it is. Emotion and intuition and a desire for remission and release come to dominate over rational prioritizing of duties and interests within an external hierarchy of values.

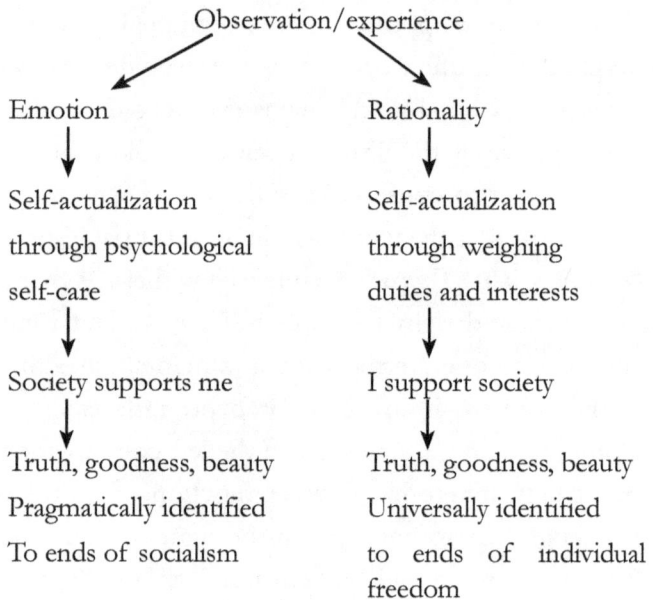

Observation/experience

Emotion	Rationality
Self-actualization through psychological self-care	Self-actualization through weighing duties and interests
Society supports me	I support society
Truth, goodness, beauty Pragmatically identified To ends of socialism	Truth, goodness, beauty Universally identified to ends of individual freedom

In the domain of charisma, left and right hemisphere are properly integrated, precluding excessively controlling left hemisphere thinking. It is the more balanced reception of the world which respects not only the drawing up from disorder and chaos, but the disorder itself as the unactualized substrate of potentiality from which all is derived. This is the domain of the divine, which remains an enigma to mankind, the source of mystery and depth which explains the otherwise inexplicable rationality of the natural order, and underwrites it with authority, the sacred order necessary to sustain in mankind a respect for the hierarchy of moral values drawn up from the potentiality.

The religious disposition identifies not just with religious creed, but with the ineffable element of religious mystery, as well. This impenetrable depth to the cosmos corresponds to an unknowable depth in mankind, the intuitive and instinctive subconscious. Charisma does not deny a subconscious, quite the contrary. Deep calls unto deep. But what takes place there? Is it the battleground of warring materialist instincts that Freud envisioned? Or is it an arena of supernatural and natural correspondence; the repository of God-bestowed conscience mixed with pre-conscious sorting of emotion?

Freud would place all of the subconscious on the level of animal instincts and desires, because he was a materialist, rejecting *ab initio* any connection to the divine. If there is a God, Freud was wrong, and the subconscious operates in God's economy. It is informed by the conscience, to which, along with divine revelation, we look for the natural law, the hierarchy of values extant in the universe as well as in the human heart.

The subconscious might also operate the "place" of formation of the axioms upon which rationality proceeds. We've considered what rationality is, but it is in a sense merely procedural. That is to say, it is not the content of thought, but rather describes the movement from thought to thought, ordered along a causative pathway, with the orientation for that progression provided by objective truth. As the earth's magnetic pole is to a compass needle, so objective truth orients rational progression of thought to itself. We call this progression "logic."

But it's quite possible to progress perfectly logically and still end up lost. It matters where you start. The starting place is an axiom: a premise that appears self-evident; which does not appear to be an inference from some other premise. It is fixed, or at least we take it to be fixed. Using physical causation as an analogy, it is ideally an uncaused first cause of a chain of inferences which follows.

Of course we can be mistaken about whether our axiom is indeed a stand-alone postulate, but the intent is to identify a first principle—that which makes a proposition axiomatic.

Oftentimes we disagree not because of a failure of logic, but because we proceed from different axioms. As between the emotivist and morality-based views,

> Rival premises are such that we possess no rational way of weighing the claims of one as against another. For each premise employs some quite different normative or evaluative concept from the others.[11]

This is typically the origin of distinctive worldviews. They differ axiomatically. People have widely varying opinions about things, but it is nonetheless possible to group them according to their baseline outlook on the world. This is how we contrast the competing worldviews of morality and psychology, to come to an understanding of the therapeutic worldview from the perspective of the moral or logos worldview.

Clearly people have different axiomatic beliefs. This is why in the past we could generally predict what a leftist's views on a subject will be, or those of a person on the right. We would say their fundamental beliefs predispose them one way or the other. Left and right are too facile, now, it appears we need more categories. But still we can listen to another's views and from them we can often predict their other views, because some set of axioms so predispose them.

But here it gets murky. If you're in a debate and you try to work through your antagonist's chain of inferences to identify the axioms on which they operate, you may find it tough going. Sometimes because of dissembling; sometimes because we don't really understand our own first principles. We might proceed from prejudice or fear, or our debate opponent may, and if so, the analysis will likely devolve to "just so" assertions that don't really reveal underly-

11 Alisdair MacIntyre, *After Virtue*, p. 8

ing axioms at all. The point is that our truly fundamental axioms are likely to be unclear even to ourselves. They seem to arise from the preconscious primordial mist, much like creation from the formless void of pre-creation chaos.

If it's true that our axiomatic dispositions are formed in the subconscious, the implications are large. It means you have a pre-rational, felt understanding of metaphysics, and of the presence of an active God or His absence, and of the relationship of individuals to society, and even of the function of society. You engage in rational processing of information from your environment, but your starting point is subconscious predisposition.

But where does that subconscious predisposition come from? Why does it form differently in you and in me? If the subconscious is the source of axiom-setting for rational thought, then our understanding of axioms—first principles—must be revisited. A first principle is a proposition upon which logical inferences begin building. But if it is formed in the subconscious like order from the formless void, then we by definition have no conscious access to it. We can't say whether the predisposition is built on hard principles or soft emotion. If you're a rightist (let's call it), your predisposition is for the solid ground of objective and universal hierarchy of moral values—a predisposition for the timeless mountain. But if you're a leftist (let's call it), your predisposition is for the liquid flow of relative and contingent values—a predisposition for the temporality of the river. These aren't first principles, but rather emotional leanings.

So if the subconscious is as authoritative on human beings as Freud and post-Freud psychology suggest, pre-axiom emotional leanings differ for those with the therapeutic as opposed to the logos worldview. In the therapeutic worldview, the desire for emotional self-care comes ahead of the desire for the order and predictability of logic and rationality. The ability to reason doesn't go out the window, however. Rather, it is employed in service to the self-care imperative. Hence emotivism, the idea that moral judgments are really just expressions of preference or attitude or feeling because it is actually impossible to distinguish right from wrong. The right course is the one that makes me feel better.

But there is also an emotional leaning for order and predictability, commensurate with the appearance of order in the cosmos and in human reason, all of which points to a Creator of natural order. Even emotionally, there must be a sense that we are not alone; that there is an ultimate authority superintending this mortal plane, and there is a yearning within, which only that Presence can requite. Promptings of guilt are understood as such, and are not confused with upsetting social alterity. Abstract justice seems to require judgment, and ultimate standards by which judgment is made, standards which are the same for everyone as a matter of equal personal dignity.

But why emotivism over morality, or morality over emotivism? Possibly the morality worldview is driven directly in the subconscious by the supernatural in some way. By God directly, perhaps, or by other supernatural influence or presence or being. The religious explanation is that God lays it on our "hearts;" that is, gives us a conscience. But even a materialist should take morality to be instinctive in the subconscious, because a materialist theory of innate morality follows from evolutionary theory: that sociability makes one more fit for survival, so that over time we evolved the Golden Rule internally, and even our sexual inhibitions.

In either case, we're right to conclude that our first principles, felt but not reasoned, include an awareness of moral absolutes in the universe. What do we do with that? We can face it directly, by acknowledging the moral universe and its implications, or we can deny moral accountability altogether. We don't rationally conclude that the therapeutic worldview makes more sense. We lapse into it because it feels more comfortable. That is not an intellectual conversion. It's indicative of having adopted the therapeutic already. Part of what actually drives us into the therapeutic worldview is avoidance of judgment. Instead of asking, and having to answer, whether our own conduct is morally right or wrong, we reject the question as irrelevant.

The therapeutic way of thinking is self-reinforcing in post-modern culture. How? Imagine this scenario suggested by Iain Mc-Gilchrist to explain the tendency to automation:

> You buy a radio set, and you soon find a couple of channels worth listening to. After a while, you find yourself listening to only one. It's not the radio set that's changed; it's you. In the case of the brain, it would not matter so much if we had settled on the intelligent channel—but we didn't. We settled on the one whose value has nothing to do with truth, or with courage, magnanimity, or generosity, but only with greed, grabbing, and getting. Manipulation.[12]

He's speaking of the brain's left hemisphere crowding out the influence of the right hemisphere, as a result of cultural conditions that cause us to emphasize one at the expense of the other, when to be fully human means to use both sides of the brain properly integrated. This is a function of the automation-producing culture we live in, of which the therapeutic worldview is (at least in large part) both cause and effect. Automation itself, algorithmic living, facilitates the therapeutic mentality, and is facilitated by it. (The implications for society as a whole are considered in chapter 14). Just as our use of the radio results in some stations never being heard, so the automated way of thinking results in some thoughts or beliefs never being entertained. This is what the therapeutic does to us. It is an emotivist rather than moral way of thinking about reality. Avoidance of moral culpability is at the heart of it, not by conscious reason but because the psychological perspective crowds it out. Moral questions are not addressed, they're avoided, and so do not become part of the architecture of axioms that inform the logos of rational

---

12 "Resist the Machine Apocalypse," *First Things*, March, 2024.

thought.

Subrational Participation

We've considered the unavoidable element of moral agency in human beings, which in turn presupposes moral realism: the objectivity of right and wrong extant in the universe. Our acts and omissions occur in a moral dimension; they are right or wrong regardless what I think about it, and regardless of my emotional disposition concerning it. But if we live in that universe of moral realism, acknowledging that we are morally responsible for what we do and fail to do, how is that reconcilable with the psychological disposition? The short answer is that it is not, but perhaps there's more to it. It is possible for individuals and even an entire culture to come under the spell of moral relativism necessary to the emotivist outlook.

The "negotiated self" after all is such because of the self's participation in the world. We become what we are because the integrated self is negotiated rather than discovered *ex nihilo*. That means we are formed dynamically in our social participation, and the social evolution of a culture is dynamic as well. This may not seem to fit a static conception of moral realism. They are reconciled by considering that the self is formed within a wide range of possible idiosyncratic personality traits, without implicating moral concerns. But more than that, we exercise agency in an environment of moral realism even in our subconscious or subrational participation in the world.

We can understand this through a consideration of Michael Polanyi's analysis of what he called "tacit knowledge."[13] It amounts to knowledge held subconsciously, because it is implicit; "tacit" by virtue of the fact that we're not actively aware of it. It is held in the

---

13 Discussed in his *Personal Knowledge/Towards a Post-Critical Philosophy*, (University of Chicago Press, 1958), and his slimmer volume *The Tacit Dimension*, (University of Chicago Press, 1966).

subconscious rather than in active consciousness. It is in the active consciousness that we exercise agency, formulating the decision to do x or not do y, and acting thereon. In our consciousness we direct our attention. We have a subconscious, but we are not actively aware of what goes on there because that's what it means to be *sub*-conscious. (For present purposes I use "subconscious" to mean also unconscious or preconscious).

To qualify this somewhat, one could as well simply speak in terms of active and aware knowledge as against implicit or tacit knowledge, bypassing the conceptual duality of conscious and subconscious, as Polanyi did. But here we invoke active- and sub-consciousness because, as noted in the preceding section, the subconscious may be the repository of certain axiomatic principles that—by virtue of being maintained in the subconscious—we're not really aware of. Polanyi suggests a mechanism for how this might work.

Polanyi explains tacit knowledge as that which you acquire without active, direct engagement. For example you know how to drive a nail with a hammer though your focus of attention is on the nail, and only "subsidiarily" on the hammer in your hand. The feel of it as you drive the nail provides tacit knowledge, acquired without active thought. You "inhabit" the hammer. (Michael Crawford masterfully describes this phenomenon, by the way, in his *The World Beyond Your Head*[14]). Your active, conscious knowledge, combined with tacit knowledge, constitutes what Polanyi calls "personal knowledge." Personal knowledge is an epistemological approach that acknowledges subjective predispositions in our apprehension of the objective external world.

In the same way you "inhabit" a physical tool like a hammer, you "inhabit" certain conceptual "frameworks" or "presuppositions" in your encounter of the world. These are conceptual axioms on which you build your conscious conception of reality. Epistemologically, it sets up a profound interaction between you and the

---

14 Farrar, Strauss, and Giroux, 2016.

world you perceive, rather than the self as dry, impersonal observer of objective facts, including moral facts.

To get just a little ahead of what Polanyi seems to be saying, it may be that the "presupposition" or "framework" you use like a hammer can include the spirit of negation sometimes referred to as "ressentiment," or critique that includes a presumption of bad faith, or a hermeneutic of suspicion.[15] This may be subtly implied, in fact, in Polanyi's subtitle: *Towards a Post-Critical Philosophy.* To be clear, axioms contained in tacit knowledge could likewise include a conservative disposition, a Burkean respect for evolved tradition and skepticism of untested change.

To go a step further using Polanyi's analysis, this could be the way in which the subconscious feeds the conscious more generally, contra Freud's theory of the functions of id, superego, and ego. Indeed, the interaction of tacit and explicit knowledge could signify the role of the subconscious as the meeting place between material and immaterial; between body and spirit. Hence the "place" where you interact with the spirit world, the "place" where your soul is fed or drained, by prayer or the occult respectively.

---

15 *The Mountain and the River,* chapter 14.

8

THE RISE OF THE THERAPEUTIC

Morality Versus Psychology

What brings about psychological man? We don't go to bed idealists and wake up the next morning selfish monsters. There has been a movement in society in which hierarchical values on a vertical moral dimension faded in significance, and became replaced over time by values increasingly formed and re-formed in the roil of social process. The mountain gives way to the river. Using again the vocabulary employed by Philip Rieff,[1] interdiction and renunciation are diminished, and release and remission emphasized.

Mountain and river should be in balance. Some individuals retain a mountain vision of objective, hierarchical values existing in ideals universally applicable to all. Others of a more emotive disposition readily discard the mountain vision to go splash in the river. The mountain disposition may obtain with insufficient latitude for remission and release; with insufficient deference to the significance of mystery, and aesthetics, and a sense of purpose. And likewise the river disposition may obtain with insufficient structure formed in a hierarchy of objective values. Neither the "form impulse" nor "sen-

---

1 Most plainly in his late-career book, *My Life Among the Deathworks/Illustrations of the Aesthetics of Authority*, (Charlottesville, VA: University of Virginia Press, 2006).

suous impulse" should be allowed to crowd out its opposite. In the thinking of Iain McGilchrist, the left-brain exercise of agentic, rational control must remain emissary to the master of right-brain big-picture contextual thinking.[2]

The inward turn in the subjective psychological realm corresponds to the unstructured river disposition in the realm of ideas. Both are consequences of the demise of objectivity. Truth and falsity, and good and evil, were once deemed hard-wired, so to speak, in the universe. In the postmodern era they have become human products, and the processes by which they came into being the dialectic; the historicism of Hegel by which we expect ongoing change in moral standards, rather than being alarmed at their mutability. Our value system is no longer understood as structured in the cosmos. It is formed in social Narrative, instead.

The postmodern era follows rejection of God. There's not an obvious date we could assign, though some will try. Rieff placed the tipping point at 1882, the year of publication of Nietzsche's *The Gay Science,* in which Nietzsche declared "God is dead" in Western culture. Some writers point to 1917 and a new cynicism following the devastation of what we now call World War One.[3] It has only been in recent years that most people, including Christians, would admit that prosperous Western countries are post-Christian, but obviously centuries of Christianity still strongly inform the post-Christian culture. The tipping point to a post-Christian society could plausibly be anywhere from mid-nineteenth to the mid-twentieth century. The marker for commencement of postmodernism should be the collapse from vertical to horizontal in our thinking, and that is best correlated with rejection of the God who sustains the vertical hierarchy of values. A reasonable moment for our purposes is commencement of the twentieth century.

---

2 *The Matter With Things,* (Perspectiva, 2021), preceded by *The Master and the Emissary,* (New Haven, CT: Yale University Press, 2019).

3 The cynicism artistically rendered in Erich Maria Remarque's *All Quiet on the Western Front* (1929).

That moment is contained within the life and rise in influence of Sigmund Freud, a significant contributor to the developing therapeutic mentality in the culture. His impact was so significant that we can reasonably consider him pivotal in that development. Before Freud (1856-1939), character was thought to be revealed in how one responded to external challenges. This was a part of the religious conception, in which we are free to exercise moral agency to attain peace with our conscience, which is imbued in us by God, the Source of moral values universally applicable among human beings.

Freud's conception of the *id* changed all that. He identified the "id" as the source of primal, innate, instinctive impulses, in tension with the superego by which we bring to bear rational restrictions on those instincts. Instead of character being revealed in how we respond to external challenges, it is revealed in how a person responds to internal tensions. It is how a person defends himself against his own potentially dangerous impulses.

Freud advocated psychoanalytic process to facilitate this, and his influence on how we came to think of human beings was enormous beyond our ability to imagine. We're all Freudians, now, because we remove God to ethereal theory or imagine Him out of existence altogether. Our moral project is therefore no longer the attempt to resolve tensions between the natural (or dust-formed) self, and the spiritual (or God-breathed) part of our being. We're to turn inward, instead, to try to resolve psychological tensions.

This is a search for a materialist explanation for the tragic sense. The failure to understand our God-imaged status opens us up to an ill-explained inner psychological tension, instead. Freud's theories were more descriptive than explanatory, but they were enough to initiate a re-framing of our sense of self. His theories fit the scientistic and materialist prejudices of the rapidly secularizing twentieth century. The Freudian construct of inner psychic tensions marked a decisive inward turn, in our thinking, toward psychological man. The tensions among the inner components of the human psyche replace the conscience, in explaining why we do what we do, and are what we are. Out with morality; in with psychology.

This was a quite fundamental shift in the way human beings understand themselves. We're cut off from God, so we're cut off from transcendent Source in formation of values and truth. While the austere verticality of transcendence is removed altogether, a form of horizontal immanence remains; a form we feel is more congenial to the inner man. Without God, one can still imagine an active moral presence in the world, but it is material rather than spiritual. It is social, and historicist, and dialectical.

What it is not is universal. To say moral values are "universal" or to describe them in terms of "universality" means they are the same for everyone. Objectivity and universality go together. Right and wrong are objective, though immaterial, features of our existence. Their objectivity makes them universal. Their universality results from their objectivity. The universality is unifying, because it means we refer to common values, a constant third reference point, in our debates.

We need to understand this in order to grasp the significance of the shift from the religious/logos frame to therapeutic subjectivity in our understanding of what makes something right or wrong. If right and wrong are generated in the flow of social process and, individually, from subjective interaction with social process, then right and wrong are not objective and not universal, which means we're no longer talking about *morality*, properly defined, at all. Right and wrong are framed in terms of psychology, rather than in terms of morality. What makes something right or wrong is no longer determined by how it compares to objective and universal standards of morality. Instead, what makes something right or wrong is determined by how it compares to a subjective and individualized standard of psychological well-being, and that, in turn, is socially formed.

Thus, in the therapeutic paradigm, "morality" has no meaning, unless the word is re-defined. For example one might describe conduct as "immoral" if it threatens individual "Identity," rather than violating an objective and universal standard of conduct such as those reflected in religious creeds. This re-definition is not just about vocabulary. It effaces the understanding of morality defined objectively and universally. It's about re-conceiving the self in relation to the world. This is sometimes summarized as "moral relativism," but the phrase is inadequate. The therapeutic paradigm does not operate on any concept of "morality" at all, if morality is understood properly as that which is objective and universal. Our plight is not just moral relativism, but the repudiation of morality altogether, the collapse of understanding that we live in a moral universe. Right and wrong are instead *socially* negotiated, and individually instantiated in the emotions.

A result of the shift from morality to psychology is that in the short run we become atomized and hostile to others. This results from the loss of commonality concerning right and wrong. There's no basis for agreement, no common third point to which to refer. In the long run, we open ourselves up to the totalitarian collective (see chapter 14), because in truth our subjectively-formed "Identity" is drawn not from esoteric spiritualism, as with old-school Gnostics, but from unreflective absorption of what the dialectical social process yields. It's still Gnosticism, but the source of esoteric knowledge is the dictate of socially generated Narrative, rather than spirit-generated gnosis. The transgressive instinct for revolution against interdicts of objective and universal morality does not make us strong individualists. We really just follow the herd, incorporating internally its evolving determination of right and wrong.

As always, the bleak secularism of this age borrows from theological ideas to construct a materialism that seems less brutal than it is; which retains a vague sense of larger meaning and purpose even if that is only the sum of humanity moving and acting in the world, generating social norms, Durkheimian "social facts" which take the place of a transcendent God. This faux immanence smooths the shift from fear of the Lord to finding values in the roil of social process. We seek psychological reconciliation with our surroundings, rather than with a God who knows my faults. This shift from vertical to horizontal in our subjective psychologies mirrors the same kind of shift in philosophical propositions. Just as postmodernism is the advent of process philosophies to replace theology, so the inner turn to psychological man is the advent of subjective emotivism to replace the look outward to objectivity, universality, and ultimately, transcendence, to form the sense of self.

As we have seen, the rise of psychological man leads inexorably to the cult of victimhood that so puzzles those who remember universal values. Its most important manifestation is in matters relating to sex; also the source of the most mischief for individuals and society. There are important ramifications for mental health—not just in the sense that psychology relates to mental processes, but in the sense that we suffer disorders of various kinds that seem new because they are.

All of this psychological distortion did not erupt into social consciousness all at once. It developed from bad ideas digested over time. We can much better understand the phenomenon of the therapeutic if we trace how it came into being, pre- and post-Freud.

Pre-Freud Therapeutic

To consider how the inward turn to the therapeutic became possible before Freud, let's condense millennia of the West into a few paragraphs. In the pagan world there was a sense of the logos and of idiosyncratic gods representing various concepts or ideals, like fertility, victory, death, and so on. There was no over-arching creator-god thought to sustain the extant hierarchy of values in the world, or of the natural order, except among the Hebrews. Both pagans and Jews had a sense of self that was outward-directed, however, in that they were not led primarily by their emotions, but by their place in the world as they received it.

The Hebrew conception of God broke out into the wider world upon the Resurrection of Jesus, the Christ. God sees all and knows all, and we are accountable to Him. Mankind is prone to evil but God's standard is moral perfection. Reconciliation to God was understood to come through the moral perfection and divinity of Jesus, and sinful mankind's *identification* with Him both in His death and in His Resurrection.

As Christians self-identified with the model of Christ, they understood themselves to be a new creation. This was a projection of self-image, imagining their own being from a perspective outside themselves. The "I" doing the perceiving distinct from the "I" that is modeled as a new creation in Christ. Not to compare ourselves to God, but we can say this is not unlike the self-identity of God declaring "I Am,"[4] and Christ's reiteration of it.[5] For God, the self-aware "I" declares its own identity. For us, the self-aware "I" declares its identity with God. We are thus drawn out of ourselves in forming a sense of self-identity. Identification with the Christ brought a self-identity that of course referenced external standards, but at the same time brought a sense of significance in the world that was available to anyone, even slaves.

We might pause to note parenthetically that this phenomenon of identification involves the duplicity of mind by which one can be both the "I" that perceives and the "I" that is the object of projected identification. This is a human capability that is not unique to the religious context. The projected identification can also be a form of victim status, as with racial or sexual minorities, or as against political adversaries, or in disordered psychological states, or as recipients of real or imagined abuse at the hands of stronger victimizers. It is likewise with the therapeutic worldview as a form of self-identification. The same mind contains both the discovering self and the

4 Exodus 3:14
5 John 8:58

discovered self.

As children of God sensitive to sin and able to avoid it and do good works, believers became aware of, and further developed, their personal sense of moral agency. Moral agency translates to conscious self-awareness and intent, in doing good and fleeing evil. Agency enhances the sense of self, requiring conscious deliberation and execution rather than, like pagans, unthinkingly doing what is expected.

There was a new sense both of significance and of humility, as children of God. This was the product of doctrine and ritual, and especially of prayer, which included introspection as an ongoing review of whether one's character was developing in a manner pleasing to God. This introspection was an inward turn, compared to unselfconscious participation in "the merry dance" of paganism, in which thoughts and actions were governed more by tradition and practice and expectations of social relations, than by agentic self-governance as we conceive it today.

In addition, obedience to Christian teaching required loving God and loving people. These precepts in turn required overcoming tribal barriers and developing empathy for others. Empathy for others means *feeling* what they feel. These elements of the burgeoning Christianity amounted to a comparatively inward self-awareness, one element in a larger sea-change in conception of self. Previously, one's self-conception began with his place in an existing order. The "individual" as we conceive it today did not exist. The birth of the individualist conception of self is best understood as coinciding with the spread of Christianity, which birthed the modern understanding of independent and individual agency.[6]

Religious re-conception of reality dominated in the West for centuries. In the middle of the second millennium *anno domini*, Western societies experienced a loosening of the religious perspective, in

---

6 A theme in Siedentop, Larry, *Inventing the Individual*, (Cambridge, MA: Harvard University Press, 2017).

favor of a drift to humanism, a resurgence of interest in pre-Christian classics and in this-world human flourishing. This meant a gradual re-direction toward what might today be called self-actualization.

The catholicity of the Christian church was challenged by schisms, most consequentially in the Reformation. Important differences in theology arose, but chief among them was that the former emphasis on mediated ritual observance gave way among Protestants to emphasis on unmediated inner sanctity. One's individual response to God was what mattered, not church authority, as much as the Catholic magisterium might promote reverence. Protestantism therefore represented a further inward turn. Eventually, further creedal splintering would render church authority increasingly questionable, but the inward, subjective turn in self-identity would remain.

The modern era is typically thought to have commenced circa 1600, with a seeking after God in His revelation in the order of the cosmos, through science. Empiricism was not in competition with faith, until sometime well into what is now called the Enlightenment, during which successes of science in understanding the material world seemed to crowd out a continuing place for religious mystery. By the late eighteenth century, many influential thinkers had concluded there was either no God, or only an impersonal, far-off God not active in the world. Self-formed authentic identity expanded as God seemed more distant.

Christianity had certainly not lost its hold at this time, but Erasmian tolerance had become religious liberty, consonant with other expanding civil liberties, the decline of monarchy, the assertion of natural law (as exemplified in the American Declaration of Independence) and the rise of the nation-state based on representative government. These developments changed individual self-identity profoundly. The self is to govern the self. The individual is self-sovereign, his moral authority superior to state, sovereign, church, and even, if he dares, God Himself.

The high-water mark for astringent Enlightenment rationalism was reached sometime around the time of the founding of the United States, 1776, though of course it's not amenable to precise dating. As though to soften its effects, and make up for the enfeebling of the mystery and aesthetics of religion, the era of Romanticism in the West had begun.[7] Recapturing some of the enchantment lost since the medieval age while retaining Enlightenment individualism, Romanticism emphasized emotion, subjectivity, imagination, and spontaneity. It was newly open to the irrational and the mysterious. We still refer to "Romantic" love, for example, to describe a pure feeling of emotional attachment to a potential mate, because the feeling is inexplicable, and seems to well up from inner depths unbidden. These are further instances of the mental dualities of self-as-observer/host and self-as-discovered/identity.

A key figure in the early Romantic era was Jean-Jacques Rousseau (1712-1778). He contributed significantly to philosophical propositions that would eventually underlie postmodernism.[8] His contribution to developing thought was not limited to propositional philosophy, however. His ideas relating to governance and property were founded on a subjective re-conception of individuals. "Man is born free, but he is everywhere in chains," he famously wrote. His sentimental writing reinforced a conception of the natural inner person as intrinsically good, with corruption and restraint and repression entering the life from the outside.

Similarly significant to the change in conception of self was Georg Wilhelm Friedrich Hegel (1770-1831). Hegel introduced the

---

7 A compelling picture of a philosophical turn toward how we conceive of self today is presented by Andrea Wulf, in her *Magnificent Rebels/The First Romantics and the Invention of the Self*, (Alfred A. Knopf, 2023). She places ground zero of the Romanticist movement in the "Jena Set" of writers and philosophers at the end of the eighteenth century, including among others Johann Wolfgang von Goethe, Friedrich Schiller, and Johann Gottlieb Fichte, all advancing an inward turn to self-examination and self-directedness, toward what we might call today self-actualization.

8 Discussed in chapters 16, 21, and 22 of *The Mountain and the River*.

historicist dialectic[9] which would later be developed on a materialist basis by Karl Marx. The discussion in preceding sections relating to the postmodern shift from vertical to horizontal are largely traceable to Hegel. History itself replaces God, in this paradigm. In the formation of self, the individual looks not to an eternal and unchanging God as author of virtue, but instead to changing social convention formed in the river of temporality. This places a person's inner formation in social process, the god of psychological man. He becomes exquisitely sensitive to every hiccup and sneeze in social ideas because society is the true source of the attitudes formed in his nascent inner being, though he may attribute it to the spontaneity of the subconscious *id*.

Perhaps the most emblematic historical event of the Romantic era was the French Revolution. Its animating force was emotional and irrational. It was Rousseau's natural man striving to be free. It proceeded on a social "spirit" of equality, much like the American founding was the "Spirit of '76." It was outwardly a bloody overthrow of aristocratic and clerical power, but it was inwardly a bursting forth of the interior man, yearning to break chains and be free. The spirit of liberation was founded on a conception of identity that twined Enlightenment individualism with the emotional passions of the Romantics. The urgent, insistent drive for liberation was founded on a self-image of the chained and repressed being, righteously clamoring to be free, and an ideal of personal autonomy. The same feeling would animate the "expressive individualism" of the postmodern era, curdling into the self-care therapeutic.

We no longer live in what is conventionally called the Romantic era, but it lives in us. It is manifested in the sense that there is an inner, mysterious component to our being that makes us utterly unique. This inner being lives in a state of repression until it is allowed to grow into the sunlight, so to speak—into conditions for that inner being's full flourishing. It is to this Romantic holdover

9 See chapter 12 of *The Mountain and the River*.

that the notion of "self-actualization" speaks, as in Abraham Maslow's mid-twentieth-century mischief-making "hierarchy of needs."[10] The Romantic era as such is usually thought to have run its course before Freud's time, but actually its psychology remained. There would have been no Freud had there been no Romanticism.

Freud

Psychology is a subset of philosophy which targets the subjective workings of mind. Of course those subjective workings are influenced in significant but unquantifiable ways by world-facts, social attitudes, and spirit, which makes the field of study quite open-ended in scope. Psychology is theoretical, but it is also practical, in that psychiatrists and therapists try to improve lives through their understanding of mind and behavior.

Because it is the study of mental states and their effects on the individual, psychology cannot be a rigorous laboratory study in the same way as physiology. It remains shrouded in mystery, though we can get to better understanding of how humans work by description, if not by explanation. Psychological practice is dependent on theory, and faulty theory can cause great harm. Mistakes of fact about human nature or physiology will render psychological practice not just ineffective, but affirmatively harmful.

Freud did not invent psychology, but he innovatively proposed theories of mind that were incalculably influential, for good or ill. He did invent a particular form of practice, which he described as "psychoanalysis." It has largely been abandoned, now, at least as it was practiced in Freud's day, but theories underlying it remain. Even among psychologists who do not consider themselves Freudian or

---

10 "A Theory of Human Motivation," *Psychological Review*, 1943. "Mischief-making" because it's often taken as a complete model of self-improvement that presupposes a socialism devoted to removing sources of repression like capitalism and the meaning-making structures of vertical Being.

neo-Freudian, the influence of Freudian theory has had a profound impact on how we see ourselves, whether we have any connection to or interest in psychology, or not. It has likewise had a profound impact on the culture at large, which in turn affects our thinking about self-identity.

Freud considered the subconscious an expansive arena for operation of intuitions, instincts, impulses, desires, and repressed emotions. There is certainly a form of preconsciousness, inchoate thoughts that do not present to our rational conscious awareness, as suggested by emotional dreams or circumstances in which we are emotionally troubled for a time before acquiring active consciousness of its source. But beyond these suggestions of subconscious mental activity, there is not much we can say.

Freud nonetheless had a lot to say, imputing to the subconscious instincts of eros and death, formed even in infancy in a child's relationship to mother and father. Freud eventually attached a name—the *id*—to this unknowable murky subconscious to which, with dubious evidence (for all his emphasis on rigorous science) he assigned particular instincts. He believed the id to be in tension with the superego of rational deliberation, which was, importantly, informed entirely by social norms and family influence. The collision of the id and the internalized superego produced the ego, the person presented to the world.

It's not hard to see why this sort of analysis might be taken at face value. There is a subconscious, and there is a rational consciousness informed by social norms, so the theory has superficial plausibility. But consider that we don't really know the scope of the subconscious. That's what it means to be *sub*-conscious. It could be as simple as the brain's sorting of emotions, or as complex and unknowable as a repository of Spirit. But left out of Freudian conception of the conscience and the superego is any natural or God-ordained source. That is, the superego is only where we internalize social expectations. Consistently with Freud's militant atheism, his theories denied any supernatural or God-ordained component to human nature.

And there are even more consequential points implicit in the theory. One is that there is no unchanging right/wrong; good/evil; moral/immoral. Social expectations necessarily will change with society, they are not objective, nor universal, nor eternal. Possibly Freud intended no philosophical breakthrough here. His writings seem to presume a static moral environment: that people just are a certain way because society makes them a certain way, and society's ideas of right and wrong are immutable. And moreover, that the psychologically formative family pattern is fixed in the cosmos. He apparently didn't foresee that the subjective turn he instigated would reverse these assumptions. Society can and does effect a shift in our perception of moral structure. Family structure, on which Freud so much relied, is not immune.

Similarly significant is the implicit loss of agency. If what we are is a complex mix of unknowable inner impulses, contesting with rational repressions imposed by social norms, there is precious little room left for exercise of personal agency. We don't pursue virtue of our own volition. Instead we are only the product of the tug-of-war between id and superego. We have little agentic influence over the kind of being that emerges from this struggle in the inner psyche.

The internal well of the subconscious is irrational, because that's what it means to be sub-conscious. In the postmodern era—again, coinciding with and boosted by Freud's rise in influence—the irrational is returned to a place of prominence, in our imagination. The hard edge of Enlightenment rationalism is softened by it, just as with religion and then with Romanticism. Postmodernism retains Romanticist notions, following upon Rousseau and ethereal visions of liberation. Religion, however, is largely abandoned. It still exists in pockets, but even among the observant its impact on the individual is significantly dissolved in the acid bath of postmodern materialism.

Religion thus leaves to the psychological inward turn the only remaining avenue for discerning the mysterious, irrational, aesthetic, poetic side to human beings that we know is there. Remember the second verse of Genesis: the rational is drawn up by God hierarchically from the substrate of the "waters" and "darkness" of the irrational and chaotic. That is the source of deeper meaning inaccessible to us in the rational consciousness. With religion discarded, the only place left to look for that vitalizing source of meaning is the subconscious, presented as a chaotic roil of waters and darkness underwriting our rationalist, empiricist, and increasingly machine-like existence. Psychology is the remaining place to escape the harsh light of dictatorial rationalism. Our pursuit of psychological explanation for the otherwise inexplicable is the new religion. The therapist couch replaces the confessional. The therapeutic worldview replaces the spiritual enchantment of the world.

In the cult of the therapeutic we seek meaning and purpose from inside, rather than outside. If there is any enchantment left in the world, it emanates from inward to outward. The whole of religious mystery begins in our inner Identity. To attack or criticize one's inner-formed identity is to attack the source of meaning and purpose. External *Authority*—God as Author of meaning—is replaced with internal *authenticity*—the personal quality of being real, or true. The concept of authenticity implies discovery within of a "true" essence, but this is a lie. What we find in there is unthinking conformity to ideology, dressed up as "authentic" identity. The locus of identity is thus found within the "authentic" inner self rather than from an external source of moral authority *over* self. Internal authenticity substitutes for external moral authority.

Questioning this substituted source of identity is a more serious affront than would be an attack on religious identity, because it is by definition personal. Critique of self-proclaimed identity is necessarily felt as critique of the self, rather than one's external affiliations. This phenomenon begins to get at the tender-hearted "snowflake" vulnerability of psychological man. The therapeutic worldview isn't just about maintaining emotional equanimity. It's about forming a sense of self from the charged interior being, in the same way a religious person of yesteryear would form a sense of self from the charged external Presence of God, the ground of *all* being. The religious person would seek to be formed by the Spirit of God. The psychological person seeks to be formed by the animating "spirit" emerging from the mysterious inner being.

That the Spirit of God is external and universal means a religious person is not personally affected by another's rejection of religious belief. The opposite is true for those who look inward for identity, in response to their religious impulse. The spiritual essence in that instance is construed as internal and personal. Rejection of the internal religion-substitute source of identity therefore means rejection of the whole of a being. You're not just attacking my religion. You're attacking me.

Freud was not the only thinker of his time concerned with subjective interiority. "Psychology" had long been an arena of philosophical thought. William James, for example, a contemporary of Freud, was considered a philosopher, and his philosophy included psychology, called by that name. His work involved explication of the workings of mind in theory, however, not a therapeutic praxis, dabbling in the neuroses of patients with talk to discern their inner promptings. Psychology was primarily a sub-discipline of philosophy, until Freud.

With Freud, it became a work-in-progress for individuals, wherein the focus was not just principles of mind and behavior generally, but application of principles to attempt healing of mental affliction. In psychological practice, then and now, there is an important distinction between serious incapacitating mental illness, and finding oneself caught in deleterious patterns of thought. Unequivocally serious mental illness, like incapacitating depression and schizophrenia, have long been within the province of the medical profession, though with limited success because cause and cure cannot typically be identified physiologically, nor treated with satisfactorily targeted pharmaceutical therapy.

Lesser impairments, like mild forms of ongoing anxiety or obsessive-compulsive behavior, might have been considered idiosyncratic quirks of personality, in an earlier day. Following Freud, they are all fair game for therapeutic intervention, to modify patterns of thought. This has had a profound effect on the advance of the therapeutic worldview more generally.

Freud was intent on making his mark in the world. His desire for fame caused him to seek an arena of effort with the widest latitude for innovation. He began by addressing what was then (in the late nineteenth century) called, variously, neurasthenia, hysteria, or neurosis. Freud developed psychoanalysis to help such patients break through certain self-inhibitions of thought resulting from excessively rigid social norms.

Although therapists today bring a range of attitudes and methods to their practices, the shadow of Freud hangs over them. The operating assumption is that some sort of repression prevents emergence of the individual's "true" self. We can't seem to get away from the absurd notion of a helpless, authentic, jailed but discoverable self, "Identity," yearning to be free. Therapists may unconsciously set about to free the client from presumptively excessive inhibiting repression rather than considering first that the client's problems may stem from excessive *dis*inhibition. Setting aside a morality paradigm for human behavior exacerbates this tendency.

Shouldn't therapy serve also an *inhibiting* function? It appears from the writings of Freud that he contemplated a static moral universe, with no idea of the moral wretchedness his theories would produce. He imagined an expansive subconscious as the repository of subliminally-experienced emotion, intuition, instincts, and impulses. That inner id would encounter the superego in dialectic fashion, producing the ego, the person's conscious outward presentation. The superego consisted, for Freud, in social norms including inhibiting interdicts. Of course social norms reflected religious moral restraints, and Freud had no truck with religion. That's not to say he was a libertine, however, quite the opposite. Rieff correctly called him a "moralist."[11] But "[t]he theory of repression became the foundation-stone of our understanding of the neuroses," Freud wrote, late in his career.[12]

Psychoanalysis therefore centered on untangling the repressions, but this would have only a remissive function. It never seems to have occurred to Freud that *renunciation* of impulses might itself be an instinct that resides also in the subconscious. If the conscience is imputed by God, such that violation of it produces guilt (as opposed to the shame of social opprobrium), then renunciation of impulses is as much a feature of the subconscious as the remissive impulse. There is then no dialectical negotiation to take place between id and superego—these are unnecessary constructs that create confusion. There is a morally right way and wrong way to behave, and developing habits of right moral thinking moves one closer to ideal. But internal inhibition of immoral thought would count as repression, in the Freudian construct.

The conscience, for Freud, reflected only the social imposition of interdicts, situated with the repression-inducing superego. Freud's approach would be to first release the repression so that the id and superego might be reconciled; not that he would do away entirely with the moral dictates of the superego. But the effect of the flawed id/superego construct was to stress release and remission at the expense of renunciation.

Can therapy (or the self-care therapeutic mindset) only ever be disinhibiting? It's hard to imagine, in today's environment, the opposite: encouragement to self-interdictory inhibition, such as by help-

---

11 Rieff, Philip, *Freud: The Mind of a Moralist*, (Chicago: University of Chicago Press, 1979).

12 Freud, Sigmund, *An Autobiographical Study*, transl. by James Strachey, (New York: W.W. Norton, 1952), p. 32, (first published 1925, and with revision by Freud, 1935).

ing the client man up, embrace stoic rectitude and reticence, and sublimate impulses to finer virtues. It seems more likely only ever moving toward disinhibition, like with those frozen Victorian ladies of yore. In the age of the therapeutic we've all got the vapors. We swoon onto the couch, lace kerchief at forehead. But now it's not the suggestion of license that undoes us. It's the suggestion of restraint. We're led by every emotional impulse and repulsed by every suggestion of moral probity. What that looks like is timorous victimhood and self-righteous entitlement. Therapy itself is an element of the downward moral spiral we're witnessing. Exclusion of moral considerations is the source of our mental health epidemic, not its cure.

Post-Freud Therapeutic

Today we've mostly moved beyond psychoanalysis as Freud conceived it. Talk therapy proceeds on other theories, but even therapists who don't consider themselves Freudian or neo-Freudian have imbibed some of these foundational principles concerning the subconscious, and what makes the self. Most therapists are irreligious, and those that therapize from a position of religious belief often do not appreciate the inconsistencies, and so may lay down Freudian cornerstones that make the whole project unstable.

This matters because people typically go to therapy to be relieved of various "hang-ups," not to learn how to shape their lives consistently with a God-informed conscience. And it matters because this is not just a matter of talk therapy practice. It is a matter of how we see ourselves functioning in the world; the self therapizing the self regardless whether we visit a professional therapist for intervention. It's a cultural issue, not just a uniquely personal one.

Therapy (and again, the therapeutic mindset, let's not be limited to talk therapy) takes morality out of the equation. We address questions of psychology from what we consider a scientific standpoint, excluding questions of morality and immorality as unhelpful and perhaps inappropriately judgmental. If morality is considered at all, it is considered as a contributor to the repressions that need untangling in the postmodern, enlightened view of personality disorders and psychological syndromes. To engage a moral/immoral dichotomy seems more the problem than the cure, in the therapeutic worldview, but that's exactly backward.

The re-conception of self accelerated by Freud was abetted in the inter-war period by Freud-influenced surrealists, with new appreciation for the imagination associated with the unconscious and irrational aspect of being. Alongside such influences were developments in postmodern philosophies, especially after the Second World War, devoted to creating meaning out of horizontal social process rather than vertical transcendently-sourced hierarchies of value.[13]

Freud's understanding of self was reiterated in the thinking of liberationists like Herbert Marcuse, whose influential *Eros and Civilization* was subtitled *A Philosophical Inquiry into Freud*.[14] Marcuse's philosophical foundations for sexual revolution and other manifestations of the cult of self-fulfillment were presented as self-identity in opposition to the acquisitive and consumerist values of a self-satisfied bourgeois middle class.

The countercultural Sixties was a rebellion against stoic, repressive self-control, presaged by the antics of the beatniks, like Jack Kerouac who, in his 1957 *On The Road*, vaulted decadence and dissipation into ultimate virtues. This was an era of "finding yourself," because the self is supposedly lost in all the conformist artificiality. It wasn't just stuffy post-war prosperity that so bothered those caught up in the rising spirit of transgression. It was a desire for freedom, but "freedom" is among the most abused words in the

---

13 Those developments were the central point of the author's *The Mountain and the River*.

14 Marcuse, Herbert, *Eros and Civilization/A Philosophical Inquiry into Freud*, (Boston: Beacon Press, 1955).

English language. What does it mean? The generations born after World War II yearned for "freedom," but what the deepening therapeutic culture taught us to want was a *feeling* of freedom, not the real thing premised on personal independence and self-responsibility. The faux-freedom really only means less responsibility and more opportunity for self-indulgence. Self-actualization meant care and nurturing of the inner id to enable it to burst forward in a noisy show of colorful creativity. What was celebrated was Whitman's barbaric yawp, shouted over the rooftops of the world. This entailed removing the barriers of stuffy conformism that so stunted the emergence of the discoverable inner being.

In retrospect, it's clear that these early cultural indicators were ushering in an era of collapse: the rapid dismantling of idealistic structure to society, causing it to fall in on itself morally. For so many individuals, too, a re-direction of energies away from virtue and toward self-actualization; release of the repressed inner being to breathe the "free" air. The individual looking outward to conform himself to external virtues was replaced by the militant self-absorbed shell struggling to feed the timorous but hungry inner being. Instead of self-actualization, the inward re-direction is a moral collapse—a black hole, sucking all life into itself.

It was into this mass psychosis that Philip Rieff spoke, in 1966, in *The Triumph of the Therapeutic*.[15] Alas, it would take some time for his observations to take root, so deep was the soil of sterile narcissism. Rieff entirely grasped that the therapeutic worldview arose because of the absence of sacred order to underwrite the interdicts necessary to structure a civilization. In this respect he observed the reality that forward-thinkers like Matthew Arnold and Friedrich Nietzsche (and others) predicted. Rieff's work on the subject is the most relevant and the most on-target. Other thinkers have contributed, however, including for example Christopher Lasch, with

---

15 ISI Books, 2007, 2nd ed., (first published 1966).

The Culture of Narcissism.[16]

Rieff's and Lasch's books have sold well, and are certainly part of the conversation, but they have not turned the tide. It would be asking a lot of a few books to do so, however, so wide and so deep is the tsunami of pop psychology self-help which continues to feed the beast. The conception of self has evolved dramatically over the last century, so much so that many people unthinkingly make self-care their life's work, and self-care means giving primacy to one's emotions. Self-control no longer counts as a virtue at all, if by it we mean control of the emotions. Emotion has authority over reason, which means it is satisfied first. We don't put emotions on hold, instead emotion guides reason. "Your feelings are valid," we hear, even when they're not.

---

16 W.W. Norton, 1979.

9
RELIGION AND THE
THERAPEUTIC

Pagan to Religious to Therapeutic

We are in a new era. Our longest realistic look-back is to pagan times, and from there we observe the development of monotheistic religion. Now religion is in decline. Does that revert us to paganism? Or to something else?

Jews as a tribe departed from the pagan upholding of child sacrifice, and sexual perversion, and instrumental usage of others—as with the gods of Molech, Asherah, and Ba'al, respectively. Theirs was a moral universe, willingly departing from the surrounding pagan peoples. Even pagans understood the moral law, however, which is after all written on the heart. Consequently, they knew they needed saving. The problem for the pagan was how? Their theology, such as it was, mitigated moral responsibility through adherence to social norms, and the inevitability of fate, and belief in transition to a vaguely understood afterlife. This wasn't sufficient to dispel the tragic sense, however. The message of the Gospel—remission of sins in Christ—came as a message of release. A load off the shoulders. This was a significant contributor to the explosive growth of Christianity across the pagan world in the first centuries after the resurrection of Jesus. The negative weight of moral significance was borne by God, not by us. Faith replaced sacrifice.

For those now trapped in the therapeutic worldview, however, there is no desire to be forgiven; indeed no Forgiver in sight and nothing from which to be forgiven. Those who have ingested the therapeutic relinquish perception of the moral law. The moral sense shifts to adherence to social norms, as with the pagans. The moral project is no longer personally seeking virtue and avoiding vice, as moral agents with moral responsibility. It's not that such moral questions are answered in a different way. It's that they're never asked in the first place. Instead right and wrong are delineated according to psychological impact. Indignation may be quite strong in self-righteous psychological man, but "morality" is no longer the right word for its provenance because morality, the word, implies objective, universal standards and a moral law-giver. The ubiquitous self-righteous indignation is over transgression of social mores, only. Virtue-signaling has always to do with environmental conscientiousness or racial sensitivity or sexual openness; never with humility, reverence, or sexual rectitude. Pascal's dictum (in his *Pensées*) is again proven true: "There are only two kinds of men: the righteous who think they are sinners and the sinners who think they are righteous."

For therapeutic man the Gospel just comes across as a message of guilt, one that would impose an impossible burden of self-restraint against the inner (and innocent) self. He does not believe the way to peace is God's intervention in our task of bearing the weight of sin. Sin is not taken seriously. Therapeutic man is likely to regard the Gospel story as, at best, a sentimental fable for children, provided its gritty story-line is properly sanitized. Therapeutic man knows the Christian story. He may be angry about its continued relevance in the world around him because it threatens his vision of self. But more likely, the re-defined conception of relative truth allows him to re-imagine its troubling moral dimension, recasting its central character as a model of postmodern Niceness.

With his wispy understanding of the God of yesteryear, thera-

peutic man has no sense of being an idolater, because he's not engaged in worshipping images outside himself. His "god" is perceived
internally, and invisibly. The difference in his outlook and that of
Jews and Christians is that for therapeutic man, the "god" also *originates* there in that internal darkness. The new god is a swirl of sen-
sation, wishes, desire, and pleasure all together in the insistent inner
id, the emerging internal being, self-righteous and indignantly so.

The pagan world was unfamiliar with Christian ideas, but of
course therapeutic man is partly formed by them. He has selectively
taken certain of them—like love of fellow man and absence of
prejudice and protection of the downtrodden—and has made of
these new internal idols, rigid absolutes with which to rule others.
Faith, hope, and love, long-held Christian values, are denatured.
"Faith" is re-cast as existentialist clinging to the this-world optimism
of "hope" for a better tomorrow until we die, and "love"—well,
"love is love." You do you. Love is confused with sentiment and
may be strongly felt in the moment, but is ultimately ephemeral and
fleeting before the god of self.

And finally, perhaps most importantly, those infected now with
the therapeutic worldview have something (disorder, trauma, oppression) other than themselves to blame for their ills, muffling the
conscience, and if the conscience nonetheless speaks too loud, psychological man remembers it is only the invention of discredited
Judaism and Christianity anyway, enculturated flotsam not yet fully
worn away in the new dispensation of the therapeutic. Psychological
man is incapable of linking the sacredness of the conscience, with
its attendant moral agency, to the dignity of the human person.

There was a sacred order to paganism, though shored up by
ancestor-worship and allegiance to rote social patterns. But paganism fostered an anemic sense of personal agency compared to that
which the monotheisms bestowed. When the Jewish version of sacred order burst out into the wider world with Christianity, this was
truly revolutionary. And yet not as revolutionary as Christianity's

collapse. There is no longer a sacred order, in the popular imagination, and so there is nothing but the churn of history to water our imaginations. The social flow of ideas across time taints perception of logos, and the taint leaches into the subterranean river of our inner psychology. We reach down there to draw up the personalized meaning we conceive to be our authentic, actualized uniqueness unadulterated by lockstep religious conformity. This can yield a sense of triumphant self discerned esoterically, but it's not spiritual mysticism therapeutic man draws upon. It is the received wisdom of Narrative telos produced in the social dialectic, absorbed and mystically concealed in the subconscious, surfacing to consciousness as gnosis seemingly revealed in the charged inner being. The therapeutic worldview thus makes us cyphers of social whim. It gradually dissolves agency, and therefore morality, and therefore dignity, and therefore meaningful participation in the world as the children of God we were meant to be.

Religion provided a kind of mediation of opposing impulses to restraint and discipline and rule-making and rule-following, on the one hand, and on the other, the impulse for release or remission; for freedom unrestrained by the tragic sense imposed by mortality and judgment. Apart from mediating opposing dispositions in mankind, religion also mediated mankind's relationship to the ineffable, by providing a necessary balance between the interdictory and the remissive inside a structure that also delivered genuine meaning and purpose to one's life.

With the demise of religion there has been a loss of appreciation for the necessity of the forms and structure generated by immutable moral categories in our world. Those moral categories meant interdicts channeling our desires toward virtue, and corresponding renunciation of impulses that would end in vice. Without such interdicts, moral forms and structure are corroded or collapse altogether. Self-indulgence is then the order of the day. There is thus a clear distinction between the religious way of encountering the world, and that of the therapeutic. Philip Rieff wrote: "religious man was born to be saved; psychological man was born to be pleased."[1] This is the fundamental divide between the renunciatory mode of religion, on the one hand, and the self-care mode of the therapeutic, on the other.

In the monotheisms, mankind is understood to be at enmity to a perfect and just God, and so people must be saved; that is, reconciled to God by a power greater than people themselves can muster. In Christianity, they must be reconciled to God by God. But why? Why does man need saving? Because without this reconciliation, he remains unredeemed. The wrath of God does not descend upon him because he doesn't finally come around to belief. It *remains* upon him because he was born into it; a sinner unable to live to God's standards.[2] Religious doctrine contains the principle of salvation necessitated by sin, and religious practice reinforces the need to minimize the sin. That practice is renunciation of natural but guilt-inducing desires.

Sin has no place in the therapeutic self-conception, however. Not that a person so affected will think he's perfectly fine, all the time. Quite to the contrary, there is an ongoing need for therapeutic self-care that is every bit as important to psychological man as avoidance of sin is to religious man. Sin and psychological harm are quite distinct, as are their opposites: avoidance of sin and self-care. Avoidance of sin means sensitivity to the conscience and respect for an external standard of behavior. The etymology of the word "sin" suggests missing the mark, like an arrow in flight going off-target.

In the therapeutic conception, by contrast, evil exists out there somewhere; the heart is innocent. This was the conclusion of Jean-Jacques Rousseau, in what he felt as a moment of epiphany. This was in the mid-eighteenth century, coming out of the dominant

1 *The Triumph of the Therapeutic*, p. 19
2 John 3:36: "Whoever believes in the Son has eternal life; whoever does not obey the Son shall not see life, but the wrath of God *remains* on him." (emphasis added).

Christian milieu in which it was well understood that the heart was "prone to wander," as a hymn from Rousseau's time put it.[3] Rousseau wasn't the first post-Christian, nor the first to consider there is some good in mankind. Obviously we see good in people all the time. But Rousseau, and presumably others who thought like him, considered the origin of evil in mankind to be the result of corrupting social influences, rather than something there inside the person all the while, as Christianity holds.

This re-conception of the origin of evil is no small thing. If the human heart is essentially good except as corrupted by bad influences, then the self is innocent of moral transgression. The only transgression in play is that of others against the pure, innocent, and guiltless self. This removes a sense of moral responsibility from one's self-conception, but also impugns others who violate the self's pure integrity. There is a direct, unbroken link between thought like Rousseau's, and the therapeutic feeling of vulnerability and self-righteous victimhood. One's conduct is a product of his psychology, which means it's not a product of his self-will. Loss of self-will, of agency, means victimhood. Things just happen to psychological man, and his psychology rather than his personal agency determines the response. The therapeutic worldview is a sophisticated form of moral evasion.

Good and Evil

But what is good, and what is evil? In the religious worldview, there is no absence of guidance. Moses didn't bring down from Sinai "the ten suggestions." There is in addition a wealth of classical guidance on what is virtue and what is vice. And of course, there is the conscience, the internal prompting of guilt in response to certain acts and omissions, a prompting authored by God, who places

---

3 *Come Thou Fount of Every Blessing* by Robert Robinson (1758).

it in our hearts. We know we've done wrong (or avoid wrong pro-spectively) when we feel this gut-level instinct attached to some kinds of conduct and not others.

There is a distinction between guilt and shame which signifies a shift from the religious to the therapeutic. Guilt wells up from in-side unbidden. It is what we feel when we know we've transgressed a universal moral law written on the heart. Importantly, it doesn't matter whether any other person even knows about it. The pressure seems to come from above though it is felt internally as a violation of conscience. An act committed in secret may induce guilt even if no one else learns about it.

Shame, on the other hand, has its origins in society around you, though it manifests internally in response. You feel shame when you act in a way you know brings disapproval of others. It could even result from an act that is not morally wrong. Often guilt and shame are felt together, where society's strictures and the moral law coin-cide. But it's possible to feel one and not the other. Because the feeling of shame derives from intersubjectivity[4] with others, it is not necessarily the result of transgression of universal moral law. That which produces guilt is evil. That which produces shame may not be.

There is ample room for confusion, however, in the world of the therapeutic. Relying on our feelings, we may conflate guilt and shame, and call evil that which violates merely a social norm, rather than a moral law written on the heart. Guilt and shame often over-lap, when they result from conduct that violates both moral law and social expectation. The feelings associated with guilt, and of shame, are similar. And if we have rejected God as the author of the con-science, there is no other place to attach the feeling that results, than transgression of social norms. In this way the distinction between

---

4 Again, conscious self-awareness combined with other-awareness combined with consciousness of others' self- and other-awareness, resulting in the consciousness play-back that creates the sense of society.

guilt and shame is lost, and cannot serve as a distinguisher between God's law and society's.

The shift from the religious worldview to the therapeutic entails a confusion in how we conceive of evil and of good. The very concepts of evil and good may seem mutable in the same way as social norms. But good and evil are immutable. For example a sexual sin that ought to produce guilt, as a transgression of moral law, may be acceptable in a society in moral free-fall. It doesn't produce shame, and the conscience may be so blunted by the internalized language of the therapeutic that we're left literally shameless in transgression of moral law.

And yet, this shamelessness does not translate to emotional strength. Quite the contrary, psychological man is rendered more timorous and emotionally frail when society dictates its version of "morality" rather than finding the real thing embedded in the cosmos. If good is rooted only in changing social norms, then so is evil. Society (not conscience, not God, not universally understood virtue) tells us what to celebrate, but also what to vilify. This leaves us vulnerable all the time that its Narrative will turn on us, making us instantly an object of opprobrium, heaping shame for "sin" that wasn't sin yesterday. This danger makes us quick to conform to what the social machine requires. We are ever conscious of the dangers of wandering out of sync to the rhythm of the midge swarm; of losing our place in the murmuration of starlings to which our allegiance is forsworn. Every step is fraught. If good and evil are not objective and universal and unchanging, but are instead subject to social fashion, then our heightened sense of vulnerability is well-founded.

And this cuts both ways. Psychological man is always potentially the victim of changing social mores, but so is everyone else, and so psychological man willingly harvests self-righteous indignation from the social transgressions of others. Moral relativism means heightened vulnerability but also heightened cruelty. Permanent estrangement from family members, to better adhere to the moment's social mores, can feel not only justified, but virtuous. The Narrative can normalize any sexual perversion and you dare not say a word. If society says bigotry is the most heinous crime, then any expression that could be construed as containing a whiff of preference for clan or tribe or nation invites an outpouring of undiluted disgust. Vulnerability and viciousness go together, as with a beaten dog.

Transcendent morals are felt within, but so are social mores, once internalized. Emotivism wears down the hard edges of both, jumbling God-ordained and socially-imposed interdicts. We can become confused about the source of conscience, ascribing it partially or entirely to social norms formed in dialectic Narrative. This can lead to a confusion of what ought to count as good and evil, because social norms and God-ordained good and evil may be in conflict. This confusion is possible, even likely, within a therapeutic worldview.

In the therapeutic way of thinking, feelings dictate what is called moral "good" and "evil." They are not moral universals, therefore, and may mutate according to social fashion. The self-care of the therapeutic means sensitivity to one's own emotions and vigilance against external threats to them. That includes the shame that would result from violation of social norms. The self-care imperative means adjusting to social norms in order to avoid psychological harm.

The herd effect should be obvious. If one's first principle is to garner good vibes through affirmation, going along with the drift of society is a must. This doesn't mean political quiescence. Quite the opposite. Political activism is a form of social joining with like-minded others. The like-mindedness inheres in jointly protecting that which makes him psychological man: the horizontal/immanent/process production of truth and values, in all things. That means radical politics based on emotive rebellion against stable categories wherever they are found; an instinct of deconstruction and teleological "progress" in service to the temporal god of the dialectic.

Moral realism is replaced by moral relativism, and moral relativism allows for social participation in what is deemed "moral" and "immoral." Political conviction and activism in the direction of deconstruction of moral absolutes is necessary to maintenance of the therapeutic worldview. It is not coincidental that psychological man drives radical politics and cultural shifts. It is a means of participation in the formation of the cultural values that replace eternal ones.

The therapeutic and the religious conceptions differ further with respect to ultimate questions of meaning and purpose in our lives. Religion answers these. The therapeutic does not. This critical difference is the reason the replacement of religion by the therapeutic is devastating for individuals and ultimately for society. "Man's search for meaning is the primary motivation in his life," wrote Victor Frankl in 1946. Rather than presenting and attempting to answer the question of meaning, the therapeutic avoids the question.

This is a legacy of Freud. We're not to be about figuring out why we are here or what is ultimately true and right and what ideals we should strive for. Instead we're to turn inward to engage in continuous rumination to the end of reconciling id and superego. Rather than look outward to compare the self to objective standards of virtue, we man the ramparts to detect threats to the innocent inner being. Achieving a healthy ego is the only meaning. Such ideals as there are exist in service to that end.

The purpose of religion is to point us to God. This is the cure for the unrest of the soul burdened with the dictates of conscience and awareness of reality beyond this mortal plane, in which resides a Person ultimately demanding if also ultimately loving. The cure is acknowledgement of sin and the need for saving. The cure is never complete in this life, but consists in continuous striving toward the model of perfection at the pinnacle of vertical values.

The therapeutic disposition offers no cure, because there is no illness—sin—to be cured from. There is no deviation from moral standard that must be addressed, but rather a balance to maintain among warring drives in the subjective inner psyche. This is a function of therapy. It does not provide meaning and purpose for human beings; it is a maintenance program only.

In the religious disposition, there is a drawing out of oneself into the dictates of doctrine but also its affirmation in community brought together by those universal—and therefore commonly held—values. The religious community of which one is a part mediates, along with doctrine and spirit, between the individual and the ineffable. Religious community is one means toward the end of opening oneself to God.

In the therapeutic disposition, means and ends are reversed. Openness to the ineffable means looking within, because it is there inside my mysterious charged inner being, not out there superintending the cosmos. There is therefore no drawing out of self. Rather, we are drawn within, to a process of ongoing self-analysis and self-care of the sacred inner being. We have a need for community, however, and indeed that need is even stronger for psychological man. Community, if given over to the therapeutic, reinforces the shift from moral realism to elastic moral relativism. Such community reinforces the turn inward for the ineffable no longer found externally in a putative God. That ineffable within and its reinforcement in moral relativism is a solvent for losing oneself in oceanic feeling of community. Social consensus, rather than universality of value, is the means, and the end is harmonious communitarianism.

But, we can lose ourselves in ecstatic feelings of community only insofar as that community is hectored into compliance with self-care therapeutic imperatives, so it poses no threat to the equanimity of the inner being. The self is not strengthened in resilience against the barbs of this world. Instead the barbs of the world must be blunted in cancel-culture thought policing. Instead of personal resilience, the world outside must be brought into conformity with a socially-negotiated standard of psychological self-care. This is what prescribes the political efforts of psychological man: fencing against threats which threaten the innocent, creative, vibrant person within, whose ultimate purpose is ecstatic community with people, rather than communion with God.

Confusion of Psychology and Religion

Religious man and psychological man stand at opposite poles. And yet, the difference is shrouded in misunderstanding. Psychological man's sense of inner tension may be conflated with the religious impulse. The transcendence of God may be deemphasized in favor of His immanence, and His immanence re-imagined without judgment.

One would think that self-confident teachers of religion would be zealous in glorifying God, which would mean preserving an understanding of the givenness of His creation, and His demand of righteousness. But we allow softer, gentler impulses of therapy to blunt the hard edges of truth. It's an attempt to tame the wild God; to try to make Him less dangerous. We understand Jesus as sacrificial Lamb but forget the Lion of Judah in our eschatology. The Holy Spirit, God present in the world, can be conflated with the psychology the atheist culture presents.

The secular world contributes to the watering down of what Christians say they believe, so that psychological man seems to be the same as religious man. Indeed, religion may be thought to compel our turn to psychological man, as both religious man and psychological man are poorly understood. The church is not immune to the persuasions of the therapeutic mentality, far from it. Christianity's messages of love, forgiveness, and forbearance have been allowed to occlude its messages of sin, evil, and need for redemption. And this to such an extent that whole denominations of Protestants have calved off the believing church to form enclaves of therapeutic reinforcement that are churches in name only. Likewise factions of Catholics and Orthodox and others.

Commentators with understanding of what has happened to the Christian church have repeatedly warned that congregants who haven't thrown over belief altogether nonetheless dilute it to the degree that it is not Christianity at all, but "moral therapeutic deism." An etiolated form of interdictory structure remains, compromised by social norms of secular society, especially concerning sexual ethics in the wake of the sexual revolution. The nuances of trinitarian Christianity are ignored, replaced with a rationalistic necessary-god deism, much like that of Aristotle and many of the Enlightenment-era intellectuals. God's immanence is thereby discarded so that a therapeutic form of dialectic faux-immanence can take its place.

The "therapeutic" portion of the new religion speaks for itself in the context of this discussion. The modern church is no longer primarily concerned with the supernatural, or virtue, or purity, or sin. Instead it is concerned with self-actualization: being the best one can be, the old lie of prosperity hawkers cherry-picking among doctrines to emphasize only what is this-world relevant. Left in the trampled dust are principles of heaven, hell, sin, confession, guilt, the crucifixion, and the demand that we take up our cross daily and bear it. These have no place in the therapeutic arena of self-actualization, in which the gritty reality of human depravity makes no appearance.

"Self-actualization" is sometimes attributed to Abraham Maslow's conception of a hierarchy of needs, in which essentials of living, like food and shelter, are satisfied first, and then various psychological needs in ascending order, culminating in self-actualization. One could debate the extent of Maslow's direct contribution to pop psychology, but certainly the concept it embodies has become ubiquitous. Its operative principle is self-self-self; I-I-I: how can *I* get what *I* need to be all *I* can be? Postmodern man in prosperous societies reflexively looks for meaning and purpose internally, in work and recreation and relationships. This way of thinking epitomizes psychological man's priority of care for the inner being.

In the age of psychological man, the therapeutic mindset has superseded the sense of sin as an explanation for missing the mark. Our actions are not construed as proper or improper according to an eternal moral standard. Instead they're construed according to a therapeutic standard: whether they contribute to, or detract from, one's mental well-being and self-actualization. If you act improperly, under the therapeutic regime, you're manifesting a disorder of the inner subjective being, rather than exercising agency in an objectively wrongful way.

If right and wrong is fixed and immutable, then people exercise agency to choose right or wrong. This makes us free. Fixed moral standards contrast to relativism, whereby we change the moral standards rather than the choices we make. In the therapeutic mindset, freedom and agency are no longer relevant values, but the meanings of the words are muddled. Freedom comes to mean "you do you," and I'll do me, able to pursue our instinctual or perverted desires rather than having the ability to renounce evil. Agency comes to mean having a choice among brand names, rather than responsibility for choosing good, or choosing evil. Moral standards become mutable according to how they affect the health of the inner being. By drifting into the therapeutic self-care model of evaluating behavior, we also drift away from freedom and responsibility for how we exercise it. It is a move from agency to passivity, and from passivity to ideological capture.

The moral therapeutic deism of the modern church is both cause and effect of the church's general passivity, in matters of doctrine and practice.[5] Passivity induces indifference to hard doctrine, allowing the anti-faith therapeutic mentality to sweep in and soften the edges of hard principles like judgment and hell. And moral therapeutic deism is hardly a set of religious principles worth putting

---

5 See, e.g., Ian Huyett, "The Problem of Christian Passivity," *Hoc Signo* (Substack), September 8, 2023.

oneself out for. It will grow no martyrs who prefer death to denying Christ. It is in fact the prevailing secular culture, but with the addition of a vaguely remembered story line of that Jesus guy. It induces passivity rather than zeal, the soft lukewarm tasteless mush about which we have been warned.[6]

---

6 Revelation 3:16-18

10
RESURGENT GNOSTICISM

Source of Identity

W e've thus far made passing reference to "Gnosticism" to describe the therapeutic worldview. In this chapter we develop the connection, considering especially the work of Eric Voegelin (1901-1985). One thesis in this chapter is that the ubiquitous references in public discourse to one's "identity" is something deeper than a statement of affiliation. It is rather a statement of discovery; the discovery of a true and authentic inner being. This conception of identity is what is meant by "I identify as x:" Not that one aspires to x, or aligns with x, but that x-ness emerges fully formed from within upon therapeutic self-exploration. It is experienced as passive reception rather than agentic assertion.

A person whose identity is formed through interaction with the objective world imagined to be Godless will experience a sense of unease or anxiety from the supposition that this identity is temporary, changeable, and formed merely from accidents of life, so there is no ultimate meaning to his existence. This state is untenable for human beings. We intuit on a deep level that there is more to us.[1]

---

1 The theme of the author's *Intuition of Significance*, (Eugene, OR: Resource Publications, 2020).

If that specialness is not explained by our God-breathed status, then it must be explained some other way. And that other way may be a conviction that there is some "real" me that is deeper than the sum of changing temporal influences. A real me that is internal, rather than a product of the meaningless external. That is the discovered self, taken as one's true Identity.

"Identity" as gnostic subjectivity presents as the only alternative to the moral realism of the logos. It seems to preserve unbounded personal control because the gnosis is an inward look rather than outward. That desire for control can be expressed in throwing over ontological boundaries to one's essence, including even the given-ness of male/female differentiation. But that leaves one's essence afloat in infinite boundlessness, an unreality of oceanic feeling. Esoterically-derived gnosis seems to provide control over one's self-redefinition. It registers internally as a spontaneous inner knowing, as with the Gnostics of antiquity. Left unanswered is the origin of that spontaneous inner knowing. It is not attributed to spirit, in the materialist dispensation of the therapeutic. Its provenance is left unanswered, but its true source is social messaging, because social mores are thought to replace moral realism. The social source of morality is not acknowledged, however, and so the source of Identity remains shrouded in mystery. Psychological man is content to leave the question of his Identity's source unanswered. It is a mystery. The kind of mystery sourced in the charism of religion, but of course religion's claim to extant moral realism has been rejected. Identity wells up within, but "why" and "how" are never answered.

The perception of inner-formed Identity is really just garbled digestion of social messaging. We learn that we are to regard ourselves each as the center of the universe, now that God is deposed, and in that position we are the measure of all things, though incapacitated and made vulnerable by unrelieved narcissism. Even the sense of self is entirely self-formed. And yet that inner being is unwittingly dictated to us, the combination of socially-approved norms which include the norm that we decide our essence. No one ever decides his inner essence is an ascetic Stylite, though he may virtue-signal just as ostentatiously. The inner essence is only ever a comfortable but vulnerable victim or victim-adjacent unactualized being, unbounded by sexual norms of the past or fixed categories of things and ideas. Psychological man is oblivious to the social influence on formation of his inner being. It is regarded as having welled up *ex nihilo* from the depths of the psyche. We make ourselves gods, and like the real God of Genesis hover over the face of the waters to draw up Identity from the formless void of the id.

Identity is not truly self-formed, however. Its provenance is mysterious only to psychological man, the postmodernist so given over to the therapeutic worldview that he lives in the delusion that ontological physical boundaries can be transcended. There are to be no interdicts, no boundaries, no form, and so no renunciation. Ultimate freedom. All release into the void. All remission of restraint. And all a repudiation of reality in its glorious architectures of hierarchy built on fixed categories of things, and meaning, starting with that first separation of heaven and earth, in the beginning. God is hated by embittered new Gnostics for His creation and all His other dear crimes.

It is further within the theme of this chapter that this mode of passive discovery of identity is a false construct placed on reality: an ideology. Further, it is an ideology that enables other ideologies. Therapeutic self-care enables the downloading of compatible identity-based ideology from the cloud, so to speak—from the radical front of the cultural zeitgeist. We may mistakenly take it to be esoterically sourced, something that is mystically just there, a kernel of uniqueness to be discovered. Though the esotericism and mystique can seem plausible to the Freudian-influenced impressionable mind, in this narcissistic age, it is a product of false Gnostic thinking.

Gnosticism is at root a way of responding to the reality of evil in the world, and the felt sense of alienation or inner unease or anxiety we all experience. We all feel a tragic sense,[2] owing not just to awareness of our mortality, but of evil and of our own part in it. Religion teaches that the tragic sense stays with us through life—we cannot be cured of it, we can only be redeemed out of it. We are brought to understand that there is indeed something wrong with us. We cannot fix it, so God must.

An alternative explanation for the sense of alienation is that something is wrong with the world. The self that emerges from within, however, is the blameless true self. That is the discovered self, true Identity. This outlook requires faith, even among those explicitly irreligious, because it taps into the longing for the ineffable, the prompt of the tragic sense that we register as religious impulse. Faith in a discoverable true self is resurgent Gnosticism.

Ancient Gnosticism

We can rightly consider the tragic sense to be of primordial origin, a tension contributing to a fearful heaviness of being that motivates but can also enervate. The motivation to sacrifice is a partial answer to this tragic sense. In the pagan pre-Christian world it was a powerful motivator, more so than we tend to appreciate now. Among the pagans the practice of human sacrifice was among other things an attempt to ameliorate the tragic sense. The reason it was prevalent then and not so much now has been the advent of Judaism and its precepts carried forward in Christianity. The first Jew, Abraham, with God's intervention signaled the departure from the moral construct of the pagan world.[3]

The history of the Jews is a vantage point from which to observe the long slow progression out of the expectation of human

2 "Tragic sense" as further defined for example in Miguel de Unamuno's *Tragic Sense of Life*, transl. by J.E. Crawford Flitch, (SophiaOmni Press, 2014), first published 1912.
3 Genesis chapter 22.

sacrifice as a way of buying one's way out of the oppressive tragic sense. Christianity exploded into the wider world because it was the sacrifice to end all sacrifices; the crucifixion bringing redemption for all time, and thereafter sacrifices (like charity, abstinence, study, saving money, disciplining children) bring blessings and joy rather than loss and never-fully-atoned guilt. Christ was the logos made flesh, the transcendent ground of being manifesting immanently, God with us. For hundreds of years mankind in the West grew into fuller understanding of reliance on God, taking Him to be the Author of every good thing, including the world He had declared "good," contrary to the vision of the Gnostics.

Still, this understanding seemed incomplete, for many; perhaps too good to be true. "Faith" replaces sacrifice, but what is "faith?" Here is how Eric Voegelin described the sense religion leaves us with even after the Resurrection:

> Uncertainty is the very essence of Christianity. The feeling of security in a "world full of gods" [i.e., the pagan world] is lost with the gods themselves; when the world is de—divinized, communication with the world-transcendent God is reduced to the tenuous bond of faith, in the sense of Hebrews 11:1, as the substance of things hoped for and the proof of things unseen. Ontologically the substance of things hoped for is nowhere to be found but in faith itself; and, epistemologically, there is no proof for things unseen but again this very faith. The bond is tenuous indeed, and may snap easily. The life of the soul in openness toward God, the waiting, the periods of aridity and dullness, guilt and despondency, contrition and repentance, forsakenness and hope against hope, the silent stirrings of love and grace, trembling on the verge of a certainty which if gained is loss—the very lightness of this fabric may prove too heavy a burden for men who lust for massively possessive experience.[4]

---

4 *The New Science of Politics*, (University of Chicago Press, 1987), p. 122, first published 1952.

These kinds of observations are attributable to many other thinkers, including but not limited to Philip Rieff,[5] but Voegelin is particularly relevant at present because, as we will see, he invoked "gnosticism" to explain the advance of ideological "speculative theories." As he suggests in this passage, the worldview of faith is perhaps a too-light undemanding burden; airy compared to the heavens teeming with pagan gods that preceded it. It is a relief to mankind but does not eliminate the tragic sense, and requires much social reinforcement. Only by seeking God can we know Him. He requires that we seek, and knock, in order to find.[6] This requires discipline. Very few have the spiritual sensitivity to take on this effort without the prompting of its acceptance socially. The social reinforcement has now faded. We can trace the decline of Christianity by benchmarks over many years (as we saw in chapter 8) and it is difficult to say what its high-water mark was, in the saturation of Western civilization. But certainly by the twentieth century A.D., social reinforcement had become spotty and anemic.

Directly upon the Christ's Ascension there was a certain plasticity to developing Christian belief, that is difficult for believers today to apprehend. Christ was the Way, not a system of belief, but the Way, to be accepted in faith, had also to be accepted in reason. Theology had to provide answers to questions, perhaps none more pressing than the continued existence of evil in the world. Gnosticism seemed to provide an answer: God was good, but the world was evil. The world was not created directly by God, therefore, but by some other semi-divine but evil demiurge. Creation of the world and mankind in it and of evil was one creative act, rather than successive creative acts as Genesis teaches. Gnosticism meant perceiving God by esoteric, inwardly-received spiritual knowledge, and repudiation of this world of evil. It was transgressive of the world-as-it-is. Gnosticism thereafter has been marked by this trans-

---

5 Especially in his *Charisma*, (New York: Vintage, 2008).
6 See e.g. Matthew 7:7.

gressive sense, which correlates to the hermeneutics of suspicion, and to Nitzschean "ressentiment," and to the revolutionary impulse vigilant against oppression, both the real kind and the kind imagined by oversensitive self-identified "victims."

Gnosticism has emerged from time to time as an attempt to explain the coexistence of both good and evil in the world. In its ancient form, the basic idea was that only the spiritual world has significance, and material things (including the human body) are of no consequence or are even illusory. Early Gnostics often lived at extremes of asceticism or hedonism, for this reason. The "real" reality is behind this flawed immediate bodily presence. We have a remnant divine spark emerging from the detritus of evil material. By it we acquire gnosis—knowing—of our true spiritual essence, and it is felt within.

We can think of Gnosticism as the instinct to unwind the architecture of ontological dualities on which the world is constructed. In the opening words of Genesis, the spirit of God hovers over the "waters" formless and void. He brings order and structure to the matterless form and formless matter. The attack on fundamental dualities, even the ontological dualities of good and evil, and of male and female, is an attempt at unwinding that order and structure. This is the object of the release impulse, at the heart of ancient Gnosticism and of postmodern gender ideology.

According to the monotheisms, the created order arrived sequentially: (1) creation of the world; then (2) creation of man; then (3) creation of woman (thus male/female differentiation); and then (4) their fall from grace. The Gnostic view was that these events coincided. The moment of creation was also the moment of differentiation of evil from good, and men from women. For this reason some Gnostic writing pays special attention to the fact of male/female differentiation, presenting androgyny as an ideal, as corresponding to the pre-Fall state of mankind.

Many radical gender activists today desire a norm of non-binary identity in place of self-identification by sex. This may seem like a peculiar extreme of gender ideology that just happens to coincide with ancient Gnostic belief. But actually it recurs in history because, short of suicide, it is the fullest expression available of the remissive/release impulse, and the most complete repudiation of the interdictory and renunciatory religious construct. It is the temporary dominance of impulses to deconstruction, chaos, and potentiality over impulses to construction, order, and actualization.

If the male/female binary can be deconstructed, then so can every other given category. The goal is a kind of ultimate expansive freedom; dissolution of the primal interdict which effects dissolution of all others. "Ye shall be as gods," said the serpent, omitting the cost. The point is to dissolve all fixed categories extant in the world which might constrain emergence of the tender shoot of true Identity. This would constitute the ultimate victory of philosophical *becoming* over *being*; an overthrow of the givenness of categories in the world. God is replaced by the dynamism of history, so purpose is now thought of as self-generated in the flow of time. This conception applies to society, but to individuals also.

Transgressive Impulse

Eventually the ancient Gnosticism faded out, but not the transgressive instinct it represents. It lay dormant, we might say, like a repressed virus, until the demise of faith and the advent of postmodern ideologies. The key element of Gnosticism, in both its ancient and postmodern forms, is dissatisfaction with the world as it is. It contains evil. And so "Gnosticism" describes a predisposition to transgressive critique of the world-as-it-is.

The transgressive element of early Gnosticism is retained in the impulse to transgression that distorts proper critical thinking. "Critical thinking" should be understood to mean testing propositions according to universal criteria beyond the subject matter itself—consistency, coherence, relevance, and so on. This is a good faith testing of ideas. The transgressive impulse curdles that idea into one of presumptive bad faith: "critical theory" as critique resting on a presumption of illegitimacy or bad faith or even fraud. It is a form of moral evasion and an assertion of power, rather than an exercise of reason.

The transgressive disposition translates to critique whereby one doesn't merely evaluate an idea to find truth, but distorts substantively to advance an ideology[7] in opposition. Ideologies can be identified as belief systems which include the element of insulating the system itself from dissent. On this understanding we can see that the "hermeneutics of suspicion" behind transgressive philosophies exemplified in atheist thinkers like Marx, Freud, and Nietzsche is actually more than merely an interpretive aid. It manifests a presumption of invalidity. It is substantively woven into postmodern Gnosticism as a purposeful dismantling and perversion of the religious impulse.

Typically the ideology that drives the transgressive instinct is not disclosed, nor even subjectively realized. It may register only as a presumption against things as they are, an unexamined discontent, a deep inner knowing; as *gnosis*. This disposition is to be expected given the emotivism of psychological man. Postmodern psychological man repudiates God, but not the religious character of gnosis. The resulting transgressive instinct drives the Gnostic to devise or adhere to a "speculative system," in Voegelin's terminology, what we might refer to pejoratively as "ideology" which substitutes for religion. An ideology is a self-contained system of thought, including systems which repudiate foundationalism, severing the connection

---

7 "Ideology," the word, is often used to mean a belief system based on fraudulent advocacy. And so it is here: it is used to mean a comprehensive belief system that rests on false premises concerning the scope of reality or human knowledge, one which carries within itself an immune system, so to speak, against critique. Voegelin's "speculative theories" refer to ideologies, on this definition. See generally, Mark Schiffman, *What Is Ideology?* (Wiseblood Books, 2023).

of Truth (not just true things, but Truth) and the world-as-it-is, wresting Truth from God so as to elevate mankind in His place.

A person caught up in the Gnosticism of the therapeutic may experience intense frustration in the desire to know and in the feeling of alienation common to mankind, and react in an emotionally transgressive direction, perceiving in the zeitgeist the narrative that Identity is gnostically discerned in the inner being. We considered in chapter 7 the mystery surrounding the formation of inclinations toward one point of view over another, and the possibility of replacing analytical axioms with subconscious disposition. Thus, your friend or child or sibling who argues for identity-formation in the discovered self may be stringing together logical statements (using the acquired language of objective logos) but with the conclusions priced-in, so to speak, proceeding from an emotional disposition reacting to this mess of a world.

The theist, by contrast, sees the evil in the world but understands it as an endemic feature of mankind—it runs through every heart. Our individual task is to address the evil within, by seeking virtue and avoiding vice. We can't fix the world without first striving to fix ourselves, and we don't fix ourselves independent of God.

There is no redeeming God, in Gnosticism, but there is certainly evil, so the goal becomes re-making the evil world through progressive material process. People in their individuality are innocent; the evil is out there, so systems of reform are devised to rid society of its systems of evil. This seems not just feasible, in a progressive, dialectical world, but demanded by the circumstances, the only "right" thing to do; the crusade being what "good" people do. Atheist materialism combined with ingrained historicism (the Marxist "diamat," dialectical materialism) will blind them to any other way of seeing the world. There is only one way for "good" people to behave, and it is to support the latest psychology-affirming socialist nostrum. Those who oppose this way of seeing the world are not disagreed with on grounds of practical principle, but on a deeply-felt sense of right and wrong. Traditionalists are not just wrong, they're evil, to the progressivist.

Transgression in its ideological specifics—Marxism, Stalinism, positivism, psychotherapy—is oriented to transgression in this general sense. It's not strictly speaking a matter of moral reform and improvement. Those are forms of progress that presuppose an Author of moral structure that is real and extant in the world, and a world that Author calls "good."[8] Instead, the gnostic transgressive systems exist to dismantle perception of the transcendent, to be replaced by a socialism that affirms the conception of good and evil rooted solely in human-generated social norms, with a high value placed on affirmation of feelings.

Historicism

At mid-twentieth century Voegelin[9] identified elements of the ancient Gnostic impulse still extant in postmodern manifestations:

> The Gnostic is dissatisfied with his situation;
>
> the dissatisfaction results from the poor organization of the world;
>
> the world needs to be saved from itself;
>
> perfection of the world will be material and historical, rather than spiritual and ahistorical;
>
> this perfection can occur through human effort; and
>
> the radical (Gnostic) can bring about the means of perfection and prophetically[10] carry it to the world.

---

8 Genesis 1:31.

9 In his 1960 essay "Ersatz Religion: The Gnostic Mass Movements of Our Time," contained in a volume titled *Science, Politics and Gnosticism*, (Washington, DC: Regnery, Gateway Editions, 1997); discussed in Riley, Alexander, "What's Wrong With the Intellectuals?" *Chronicles Magazine*, February 2024.

10 "prophetic" was not Voegelin's word, it is an inference.

This last step corresponds to psychology because the esoterically prophetic solution is felt in the inner being just as with Gnostics of yore, who felt they acquired it spiritually. The inner subjectivism of psychological man is always in process; a microcosm of the Hegelian/Marxist historicism taken to be the substitute engine for "perfection of the world."

Therapeutic man is gnostic because meaning seems to emerge unbidden from the vibrant inner being. But that meaning, including the god Identity, is only a product of his divided mind.[11] One part is set at a remove from active consciousness, unconsciously imbibing prompts of the zeitgeist. The other part navigates the being-ness of the world, using the acquired language of objectivity. *Geist* is god, for psychological man. History generates meaning, it does not come from on high. This-life temporality is all-in-all, but mankind is constructed (by God, actually) to require meaning and purpose, so without Him we distill meaning from social movements, the new truth-generating god.

On this view, history doesn't just mean the facts before this moment. It is active and agentic. It is the flow of ideas over time within society, and so it corresponds, one-for-one, with membership in society. God is replaced with small-s socialism, and evolving social dictates are received as authoritative in the inner being, there to well up and be received as special knowing, absorbed with utter confidence and utter certainty.

The mutability of resulting ideals does not render them suspect, in the postmodern, therapeutic imagination. To the contrary, movement and flow is the norm. Therapeutic man viciously recoils at the suggestion of moral judgment, with its rigid eternality. This fact is confused, however, by the movement and flow applied to language itself. Words are re-purposed continuously, so that "morality," the word, is re-applied to its opposite, the evolving norms of radical socialism. What society says moment to moment is god, now.

---

11 As described in chapter 3.

In this way radical politics and the therapeutic worldview become symptoms of the same disease.

To further understand the "material and historical" formulation of postmodern Gnosticism, let's take a step back in the history of philosophy, to Friedrich Hegel. Writing at the end of the eighteenth century, he introduced the dialectic, which we can simplify as process philosophy: meaning and purpose generated socially and temporally, a phenomenon of Becoming, rather than statically and eternally emanating from Being.[12] This facilitated the chief departure of modern Gnosticism from the ancient: perfection of the world as a materialist phenomenon, rather than spiritual, consistent with the dialectical materialism of Marx.

We have hitherto placed the dawn of the postmodern era at the turn of the twentieth century. For reasons identified in chapter 8, this corresponds to the influence of Freud, most relevant for understanding the therapeutic worldview. It also corresponds to the beginning of influence of William James, also a psychologist. James spotted the resurgence of Gnosticism in Hegel, in his 1896 essay *Will to Believe*.[13] Gnosticism he regarded as something like determined desire to know, placing it an antipode to "agnosticism," with the practical resolution to this duality being theism. He equated Gnosticism to process (hence his citing Hegel) by which the being-ness of things is ruled "out of court" so that the system must be allowed to stand on its own. Marxism is an example of such a system, in that it ignores that which lies outside the system itself: namely, the objective source of the supposed gnosis. James imagined it as devouring the object of knowing, disregarding eternal Source for all knowing, essentially making ourselves Being itself, or God, in our

---

12 More thoroughly developed in the author's *Dangerous God, A Defense of Transcendent Truth*, and *The Mountain and the River/Genesis, Postmodernism, and the Machine*, (New English Review Press, 2021 and 2023). This is the transcendence/immanence tension extant at least since Plato and Aristotle, a paradigm usefully applied from time to time in philosophy since.

13 *Will to Believe*, pp. 134-142.

knowing.[14]

Likewise, incidentally, Eric Voegelin, who called the "speculative theories" of post-religious ideologies, like Marxism, an "intellectual swindle" because they deny the natural order. For Voegelin, it is so obvious that we encounter the world as well-ordered, that to deny this starting point for truth is to suspend in mid-air, so to speak, the whole resulting ideology.[15] Voegelin did not spell out why this is self-evident, in his discussion of Gnosticism, but it might go something like this. The order of the world is manifested in the predictability of cause and effect in nature. This predictability discloses the objective rationality to the cosmos, rather than chaos. That is, the logos. Our ability to apprehend the orderliness of the cosmos reveals a corresponding orderliness of thought in the subjective mind. As a compass needle points north, so the progression of inferences points toward objective truth. There is thus a correspondence between order in the objective cosmos, and rationality in the subjective mind. The objectively existing order to the cosmos bespeaks rationality: an ordered Mind to create and superintend the ordered universe. Voegelin: "Gnostic man no longer wishes to perceive in admiration the intrinsic order of the cosmos."[16] He appeared to consign to discredited "positivism" theories that depart from a correspondence theory of truth.[17]

Disregarding this feature of existence is a departure from the Judeo-Christian understanding that evil is not correctible apart from God through a process of individual or social perfection. Disorder comes from within, in the form of original sin. It is also a departure from the pagan, Hellenic understanding of the logos, the active contemplation of the orderliness in the world. This is a fundamental

---

14 Ibid.

15 See Science, *Politics and Gnosticism*, Regnery 1997, pp. 10-22 (first published 1952).

16 Ibid., p. 7.

17 The principle in philosophy that truth corresponds to the way the world is. Postmodern philosophies depart from this long-held principle, finding truth to be generated instead in social processes. And as with truth, so with morality.

182 ～ *The Discovered Self*

shift in thinking important to understanding the therapeutic world-view: that our angsty tragic sense originates not in our own nature, but in the world out there, just as with the Gnostics. The necessary corollary is that the self is pure, but vulnerable to the corruption of the world. In this way the chickens of Rousseauean romanticism come home to roost.

Returning to James, note that his critique of Gnosticism necessarily encompasses not just Hegel's dialectic, but all process philosophies which dominate the Godless postmodern era, including those giving birth to, or culminating in, the dangerous gnostic philosophies later identified by Voegelin (non-exhaustively) as progressivism, positivism, Marxism, psychoanalysis, communism, fascism, and National Socialism.[18] These have in common a rejection *ab initio* of transcendence, and consequent collapse into process production of propositions, and relativism in morals.

Voegelin reached back before Hegel for conceptual historicism in gnostic movements, to Joachim of Fiore (or Flora)(1135-1202). Joachim theorized three ages, or realms, based on the Trinity: Father, Son, and Spirit. The age of the father was pre-Christ. The age of the Son was the first 1260 years following His Advent (why that number specifically is owing to interpretations of apocalyptic literature). The age of the spirit following would involve development of a monkish, contemplative utopia. Voegelin, in 1952:

> In order to lend validity and conviction to the idea of a final Third Realm [as with Joachim], the course of history as an intelligible, meaningful whole must be assumed accessible to human knowledge, either through a direct revelation or through speculative gnosis.[19]

Joachim's concept of three ages, or realms, presages Hegelian

---

18 "Ersatz Religion," section I, contained in *Science, Politics and Gnosticism*, (Regnery, 1968), p. 57.
19 *The New Science of Politics*, p. 112.

historicism, the idea that history itself is a dynamic evolution toward some enlightened goal. Thus Voegelin equates process ideology to Gnosticism on the basis of the living, breathing dynamism of history.

This is the essence of progressivism, the idea that history is formative, rather than formed; that it is moving us toward some more perfect society. There's no fixed goal, no ultimate Being, no Christian apocalypse (or "unveiling"). There's only the dynamism of history itself to explain who and what we are. This immanentizing flow still had a spiritual element with Hegel, but then along came Marx, to strip historicism of spiritual impulse. History itself replaces God. The temporal replaces the eternal.

Material Esotericism

Early Gnosticism was spiritual in nature. It held that a demiurge created the world; a spiritual esotericism generated the gnosis of inner enlightenment. If the therapeutic worldview in the secularized postmodern era is a form of Gnosticism, therefore, it must be either an unacknowledged return to spiritual esotericism, or else spirit is replaced with a materialist esotericism psychologically veiled from one's self. Let's consider first the materialist version.

On the materialist view, the inward psychological turn by definition does not derive its dynamism from spirit, but from progressive, social, historicism, the God-substitute. A prerequisite to being caught up in the therapeutic worldview is ignoring or actively rejecting God and any concept of the supernatural. The individual, in his subjectivity, believes himself impervious to spiritual influence and looks within for its substitute in psychological dynamism.

Therapeutic man is Gnostic because meaning seems to emerge unbidden from the vibrant inner being esoterically. The inner being is thought to have no spiritual component, however, so it must be formed in the body, *sua sponte*, or must find its way to mind socially.

The brain cannot generate Identity unaided, and so the discovered self, if of purely material origin, must have an external material source. The esoteric nature of that source results from mental process which distances source from active self-awareness. The god Identity is a product of divided mind. One division is set at a remove from active consciousness, thereby unconsciously imbibing prompts of the zeitgeist to which psychological man is newly open. The other navigates the being-ness of the world, using the acquired language of logos objectivity. What is expressed in logos terms is actually an expression of self-interested psychological need for social solidarity to fill the hole left by God's removal.

To grasp this we must keep in mind our capacity for double-mindedness, as discussed in chapter 3, and how it manifests in therapeutic man. The self talks to the self, as when we "talk ourselves into" working out rather than going for a drink, the self in tension with the self, including on matters more momentous than self-discipline toward physical health. In our desire for social oneness, like a salt doll cast into the sea, we can subtly discern and adopt social direction without acknowledging it. It can drive us from within the psyche and manifest as self-expression, the self "discovered." We delude ourselves with ease, and routinely, if we are not vigilant, and so we are especially vulnerable to this self-delusion if we first throw over devotion to objectivity of truth and relax into the flow of relativism. It is entirely within the capabilities of complex human psychology to overlook the source of external influence, yet absorb it in a way that hides its origin from self.

All the while, psychological man can speak in logos terms as a second language, so to speak, while his primary way of reacting to the world is emotive. This is an additional feature of his reflexive double-mindedness. Taken to this extreme by psychological man, it manifests the instrumentalist element of the therapeutic. The emotivist outlook is not, to reiterate, merely emotional. It camouflages the calculated instrumental usage of others. The primary operating principle for the emotivist is satisfaction of self-interest ahead of principle. Self-interest is unique to me; principle is universal.

Acting on principle results in social harmony. Acting on self-interest obviously does not, and so the language of logos is employed as camouflage. My desire to follow my own base instincts, heedless of consequences to others, can be expressed in terms of rights or freedom or authenticity. In politics, the emotivism of the therapeutic leads us to vote self-interest (over principle), and expect others to do so, and this becomes normalized. Buying votes through redistributionist programs, for example, begins to look normal. In private interactions, the emotivism of the therapeutic means using others instrumentally, in unceasing manipulation, and an expectation of being manipulated in return. This bleak vision results in never being released from the vicious cycle of instrumental interactions with others and with society. And it is reinforced in therapy, because moral right and wrong are eschewed in this environment. Principle is not allowed to overcome self-interest, and therapy begets therapy, a self-reinforcing, downward-spiraling cycle to misery and constraint, rather than freedom.

All of the "speculative systems," ideologies Voegelin rendered "Gnostic," are instances of pragmatism, sophistry employed to serve the simple idea that ends justify means. The ends are invariably some form of gnostic transgression against the given-ness of things, starting with the ground of all being, the creator God of the universe. All follows from there: the (gnostic) disappointment with how the world is, and the misguided belief that the social dialectic will in time fix it. Transgression in its various ideological specifics—Marxism, Stalinism, National Socialism, positivism, psychotherapy—is oriented to transgression in the general sense of rejection of God, or what Philip Rieff called "sacred order." Gnostic transgressive systems exist to obscure our perception of the transcendent, flattening the structure of moral values and releasing them to the dynamism of temporal flow.

All of these anti-religion "progressive" systems of belief have within them immune systems of sophistry to deflect criticism of the system, detaching the system from reality, from being, and in particular the ground of all being, the transcendence which is its enemy. Hence Voegelin's description of the ideology-creators as "intellectual swindlers." The ideology in this way is believed to stand on its own, ungrounded in Being itself, and therefore not sustained but rather continuously regenerated in the movement and flow of Becoming. This is a material process, not a spiritual one; a matter of muddled psychology unenlightened by acknowledging capital-T truth.

Of the ideological transgressive systems, we are particularly concerned here with the therapeutic. Premised as it is on emotivism, it means there is, in the words of Elisabeth Lasch-Quinn, "the loss of any shared vantage point and basis for judgment beyond individual subjective desires." Therefore, "[w]hile emotivism can come in the guise of emotion, it often works in service of or as a cover for calculated self-interest."[20] Its prevalence means destruction of culture. Citing Rieff, Lasch-Quinn notes:

> Absent a sense of communal purpose that makes our efforts to rein in self-gratification understandable and manageable as guidelines for behavior, cultural chaos ensues. The unmoored self is left with little in life to go on apart from "manipulable" feelings. Paving the way for political and personal instability, such conditions invite susceptibility to political manipulation and a chronic sense of insult, offense, and disrespect that threatens community and individual happiness.[21]

Consequently, under the regime of the therapeutic, the personal is indeed the political, alas. We have considered at some length the

20 "Ancient Philosophy's Return Amidst the Triumph of the Therapeutic," *Church Life Journal* (McGrath Institute for Church Life), May 25, 2021. This article is excerpted from the introduction to her *Ars Vitae*, (University of Notre Dame Press, 2020). 21 Ibid.

impacts of this ideology on the individual, but it is a collective phenomenon, too, with collective consequences. Those in thrall to the therapeutic mentality bring down society; then society past the therapeutic tipping point brings down individuals within it. With its signal element of emotivism, the therapeutic renders its victims vulnerable to ideologies that share the transgressive impulse, doubling and tripling down on the felt sense of "insult, offense and disrespect," its victims in an ever-downward spiral that can't be overcome without breaking entirely not only from the manipulations given and received within the therapeutic, but all the other God-denying transgressive movements that the therapeutic delivers one to, the ism's of progressivism, communism, antisemitism, and illiberalism more generally. The therapeutic worldview delivers us to subjection within the managerial state; to the tender mercies of Nurse Ratched in ever-blooming protean expressions of collective social power. This includes the state, certainly, but also other allied Machine manifestations primed to dictate how we are to live and even what kind of creatures we must be. (As will be fleshed out in chapter 14).

In this environment, social Narrative takes on a distinct reality that we imagine to be akin to divinity. Gnosticism thus helps to explain the ongoing partnership between the therapeutic worldview and radical politics. Upon rejecting God, there is still an instinct for the transcendent with no way to satisfy it, other than to look to the this-life immanent for higher purpose. Thus the receptivity of psychological man to products of political dialectic. An instance of this is the neo-Marxist oppressor/oppressed lens through which one views this-life utopian development. Absorption of Durkheimian "social facts" isn't a purposeful mental process. The social facts are thought to be divined from the ether and therefore self-evidently true. This is the esoteric source of the discovered self, of "Identity" materially rather than spiritually derived. The perception of inner-formed Identity is garbled digestion of transgressive social messaging.

To say transgressive Gnosticism is substantive ideology is not to say necessarily that one studies textual propositions of a modern gnostic system and becomes persuaded to the truth of the system. It is more likely felt, than propositionally accepted. As one might expect, this is likely especially true for the ideology of the therapeutic worldview (Voegelin's "psychotherapy"), its emphasis being on emotivism generally rather than rationality. It would need scant reinforcement if one is predisposed to it emotionally. The axioms for the gnostic system might lie not in analytical, rational propositions, but in a feeling of frustration or simmering anger or alienation; revulsion at the world-as-it-is. Voegelin himself seemed to recognize as much, in his *The Ecumenic Age*[22] written in 1974, long after his early forays into modern Gnosticism. Michael Franz commented:

> Voegelin's mature analysis locates Gnosticism in the consciousness of particular individuals who fail to bear up under the tensions of existence . . . and who react aggressively against the uncertainties and limitations of creaturely existence by seeking to abolish them through gnosis.[23]

This is not a matter of systematic ideological persuasion, but rather the nostrum that we "trust our feelings," denying the natural "limitations of creaturely existence." The veiled ideology is that uncertainties and limitations of any kind are anathema to personal freedom, those inextricable from "creaturely existence." This unacknowledged ideology is an attempted end-run around "tensions of existence," likely because of lack of the resilience that might have been formed in love, as against the tragic circumstances of evil and death and hate and indifference, the oppressive weight of the tragic

---

22 Volume Four of *Order and History*, (University of Missouri Press/Louisiana State University).

23 *Voegelin View*, a publication of the Voegelin Society, "The Concept of Gnosticism and the Analysis of Spiritual Disorder," March 14, 2020.

sense no longer tempered by religion.[24] The individual falls prey to ideological presumptions without even recognizing the system of which they are a part. So, for example, a person might deny ontological sex differentiation not because he's worked it out rationally, but because it is part of an ideology of vague openness and unconstrained personal freedom which hides "the uncertainties and limitations of creaturely existence," including the unshakeable tragic sense.

Spiritual Esotericism

Moving on from the materialist explanation for veiled esotericism, it would be prudent to consider there may well be a spiritual component, after all. The spiritual element may not be benevolent, as with the imagined divine spark of ancient Gnosticism, but rather may be a spirit of delusion participating in the division of mind by which we find esoteric meaning within.

Even avoiding talk of angels and demons, one can see "spiritual" knowledge is in fact found by psychological man, in discovering the true self within. This approach doesn't incorporate the whole demiurge-made-the-world idea, and so spirit is not contemplated in that sense, but it does incorporate the atheist therapeutic's inability to deal with the tragic sense, especially the fallen-ness of the world and of individuals within it. Mankind's desire for knowing the source of good and evil, for gnosis as with the first couple in the Garden, is the reason for the Fall. It created the angsty tragic sense which all Gnosticism since has tried to reconcile without invoking the one way to live that God provided. All ideologies not rooted in sacred order are "Gnostic," because they rely on untraceable inner

---

24 Autism, possibly resulting from less than ideal left- and right-hemisphere integration, may make one particularly susceptible to the frustration resulting from inability to bear up to the tensions of existence, and thus more susceptible to transgressive ideological suggestion, but that is a speculation beyond the scope of this book.

knowing, whether we attribute the gnosis to spirit or to materialist psychology.

Based as it is in temporality rather than eternality, the therapeutic worldview makes one susceptible to the radical political ideologies that are the froth on the waves of temporal ideological movements. The subrational consciousness is invoked to assist in the veiling of Identity's source. Instead of looking overtly outward to spiritual guidance, as when we pray or look to revelation, the therapeutic involves looking inward for mystic revelation. This looks like a spiritual quest, the only difference being that we first grant to internal, temporal, psychological process the same authority previously acknowledged in God.

If there is an Unseen reality, a "place" which coincides with this material world but also extends beyond, then the gnostic prompts to human imagination may initiate in that immateriality; that is, its source may be demonic.

11

Narcissism and Other "Disorders"

What Is Narcissism?

What is a "narcissist," and how does narcissism relate to the therapeutic worldview? Here's as good a description of narcissism as any, found in a lament by Nigerian feminist author Chimamanda Adichie:

> In certain young people today . . . I notice what I find increasingly troubling: a cold-blooded grasping, a hunger to take and take and take but never give; a massive sense of entitlement; an inability to show gratitude; an ease with dishonesty and pretension and selfishness that is couched in the language of self-care; an expectation always to be helped and rewarded no matter whether deserving or not; language that is slick and sleek but with little emotional intelligence; an astonishing level of self-absorption; an unrealistic expectation of puritanism from others; an over-inflated sense of ability, or of talent where there is any at all; an inability to apologize, truly and fully, without justifications; a passionate performance of virtue that is well executed in the public space of [social media] but not in the intimate space of friendship.
>
> I find it obscene.[1]

1 www.chimamanda.com/news_items/it-is-obscene-a-true-reflection in three parts/

You've probably met the person she describes. She wrote of "certain young people," but this combination of awful traits is not limited to young people. Because the way of thinking that produces this kind of person has become so much more prevalent in recent years, however, it may be more obvious in a younger demographic. Those traits are the opposite of maturity, and indicate a complete buy-in to "the therapeutic."

Psychological man places process ahead of substance, just as in the world of ideas the river inclination is put ahead of the mountain. Emotional evaluation is the process, and so the substance is whatever feels subjectively most satisfying. This is how rational thinking is distorted and subverted by the therapeutic.

For this reason we should not be surprised to encounter the kind of negative character traits recited by Adichie. From the inside they presumably make some sort of sense, but from the outside looking in, betray a depthless self-absorption and the absence of empathy necessary for healthy relationships with others. Zombie-like, together yet alone. The tell is that all is "couched in the language of self-care," self-care being the entire point for therapeutic man.

Narcissism can be understood better by its effects than by its symptoms in the abstract. Here's Marilyn Simon:

> Narcissism isn't merely an issue of having an inflated ego. It is the condition of being enamored with one's idealized projection of oneself to the exclusion of reality and of one's real self. This occurs not because one is vain, but because one is too fragile to admit failings or fault. It has nothing to do with self-love, but rather with being locked in a solipsistic gaze with a fantasy of one's self. Contemporary culture has taken classic narcissism and turned it into a new moralism. What we deem goodness now is that everyone else affirms the delusions of one's wishful thinking as objective truth. . . . [O]ur self-positive, identity-affirming culture as a whole, would suggest that not only is Narcis-

sus correct in falling in love with a projection, an unreal and unreachable image of himself in a pond—something the Greeks thought was quite bad enough—but also that the rest of the world must affirm his reflection as the real thing and celebrate his dead-end obsession with it.[2]

According to the Diagnostic and Statistical Manual of Mental Disorders (DSM) put out by the American Psychiatric Association, narcissistic personality disorder is a pervasive pattern of grandiosity (in fantasy or behavior), a constant need for admiration, and a lack of empathy, as indicated by criteria like grandiosity, self-importance, preoccupation with fantasies of success or power or brilliance, a belief in one's specialness or uniqueness, being misunderstood except by high-status people, a need for admiration, a sense of entitlement, exploitative behavior, a lack of empathy, envy, and arrogant or haughty behaviors or attitudes.

This is descriptive, but not really explanatory. Worse, it's a description that fits every human being on the planet, to one degree or another, except in its use of unhelpful qualifiers like "pervasive," "constant," and "excessive." These are unacceptably fuzzy descriptors for something so important as the ostensible difference between ordered and disordered; between mentally healthy and mentally ill.

If you try to flesh out the boundaries of narcissism as disorder by listening to people who present themselves as knowledgeable on social media platforms like youtube, you'll find an unending parade of putative experts ticking off the same vague checkpoints so you can privately diagnose your hated boss or spouse or parent and put them in a mental box marked "disordered" and thereafter consider them categorically contemptible. The give-away to the pointlessness of armchair youtube therapists is that the diagnosis always seems to be directed to bothersome others; seldom to the listener himself or herself. The point of listening is to protect yourself from narcissists,

---

2 "The Attack on Beauty," *Quillette*, December 1, 2020.

194 の The Discovered Self

rather than the more worthwhile goal of not being a narcissist your-self. Perhaps the first symptom of narcissism is identifying others as narcissists.

Moreover, as the entire culture heads together downhill to ter-minal navel-gazing, of what use could vague descriptors like those for narcissism-as-disorder be? The suggested boundary between or-dered and disordered is itself shifting. We have to read descriptions like that for narcissism and ask "compared to what" because it is necessarily relative to the state of the culture at the moment. The DSM "disorders" presuppose a morally static universe, much life Freud did. They don't take into account, therefore, the effect thera-py itself has on the standards and definitions, just as the live therapy environment insufficiently accounts for its own effects on clari-ty-seeking clients.

The main trouble with the DSM descriptions for "personality disorders" like narcissism is that they attempt to address in psycho-logical terms what isn't a matter of psychology at all, but of moral-ity. Indeed, this is the key symptom of the disordered therapeutic age: that we attempt to re-categorize moral failures as psychological maladies. Sin as syndrome.

This is a large mistake. For one thing, sin is real, we conceptu-ally discard it at our peril. For another, sin is necessary to a self-con-ception that has moral agency. There is no personal dignity without moral agency and proper exercise of it. Self-as-syndrome is a mas-sive cop-out, a pathetic attempt to dish moral responsibility onto the material universe by re-defining ourselves on coordinates of vul-nerability and victimhood. Rather than admit failings and the need for saving from them, we deny them, cleansing ourselves of our own sin by the baptism of ideology, making of ourselves our own Messiah.[3]

What might actually be helpful is a description of virtues and

---

3 Recall that "ideology" as used here is not merely a system of ideas, but a comprehen-sive way of looking at the world that absorbs individual agency.

vices relating to the selfishness that the "narcissism" diagnostic is intended to get at. If you know someone who is selfish, in the sense of putting himself first and lacking empathy and so on, which is the more humane and more accurate way of thinking about them: moral fallibility common to all mankind, to be addressed in striving for greater virtue? Or diagnosis of mental illness?

Hopefully the ready answer is to shift to the moral paradigm and away from the therapeutic. The moral paradigm means it's not you, it's your conduct, and you can right the ship by striving for moral virtues that apply to all, rather than categorizing yourself as helplessly disordered. Seeking virtue is an exercise of agency, by which we can change and improve, in contrast to passive acquiescence to psychological "disorder" which marks us as ever after vulnerable and in need of therapy.

Psychological man has lost the thread of logic which tells us we can love a person but not their sin. We can differentiate between the dignified person and their sometimes sinful conduct. In the therapeutic morass, this isn't possible. The personal is political. The ideology is the person, and vice versa. Disagreement is denial of personhood. There must be absolute unanimity on the principles of "identification." Ideological dissent is considered hate. This is why you're considered a "transphobe" if you disagree with the principle that people can change sex. This is why you're considered a "homophobe" if you think sex has a moral component. In a morality paradigm, a person who sins is not irredeemable. He can repent and seek virtue. In a therapeutic paradigm, there is no sin to be tainted with, but there is syndrome, so we then live in a perpetual twilight of shifting disorders, vulnerable and afraid, the insect of Kafka's *Metamorphosis*.

With the therapeutic perspective you "identify" with your diagnosis. It means you're stuck with an illness which then defines you. You're captive. As an element of identity, the diagnosis is integral to you, not conduct which you have the power to correct in the pursuit of virtue. It's pathologization of what should be morality. It means the therapeutically diagnosed individual is infected by an outside agent. It's not his fault; someone else is to blame. The diagnosed person "is powerless over his or her disease and has no responsibility for its onset."[4]

This is no small concern for the individual who self-identifies by diagnosis, of course, but it also has a society-wide effect. Diagnosis-as-identity becomes normalized, further contributing to the therapeutic mindset. As many as 42% of the rising generation has received a mental health diagnosis![5] So common is it to self-identify according to diagnosis that some people openly include mental health disorders in their short-version bio, in interactions with others or on social media.

Identity may be taken on by the individual, but it is thereafter to be respected by others, in the ethos of the therapeutic. It is unchanging, because that's what "identity" means. Just as identifying as gay or as being on the autism spectrum or as non-binary, identity with a mental disorder means you place yourself in the prison of that identity. Even if you develop some recognition and avoidance techniques for what are described as indicators of "narcissism" or some other applicable "disorder," you conceive it remaining as part of your deep identity.

To "identify" as one with narcissism personality disorder is to say attitudes like self-importance and low empathy are immutable traits, meaning you can't purpose to change them significantly, as a matter of self-improvement or simply maturity. To say "I am a person with narcissistic personality disorder," instead of "I'm sometimes selfish" signifies this shift to identity rather than sin. Psychological maladies seem immutable—you're stuck with it and there's no right or wrong associated with it. You can't help it, but neither

4 Nolan, James L. Jr., *The Therapeutic State*, p.15, citing Stan Katz and Aimee Liu, *The Codependency Conspiracy*.
5 Hymowitz, Kay, "When Every Day is a Mental Health Day," *City Journal*, February 27, 2024, a review of Abigail Schrier's *Bad Therapy*.

can you rise above it. Self-identity around mental disorder is a way to escape a sense of moral responsibility, so as to keep the inner being pure. That's why people drift into it.

But it's a two-way street. In the morality paradigm: moral responsibility but with the ability to recover. In the therapeutic paradigm: no moral responsibility, but with the failing indurated into "identity." If bad conduct is a "symptom" of mental disorder, then you're not morally responsible, but the cost of preserving the seeming innocence is loss of agency. If on the other hand bad conduct is seen as a moral failing, then you *are* responsible, because a bad person is a person who does bad things. But that comes with agency, the freedom to change, and freedom from the prison of "identity." With agency comes dignity, as we've previously noted. These elements of our existence go together always.

Which is better? To try to preserve the inner self as inviolately innocent by identifying with a mental disorder? Or to be guilty—as we all are of something—but with the ability to turn from it? In the first instance you're innocent but captive, lacking agency to choose a better way, mired in an inescapable category of disorder. In the second you're guilty but retain agency, and therefore dignity, unchained to ideological category, so you're free to become better without the sin attaching to you permanently. Sin is something we do, not something we are. Identification is what we are.

Note also the mechanistic thinking that accompanies diagnosis-as-identity. Because of the immutable nature of the "disorder," you just are that thing, and it's not something you control through repudiation of vice and embrace of virtue. It's just what you are, your very humanity. You're siloed in with others who have that diagnosis. You're a person with brown hair, brown eyes, and anxiety disorder. You are categorizable as a certain sub-species of human and can be dealt with accordingly by the collective.

In moral language, rather than psychological language, how would we describe the person that could be diagnosed as "narcissistic?" Probably with a word like "selfish," but, in the spirit of the DSM's use of many vague words, we can go beyond "selfish" to identify virtues and vices that are particularly implicated in the sin of narcissism. Here's a start: compassion, empathy, humility, forgiveness. Indifference, callousness, hubris, resentment.

These are perhaps not explanatory, such as by explaining *why* a person is compassionate or indifferent and so on, but then neither is DSM psychobabble explanatory. So in what way is the language of psychology an improvement over the language of morality? Answer: It's not, unless the goal is to subtly shift our framing from pursuit of objective and universal moral ideals, to manipulating the person as a component unit of a larger social machine.

If your child grabs a toy from another in kindergarten, what is the right response? Do you admonish the child to be normal? To not be exaggeratedly self-important? To have empathy? No, of course not. But you might say "don't be selfish," leaving it at that because really, that's enough. It is part of the paradigm that we should pursue virtue and avoid vice. Or if they're ready you may go a little further, and say "how would you feel if someone grabbed a toy from you?" "Do unto others as you would have them do unto you," we've heard somewhere. It's moral and creedal, but it carries a lot of weight, including the demand for empathy, an essential narcissism preventative. There's still that need for admiration, but admiration can be earned with virtue.

The Narcissism Epidemic

As to narcissism associated with the therapeutic worldview in the culture, we might begin with *The Culture of Narcissism*, Christopher Lasch's popular book published in 1979, and relate it to Philip Rieff's insights in *The Triumph of the Therapeutic* written more than a decade earlier. Lasch clearly read Rieff, but didn't seem to regard himself as building on Rieff's work. Though he acknowledged "the rise of the therapeutic," he didn't seem to regard it as inextricably linked to the cultural disorder of narcissism he described. It's also not clear that Lasch understood the impact of the loss of religion, as did Rieff. Rieff saw the therapeutic worldview birthed by Freud as replacing the worldview of faith. Lasch embraced Freud uncritically.

We can nonetheless observe substantial overlap in Rieff's and Lasch's contributions, yielding the conclusion that (1) the culture of narcissism, (2) the gnostic conception of "identity," and (3) the therapeutic worldview, are inseparable features of the same phenomenon, and it is essentially religious in nature.

Many people use the word "narcissist" promiscuously, airily diagnosing people they don't like with it. It's easy to roll the eyes at this, because surely it means more than selfish lack of consideration for others. Even after reading the most famous book on the subject, however, we find that's pretty much what it does mean, even in therapy circles. We can become frozen in a childish state of emotional helplessness, in which rationality serves emotion rather than the other way around. That's essentially narcissism understood as a psychological disorder.

Lasch does provide some helpful insights, however. If you think back to the myth of Narcissus, you recall he saw his reflection in a pool of water and fell in love with himself. So sure, that's unremitting selfishness, squeezing out any possibility of fellow-feeling with others. We might think of that as the right-wing version of Narcissus.

But there's an opposing perspective. Narcissus doesn't recognize himself in the reflection. So you could say he's not really falling in love with himself, instead he's unable to distinguish himself from others, so there's no "other" to love. A left-wing version of Narcissus. Not self-love, but absence of self-boundary. A merger with society that negates the ability to love a particular member of it.

In *The Minimal Self*, Lasch wrote:

> As the Greek legend reminds us, it is this confusion of the self and the not self . . . that distinguishes the plight of Narcissus. The minimal or narcissistic self is, above all, uncertain of its own outlines, longing either to remake the world in its own image, or to merge into its environment in blissful union. The current concern with "identity" registers some of this difficulty in defining the boundaries of selfhood.[6]

It seems both desires are really operative: a desire to remake the world, and a desire to blissfully join with it. These are antagonistic desires, obviously, yet psychological man pursues both. Hence his frustration and anger at those who resist conformity with the therapeutic hive mind. This is of a piece with the epidemic inability to recognize boundaries in general. In direct contrast to the cascading and interlocking dichotomies set up in Genesis, postmodernists want to extinguish alterity[7] in its every manifestation, even that between male and female. There is no ontological feature of selfhood, in this way of thinking. Existence precedes essence. It is an insistence on god-like ability to form the self *ex nihilo*. An attempt to return again to the formless and void chaos of potentiality from which God created the world (Genesis 1:2) in the differentiating duality of binary oppositions (Genesis 1:1). It's an attempt at a do-over on creation, this time without the external agency of God. We're to imagine Him out of existence, and replace Him in our imagination with mankind, collectively, as the source of human agency.

Lasch was a committed Freudian, and Freud was a committed atheist. Indeed, Freud's theory of warring inner impulses takes the place of faith, as Rieff compellingly argues. The Freud/Lasch conception of selfhood starts with God dead. If there is no God, the mysterious life force must have another source. And so it is under-

---

6 *The Minimal Self* (New York: W.W. Norton, 1984), p. 19.
7 See chapter 13, *The Mountain and the River*.

stood as a social phenomenon, rather than the putative God speaking to individual hearts. The socially-derived life force is generated immanently rather than transcendently; in the roil of changing social process rather than fixed eternality. It manifests as Narrative. We embrace it, if we do, because we seek, in place of God, the ecstasy of oceanic feeling, the communist fantasy of unbroken community with all mankind.

This concept of oceanic feeling may help us in understanding the inward turn. Freud discussed it in his 1930 *Civilization and Its Discontents*,[8] which was really a follow-on to his earlier *The Future of an Illusion* (1928).[9] The "illusion" was religion, and Freud's purpose was to explain its necessary demise for what he thought a proper understanding of the psychological self. His replacement of religion with his own theories of psychology was quite deliberate.

In chapter 1 of *Civilization and Its Discontents*, Freud dismissed the notion of a religious impulse as evidence for the validity of religion. Consistently if not coherently, he likened the religious impulse to the infantile desire for unbounded oneness with mother; to desire for "oceanic feeling" with the undifferentiated outside world.[10] This is curious because his source for the idea was in correspondence from a friend, Romain Rolland, after publication of *The Future of an Illusion*,[11] in which correspondence Rolland cited the nineteenth-century religious mystic, Ramakrishna, as a source for this idea, in his illustration of a salt doll released into the ocean, to become one with it.[12] This suggests a desire for undifferentiated immersion in society, however; not the angst of separation from God experienced as a

---

8 Transl. by J. Strachey, (New York: W.W. Norton, 1961), first published 1930.
9 Transl. by W.D. Robson-Scott, (Mansfield Centre, CT: Martino Publishing, 2010), first published 1928.
10 *Civilization and Its Discontents*, p. 24.
11 Ibid., footnote 2.
12 See *The Mountain and the River*, p. 239.

sense of alienation[13] or an intuition of extra-worldly significance[14] or unrequited yearning.[15]

The difference is instructive. Freud himself construed Rolland to mean "a feeling as of something limitless, unbounded,"[16] but given Rolland's salt-doll illustration, that feeling is more obviously a this-world desire to overcome alterity and so also tensions with one's fellow man. It is a temporal consideration only, despite Rolland's hint also at "eternity."[17] Freud confused two distinct intuitions. On the one hand, small-s socialism, a communistic desire for humanity's oneness; and on the other hand, a sense of lostness from the ineffable, transcendent, Source of life. These are not the same thing, and if we understand the difference, we also understand much of what ails postmodern man. God is not society; society is not God. But the confusion is understandable if, like Freud, one has rejected God *a priori*. If there is no God, the felt sense of angst or alienation or longing is answerable, if at all, only in a turn to a socialism that discourages difference and attempts to manufacture brotherhood out of sheer desire; which conjures *fraternité* just on our insistent say-so. The confusion appears quite common, given the strong correlation between atheism and radical socialist politics.

If there is a God, however, then we cease looking side-to-side for peace, and instead look upward, to transcendent Source for ideals that have the unifying effect of bringing us together organically and without coercion, motivating us to willingly defer to values universally applicable. This happens naturally upon obeying the distilled two-part summary of God's law: that we are to love God and love our fellow man. It means we are to look upward to God-spon-

---

13 The tragic sense, for example as explicated in chapter 6.

14 See Norton, Albert, *Intuition of Significance*, (Eugene, OR: Resource Publications, 2020).

15 See Plantinga, Alvin, *Knowledge and Christian Belief*, (Grand Rapids: Eerdmans, 2015).

16 Ibid., p. 24.

17 Ibid.

sored universal values, and understand them to be universally applicable in dealings with our fellow man, so there are viable rules of engagement, so to speak. Love is possible.

For Freud, the inward turn to psychology, and explicitly away from religion, made sense as a way to assuage the feeling of inner dissonance, even if he misdiagnosed its source. But because he misdiagnosed its source, and because of his influence on the culture, he set up an inevitable course to cultural narcissism, as surely as tipping the first in a line of dominoes.

The "oceanic feeling" Freud confused with a desire for religion over-simplifies what the myth of Narcissus and Echo teaches us. An echo is a reflection in sound, and a reflection is an echo in vision. The story of Narcissus and Echo contains two ways, reflection and echo, of seeing the same issue of the one and the many; of unity and multiplicity—of one moral law and its application to the many; of unity in shared values and multiplicity of their application. Freud would throw it all in together: all multiplicity; all unity; all of us in an undifferentiated sea of pulsing emotion.

One way to understand Narcissus is simply that he's obsessed with himself. But he's obsessed with himself because he's unable to differentiate himself from others. There's no boundary, and so the reflection he sees is inaccessible. It's a reflection of all humanity. One cannot love another without seeing the other as Other. Alterity (Otherness) enables, rather than prevents, love. The tale is incomplete without considering also the plight of Echo. She's completely *un*obsessed with self, so immersively obsessed is she with Narcissus. She also is unable to differentiate Narcissus from others, but for the opposite reason: she sees only him.

Both are concerned with unity and multiplicity. Narcissus sees and rejects all, but in seeing himself reflected back to himself, wants only himself, which he cannot have because the self is undifferentiated from others. It is therefore a reflection of all. We know from the full version of the myth that he can accept no other, and now he finds that what he thinks he wants is unattainable, because the self is a mere reflection. It is all of mankind. It spurns the real Narcissus. Oceanic communitarianism is impossible.

At the same time, entire immersion in self-isolation is impossible. Like Narcissus himself, Echo rejects all and sees only Narcissus, but in seeing him she reflects (echoes) himself back to himself, partially, and so prompts his rejection. Her echo in a sense spurns Echo.

This is the real significance of the Narcissus myth, and helps us to understand the reason (1) narcissism, (2) the gnostic conception of Identity, and (3) the therapeutic worldview, should be understood as inseparable features of the same phenomenon. It is the curdled inward turn which is also a sensitivity to social influence, an emptying out of self in the name of finding self. Like Narcissus, psychological man seeks to find himself in society's reflection, but that ephemeral "self" is false and so ultimately unattainable. We become transfixed in what we imagine is the true inner self reflected back to us by society. The false reflection is the inchoate, innocent, and tremulous inner Identity. A true inner being and unique, we feel, but it isn't really. In our imagination we take the ephemeral reflection as true essence, and believe it is manifested in unique Identity.

Though social process is the actual source of Identity formation, Identity is nonetheless thought to originate *ex nihilo* from the sacred inner being. Psychological man thus misperceives the source of his Identity, ascribing it to mysterious tensions of the inner id, not grasping that it's mere internalization of social dicta. We look to society around us for Identity but at the same time have imbibed a false Freudian vision of the ego emerging in part from the roil of the id's inner subconscious turmoil. Psychological man mistakes the collective's vision of him for inner spontaneous eruption of Identity. The reflection for the reality, as with Narcissus. The echo for deep meaning, as with Echo. In this way psychological man gives himself over to the collective, and is ready grist for the totalitarian mill. Freud evolves to totalitarianism.

Because the emerging Identity is sacred, it must be protected from the threat of an angry and absolute far-off God, antipode to the divinity within. One's true Identity is misperceived as timorous and frail, blinking away dew in the first fresh hour of morning. But it is actually a self-delivered orc, grinning malevolence in the fading twilight of civilization. We don't see ourselves creating this entity; rather we only discover it, and then protect it and nurture it and offer it up to the social river in which "we live and move and have our being,"[18] replacing both pagan gods and the one true God with immersive socialism. From a religious perspective, this is an occult undertaking, opening oneself up to demonic presence.

The mirror is suggested here as an icon for the therapeutic worldview, in much the same way as the cross is an icon for Christianity. Likewise Lasch, concerning narcissism:

> The narcissist depends on others to validate his self-esteem. He cannot live without an admiring audience. His apparent freedom from family ties and institutional constraints does not free him to stand alone or to glory in his individuality. On the contrary, it contributes to his insecurity . . . . For the narcissist, the world is a mirror, whereas the rugged individualist saw it as an empty wilderness to be shaped to his own design.[19]

I don't know how therapy would help such a person. Nor does Lasch:

> As a psychiatric patient, the narcissist is a prime candidate for interminable analysis. He seeks in analysis a religion or way of life and hopes to find in the therapeutic relationship external support for his fantasies of omnipotence and eternal youth.[20]

---

18 Acts 17:28.
19 *The Culture of Narcissism*, p. 19.
20 Ibid., p. 54.

The reference to "omnipotence and eternal youth" goes back to Lasch's take on the myth of Narcissus in his effort to give substance to "narcissism" as a diagnosable disorder and one that has overtaken the culture. Citing Otto Kernberg,[21] he says the reason therapy is undertaken at all despite its ineffectiveness with emotionally shallow narcissists is because of "the devastating effect of narcissism on the second half of their lives."[22] Short-term emotion-driven responses to the trials of life yield severe long-term self-damage.

The narcissist doesn't resist therapy. To the contrary, therapy is the liturgy of his replacement religion. Not just submitting to "counseling," but in the assumptions about reality the therapeutic mindset fixes. Social process, rooted in a therapeutic worldview, replaces fixed truths. Its flow generates a conviction that subjectively experienced psychological well-being is the point of existence. It is the warm comfortable bath reinforcing emotional subjectivism, the alpha and omega of reality for the narcissist. This understanding of reality is in opposition to the paradigm of unchanging ideals to which we should aspire, once drawn out of our childhood psychological cocoon.

A narcissist isn't interested in virtues of resilience or endurance, or in taking up one's cross daily. There is no satisfaction in honoring virtue through the weathering of pain. He wants ecstasy. The etymological basis of "ecstasy" suggests being taken out of oneself (ex-stasis), which is why we might say someone deep into worship of God is caught up in religious "ecstasy." It's likewise used in the quasi-religious therapeutic, to mean communion with one's fellow man, as when we read "ecstatic feelings of community," a phrase equivalent to social "oceanic feeling."

Abandoning God opens us up to a conception of existence that folds all into all. We can come to think of ourselves as an undif-

---

21 Ibid, p. 52.
22 Ibid., p. 54.

ferentiated continuum of humanity, a form of oceanic religious feeling. But it's not the transcendence of monotheistic religion. It is an extension of the immanence of pantheism but with its spirituality extracted and replaced with the "divine" presence of society, the omnipresence we embrace because we must replace God with some alternate object of belonging. We must have our religious ecstasy, one way or another.

The Mirror as Icon

The magnificent but quiet cathedrals of Europe are symbols of a former sacred order. They are each full of icons which bring to the willing mind the entirety of the Christian story. The countryside, too, is in many places full of such icons. At a high spot on the approach to Mount Seceda in Südtirol, for example, you may step off the *umlaufbahn* and walk all around, enthralled at the scenery, and at some point look up and be startled by the larger-than-life wood-carved crucifix that looms over the whole scene—as if the real Christ were right there, above you the whole time, but you don't see Him until you happen to look up. When you finally see, it changes everything.

Tourists to the mountains of northern Italy and Austria will find innumerable crucifixes and other religious icons at road turnings, lonely mountain paths, rocky outcroppings, and hollowed-out places in rock walls and even tree stumps. Through such icons we're invited to consider the sacred order they represent—or once represented—and by extension also the mystery at the boundaries of our materialistic understanding. We may imagine the icons standing vigilant at night and in inclement weather, when no one observes, but nonetheless imparting unto the world a message of timeless love breaking into our time-bound world.

In his *Twilight in Italy*[23] D.H. Lawrence described their effect. At first, he thought of them as ignorable sentimentalism:

> But gradually, one after another looming shadowily under their hoods, the crucifixes seem to create a new atmosphere over the whole of the countryside, a darkness, a weight in the air that is so unnaturally bright and rare with the reflection from the snows above, a darkness hovering just over the earth. So rare and unearthly the light is, from the mountains, full of strange radiance. Then every now and again recurs the crucifix, at the turning of an open, grassy road, holding a shadow and a mystery under its pointed hood.

"A shadow and a mystery" suggests the ineffable, the still, small voice of religious impulse, persisting in the face of Enlightenment rationalism. Even in dismissal of the icons, we may find in them a lost memory of the deep of human experience; a primordial emergence from chaos; reality beyond a flat encounter of the world in its physical dimensions only.

Protestant Christians were of course to be iconoclasts, but the significance of the centuries-long Protestant/Catholic stand-off is entirely moot in our post-Christian world. There are of course important theological differences, but they're pointless family squabbles compared to the raging war between those who believe and those who don't; between those who see God superintending the world on the basis of unchanging moral values, and those who see nothing but the liquid flow of values socially derived.

The collapse from formative vertical orientation to formless horizontal takes place now subjectively and psychologically; not merely propositionally and philosophically. Internal well-being pushes out external virtue, as the principal guidance for how to live a life. The post-Christian world around us reverts not to classical paganism, which at least involved a sort of superficial reverence, but

---

23 New York: Viking 1958 (first published 1916).

to an unapologetic worship of the self and its full "actualization," amen. We are worse than the pagans ever were. At least they worshipped something besides themselves.

The presence of the mountaintop crucifix (and innumerable others like it) should make us wonder what our signifiers of religious impulse should be now. With Christianity subtracted from the world, what icon takes its place? How about a mirror, at every road juncture, footpath, and high place? Like Narcissus we freeze in scrutiny of our own image. We are our own gods.

In his book *Don't Follow Your Heart*,[24] Thaddeus J. Williams describes the elements of today's "religion of self." It is a creed of unremitting narcissism, taking us down a black hole of self-worship. This is the religion for which the mirror is icon. The locus of self-formed identity: flat, sterile, empty, substance-less, unconnected to other life. A simulacrum of embodied self, reflecting, quite literally, the self back to the self as all of one's genesis. It is transitory, fleeting, existing on the bubble of *now*. Look away and it's gone. At least the crucifix could be venerated for the eternality of values it represents, and the *embodiment* of those values in the person of the Christ, who lived, died, and was resurrected in history.

The crucifix versus the mirror. The Otherness of God versus the sameness of me. The crucifix recalling us to a story outside ourselves, a reminder of the order in the universe and in our apprehension of it that tells us there is more going on than the temple of self, snatching at evanescent meaning from the roil of social process. The mirror reflecting the insistent *now* of self-image, embodying nothing, calling us to utter devotion to self. The fleeting nature of the mirrored self-image corresponds to the temporal *presentism* of this age. We're expected to look at everything old dismissively, and everything new receptively. The ethos is, in other words, "to hate everything except the latest thing," as Anthony Esolen puts it. We

---

24 Williams, Thaddeus, *Don't Follow Your Heart*, (Grand Rapids, MI: Zondervan, 2023).

210 ~ The Discovered Self

don't really just check the "none" box. We turn and worship something else. That something else in this age is the self, for which the mirror serves as icon.

An enemy of the *logos* understanding of objective truth and value is the therapeutic worldview. It is insidiously installed; a stronghold of imperturbable desire and unbounded self-absorption, rising in our very midst in every distortion of sexuality, fixation on prestige, and self-admiration. Our iconoclasm now should be directed at the icon of self-worship: the mirror. Our world is full of these symbolic mirrors, and we must shatter them all.

12
THERAPY

What Is Therapy For?

For those altogether outside the strange new world of therapy, it can seem bewildering. We vaguely associate it with mental illness, but most therapeutic activity is not really about mental illness, properly understood. Rather it's about addressing negative thought patterns that could perhaps be improved upon through talk therapy that encourages some thought patterns and discourages others. It's important to make the distinction between incapacitating conditions that require significant psychiatric intervention, on the one hand, and talk therapy to assist in addressing negative habits of mind or social discomfort, on the other. The therapy to which the therapeutic worldview points is the latter.

Until recent years, "mental illness" referred to serious psychological maladies as distinct from the wide range of human foibles we would normally put down to individual idiosyncrasy. That's changing. Degrees of mental illness exist in everyone, it would seem.[1] Everyone, all the time, is a candidate for therapeutic intervention.

---

1 See, e.g., Rufo, Christopher, "The Cluster B Society," *City Journal,* September 24, 2023. The pervasiveness of diagnoses for relatively minor "disorders" is recounted in Abigail Schrier's *Bad Therapy.*

The presumption seems to be that we're all in need of it. That means our troubles are understood reflexively as the subject of psychology rather than of morality. We're more likely to think of ourselves in machine-like terms, something to be worked on and tuned-up; reactive rather than agentic.

What does it say about us that we are all candidates for therapy? It's true that everyone needs help and advice, now and then, in the exercise of appropriate humility and diligence. But to say therapy, or at least the therapeutic outlook, is for everyone is to say that everyone suffers from mental illness, or if not mental illness presently, then a kind of inherent mental or emotional instability that can tip over to mental illness at any moment and on slight provocation.

We don't think in terms of crazy and sane, anymore, because such terms imply a sharp distinction. In the therapeutic worldview there is no such sharp distinction. The presumption seems to be that everyone, all the time, is in need of emotional coddling to weather the storms and vicissitudes of life. Emotional strength and resilience and dependable self-reliance are severely devalued as virtues. We are all presumed to be in a floating and fluctuating state of mental health, all the time. Stoicism is an anti-virtue. Indeed, a vice, if it means we resist therapy. In that event stoicism is outed as defiant stubbornness because it manifests as resistance to the right-think of the therapeutic.

Toxic Therapy

"Therapy," in its broadest definition, means care due to injury or illness, as with physical therapy following an injury, or drug therapy for certain kinds of illness. But the word is also applied to interventions for purely mental conditions. The reason for pointing out this context is that all therapy, to be therapy, must be toxic. Physical therapy temporarily inflames injured muscles and joints, but it also strengthens, to hasten one's recovery. All internal medicines are toxic, as is necessary to attack inflammation or certain of your biotics or chemistry. The toxins of a good drug can also damage healthy tissue or wipe out good bugs, which is why dosage is so important. To be helpful, therapy of any kind must also be potentially dangerous.

Mental therapies can also be toxic. Ordinarily mere talk should never be considered toxic—offensive or enraging or fraudulent, perhaps, but not toxic. One context in which it can be toxic, however, is therapy, not only because of the peculiar relationship of therapist and client, but because of the underlying premise of ministering to the psychological self. The point is to open oneself up to the therapist so the therapist can then guide the client toward better thinking or practices. That can be toxic if the talk leads the client ever further into an amoral and psychological understanding of their own interface with a world that is actually structured on morality and the logos of objective truth breathed into the world.

The shift away from a moral perspective—moral evasion—is a mainstay professional principle of therapy. The idea is that imposing judgment would inhibit the client's opening himself up in a way believed to initiate healing. Moral considerations are thought to imply judgment, and as such considered an impediment to sound therapy. Therapy therefore usually proceeds on an amoral premise. An amoral but perforce false version of reality thus underwrites the whole enterprise.

It is strange to think how a therapist could ever help by skirting questions of morality. The moral dimension to the client's thought patterns and conduct and decisions in life is absolutely central to advancing psychological well-being. It is inconceivable, from a moral perspective, how this could be left out of talk-therapy discussion, but it routinely is, in our post-Christian world. Indeed, for most secular therapists it is an article of professional faith that they avoid anything that might be taken as morally judgmental. "The idea that 'we as therapists shouldn't talk about right and wrong' has become the very different idea that there is no right and wrong in the first place."[2] How could it be otherwise? Therapy typically moves the client away from the very thing they most need: embrace of the moral structure of the world, and the meaning-making tragic sense.

Ultimately, this avoidance is just demoralizing. Quite literally, because it means the bringer of normalcy, the therapist, excludes the moral dimension from reality. It is a one-on-one practice of what in philosophy terms is pragmatism:[3] the idea that truth is found in what works. As with cultural pragmatism, one must obviously ask: "works for *what*?" In public discourse it's whatever advances the critical deconstructive hermeneutic, reducing Narrative to relative and situational ideas of right and wrong. In the private therapy sphere, it's much the same. The answer to the question "works for what," is whatever makes the client feel better, and that is wrongly believed to be *self*-actualization of *self*-generated values. If values are self-generated, they're not out there fixed in the cosmos where they can be sought after. Instead they're whatever I as the client make them out to be, with the guidance of amoral therapy. It has the effect of denying the moral agency of the person,[4] encouraging them in ongoing moral evasion but also the conclusion that they can only feel better, they can't actually *be* better; it's beyond the reach of their therapy-stunted agency. This seems inescapably a counsel of despair.

Therapy has become a way of life, for many people, and even those who aren't purposely engaged in active therapy are nonetheless engaged in transactions that have elements of the therapeutic about them, such as in teacher/student "social emotional learning" sessions, "life coach" or "career coach" sessions, or even informal

---

2 James Mumford, "Therapy Beyond Good and Evil," *The New Atlantis,* No. 68, Spring, 2022.

3 See *The Mountain and the River*, chapter 21.

4 Much like the excesses of the "gentle parenting" movement. See, e.g., Marilyn Simon's December 23, 2024 *Submission* Substack, "The Cruelty of Gentle Parenting. "

friend-to-friend or boss-to-subordinate sessions in which one presumes to advance psychological principles to help the other, while sidelining altogether moral values.

The toxicity inheres in the amoral psychologizing context in which specific problems are marinated. The goal is to become a better-functioning me, better self-actualized and emotionally confident. That sounds good, on the surface, but note it leaves out building character. "Character" evidently has to be defined, now, to be understood. It means having virtue. So let's define "virtue," too. One who is virtuous is one who aligns with—dare we say "identifies" with—certain positive traits that are conspicuously impersonal, which is to say not unique to me, but objectively extant in the cosmos; universal in the sense of being the same for everyone. These are traits that were routinely taught and intuitively grasped, once upon a time. Traits like those once emphasized in the Boy Scouts: trustworthy, loyal, helpful, friendly, courteous, kind, obedient, cheerful, thrifty, brave, clean, and reverent. Virtues like these are external and aspirational. Psychological practice is internal and procedural.

There is a seemingly ubiquitous call to "destigmatize" therapy, so as to reduce hesitation to seek it out. But few people anymore actually hesitate to enter therapy. Stigma attaches more to therapy resistance, than to therapy. And the hectoring to destigmatize therapy has consequences. Most pertinently, it reduces a barrier to the amoral psychological worldview. For someone obviously in need of therapy, stigma is outweighed by benefit. But for others, reducing stigma just means further normalizing of a destructive me-first, self-care life purpose.

Seeking therapy when there is no serious mental illness has moral implications: against internal fortitude and for heightened vulnerability. Therapy may do more harm than good, in many circumstances. To put it bluntly, some level of stigma is good. If it serves as an impediment to seeking therapy, it also serves as a reinforcer of the need for resilience, which can be strengthened through personal determination and due sensitivity to moral concerns. This is not to say all therapy is bad, to reiterate. But it is to say that therapy is harmful if it ignores or treats as irrelevant the moral dimension.

And, it must be said, much therapy *is* bad.[5] Too many bad theories are tossed about by busybodies who feel they've acquired esoterically the intricacies of the human mind by reading pop psychology. Therapy is ubiquitously an engine of hard-left progressivist ideologies.[6] "Trauma" is in the very air as the root explanation for every discomfort, and it turns out trauma doesn't even mean trauma. It's used to mean experiences that aren't violent or sudden but are considered emotionally abusive or neglectful over time and after-the-fact—basically circumstances that seem negative in retrospect, available to provide cover for explaining emotional vulnerability in the present. Practically anything can be deemed "traumatic," or "abusive," or "toxic," and calling it such doesn't really help the person who claims it. To the contrary, it wears away at the resilience necessary to weather the inevitable interpersonal difficulties of life. It encourages self-delusion. It lifts the load of personal responsibility for present circumstances because of events now deemed in retrospect traumatic or abusive. And dumps them onto someone else.

This is perhaps nowhere more obvious than in the "child within" movements of recent decades, along with the vogue for codependency counseling and trauma recovery, which put forward the notion that the inner "child" in all of us is abused and therefore weak and in need of special nurture and care; that all parents are abusive; and, looking back to Freud, all psychological maladies originate in childhood and especially in one's relations with mother and

5 Abigail Schrier does an admirable job explaining "bad therapy" in her 2024 book by that title.

6 Ryan Rogers, "How Mental Health Therapy Became Fluff and Wokeness," November 15, 2024, Substack *The Multilevel Mailer* (continued in 2 additional parts) and Ryan Rogers' *The Woke Mind*, 2025.

father.[7]

The trauma industry produces dubious theories like repressed memory and "complex" intersectional disorder theories. These have been discredited[8] but continue to be given life by people desperate to explain away their vulnerabilities without taking any responsibility for them. Culture shapes the symptoms of patients, as does therapy itself. Trauma-induced repressed memory makes for a good movie plot, but is an unsound theory for meddling in real lives. It is too often invoked to lay blame for one's troubles on someone else. Always on someone else.

Being guided by the prescriptions of therapy can induce bad—that is to say, immoral—conduct on the part of the therapy client. So much of it involves diagnosing not the client himself but people in the client's life who might have negatively affected him, or even "traumatized" or "abused" him. This is part of the search for the genesis of harm to the client, ostensibly so that the client can begin a process of healing. But it's too often not healing which results, but deeper vulnerability, broken relationships, and erosion of empathy for others. A downward spiral, rather than improvement.

If, in therapy, the discussion involves other people in the client's life newly discovered to have been "abusive" or "traumatizing," or who perhaps themselves meet vague DSM criteria for disorders, that should be a huge red flag that the "therapy" will do more harm than good. It prevents moral self-examination by the client because morality is not the issue, mental health is, and only the mental health of the client. It can mean erection of self-defeating boundaries, a retreat to the castle keep to reinforce the buffered self in resilience-destroying tremulous victimhood.

Such "boundaries" are likely offensives, in actuality, ruthlessly

7 See, e.g., Torrey, E. Fuller, *Freudian Fraud*, (HarperCollins, 1992), pp. 207-213.
8 As pointed out in Schrier, Abigail, *Bad Therapy*, (Chicago: Sentinel, 2024), see also Ley, David, "Forget Me Not: The Persistent Myth of Repressed Memories," *Psychology Today*, October 6, 2019; and Watters, Ethan, "The Forgotten Lessons of the Recovered Memory Movement," *New York Times*, September 7, 2023.

and cruelly sundering relationships, all because this is wrongly deemed therapeutically necessary. Therapeutic prescriptions are never value-neutral, including those spewed into the culture in a never-ending odorous stream of self-help, self-examining, you-first, pop-culture counseling. Most of this is in defiance of the actual moral universe we live in. Some small part of it may suggest you acknowledge the little monster within. The rest is poison.

You can't change other people, you can only change yourself. Changing yourself might involve developing coping strategies for troublesome other people, but that's quite a different thing than diagnosing those other people from afar in order to cement one's self-righteous resentment and self-justifying grievance. If there is someone close to the client with whom the client has a difficult relationship, and who shouldn't, *on moral principle*, be avoided (parents, siblings, friends, perhaps the boss), the therapy should be directed to the client's more healthy interaction with the person. Instead, the therapy is often turned outward, so to speak, to vilify others in service to cocooned emotional protection of the client. This weakens, rather than strengthens, the client. Moreover, it is inherently unreliable, a trial and conviction of others based entirely on the client's suspect perception, made irrefutable by the presumption of amorality in the therapeutic context. It is ultimately damaging to the client. It likely deepens a downward spiral, and often removes from the client's orbit those who might actually be in a position to help. It is morally wrong.

The shift from sin to syndrome is not without consequence. Moral culpability presupposes moral agency. The absence of a sense of moral culpability, when it should exist, means passivity or moral obtuseness. To treat someone as a sinner is to acknowledge their moral agency. To treat them as if they are in the grip of a syndrome is to acknowledge only helplessness. It is disempowering. Aside from fragility-producing psychological vigilance, condemnation and retribution are the only ways forward. Sin, on the other hand, means an opportunity for repentance, forgiveness, and restoration.

Moreover, ordinary features of human existence can be regarded as pathological. Let's consider anxiety, for example. Not the kind of enervating and incapacitating anxiety that recognizably impairs one's normal interaction with others, but rather the kind of anxiety every one of us experiences on a daily basis commuting to work or navigating bureaucracy or even negotiating with a spouse. That kind of general anxiety could be said to impair one's normal interaction with others, perhaps, but it is the kind of thing we must willingly assimilate into our experience to be minimally functioning people. And yet, it can be elevated, in the psychologically over-sensitive mind, to a syndrome to be treated through anxiety avoidance rather than normal life tension that may require greater strengthening to capably weather. Exposure to risk and harm makes one psychologically resilient. The opposite is also true: removal of all risk and harm makes one fragile.

Therapy clients can become impervious to the feelings of others, so concerned are they with building and maintaining control mechanisms to avoid additional psychological trauma to themselves. It amounts to a shift of responsibility from self to others out there, further siloing the client and reinforcing pathological solipsism. This makes a person worse, not better. Contrary to the assumptions built into most modern therapy, it just isn't all about me.

Therapeutic Conformity

With the thinning between mentally well and unwell, does it make sense anymore to tolerate idiosyncrasy? Perhaps conformity is the signal for mental health. Maybe we're all crazy, or maybe none of us are. In the new dispensation, who's to say our disagreements are not matters of mental health, rather than disagreements of principle? Is a trans person mentally ill? How about one who affirms another's transition? How about one who opposes the ideology that demands affirmation? Were all the Germans under Hitler mentally ill? In the age of the therapeutic, how do we say any dissenting opinion is a rational conclusion, about, say, politics, or culture, or religion, or common sense, rather than an indicator of mental illness? Wrongthink is deemed an occasion for therapeutic re-education, rather than debate. How can individual dignity be maintained, in this environment, to say nothing of critical thinking and freedom of independent thought? How do we say anything is right or wrong in any absolute sense, rather than a violation of the cardinal sin of resistance to thought-conforming therapeutic?

Too often, we can no longer simply disagree, without one or both of us falling afoul of the therapeutically-approved answer. The point of therapy is to move you to the "right" way to think and feel, the one socially approved. Therapy thus functions to induce conformity to the prevailing social narrative, which is another reason we should be suspicious of its application to ordinary stressors of life. Insistence on talk therapy for people who are just quirky (that is, all of us) can become an engine of postmodern and posthuman automation.

"The therapeutic" means not just an attitude or frame of reference or disposition. It is not just an idea, or a set of ideas. It is rather an ideology in the pejorative sense: a system of cohering ideas built on false ideals or mistakes of fact about human nature; one that cancels rather than encourages critical examination. The failure of critical examination may be an element of the ideology's principles itself, or it may be implicit, as with devotion to an abstraction without grounding in the reality of facts of human nature or the natural order.[9] Postmodern ideological intolerance takes the form of undermining the intellectual tradition of critical thinking,[10]

9 See, Crawford, Matthew B., *Archedelia* substack "What is Ideology," March 15, 2024.
10 The salutary practice of testing according to criteria beyond the subject matter, evaluating for consistency, coherence, relevance, and so on; as distinct from the "critical theory" of ideology that is only an assertion of power, a disguised attack rather than genuine scholarly critique.

and in turn enables the toxic sentimentality of the therapeutic.[11]

For psychological man, ideas are evaluated by the measure of emotional well-being, rather than according to their place in a rational universe, rationally considered. Relationships to people and institutions and authority are governed by the criterion of subjective psychological harmony. Our well-being is no longer conceived as the product of aligning ourselves with ideals, the moral best version of ourselves. It is instead the result of aligning everyone out there with the therapeutic mindset, the victimized and fragile worst version of ourselves. Talk therapy is employed to aid in this project, to address an ever-expanding array of disorders and neuroses, but also as a necessary-seeming aid in emotional processing of events according to therapeutic criteria.

In this environment maximizing human potential means the therapeutic approach extends well beyond those who self-identify as disordered in some way. Talk therapy is, for many, the default mechanism for improvement on nearly any upsetting event or feeling of weakness against the trials of a demanding world. Talking through difficult relationships and self-imposed limitations is taken to be the mechanism for getting us fit for the fight—reinforcing a machine mentality by which the self is subjected to tune-up and repair according to social norms represented in the prescriptions of the therapist.

The therapist in this scenario serves as the arbiter of social norms. What is the point, after all, of going to a therapist? It is to move you toward a more ideal self, painfully if necessary. In practice it is more often a palliative self-exploration and affirmation, rather than a program of self-confrontation. But in any event it is at least presented as movement toward some ideal, and that ideal is necessarily supplied by the therapist. Not that the therapist necessarily tells you outright what you should or shouldn't think. Rather, that

11 See, Davidson, Bruce, "The Fall of Critical Thinking," Brownstone.org, March 24, 2024.

certain attitudes are reinforced and some discouraged according to the therapist's vision of normal.

How could it be otherwise? What set of goals *should* a therapist move the client toward? The "normal" ones, of course. The point of the whole exercise is to address the client's understanding of abnormal or unhelpful or distressing interactions with the world. A therapist doesn't conform himself to the map of reality created by the client. That would be contrary to the point of therapy because the client is, after all, in therapy in the first place because he feels his own map is distorted. The therapist intentionally moves the client toward an ideal of normalcy that is supplied *by the therapist*. In this way idiosyncrasy is driven out by social prescription, and is replaced with conformity for the sake of conformity.

This is not only a move toward whatever society considers "normal," it is also a move toward what individual therapists believe should be normal. The entire profession is rife with ideological purpose put ahead of individual client well-being. Many therapists proudly announce and even advertise their ideological requisites, as with "feminist" therapists. At least they're telling you up front certain of their beliefs that they're more than willing to redirect clients toward. Ideological neutrality is impossible, in this environment, which is to say most therapy is an exercise in indoctrination: affirmation of the irreligious, progressivist zeitgeist. Outside of the explicitly religious context, like interactions of priest and penitent, or pastoral counseling, therapy is conducted entirely on a presumption of therapeutic dialectical materialism. It is ideological at its core.

Therapeutic Industrial Complex

Apart from explicitly religious-driven therapy, the ideals to attain through therapy are derived from the ether—the fluid social norms to which we're expected to aspire. The fluidity in social norms results from explicit or implicit neo-Marxist process philosophies, by which the postmodern world abandons transcendence, with objectivity and universality of values collapsing right behind.[12] An irreligious therapist likely lives in Zygmunt Baumann's "Liquid Modernity,"[13] and if the client expresses a differing vision of normal, at best the client's vision will be folded in dialectically. No overt contest of will or propositions need take place.

The only way to discern deviations from normal is to draw inferences from what a person says or does. And to do that, we must have some idea in mind already of what constitutes normal and what constitutes a deviation. Attempts to objectify standards and deviations therefrom are made by experts in the field of psychiatry and psychology, as with the Diagnostic and Statistical Manual of Mental Disorders (DSM) put out by the American Psychiatric Association. The very existence of such a catalogue implies that there is such a thing as a normal human being psychologically. Symptoms of "disorder" imply a default "order" to human beings.

No one is properly "ordered" by such vague standards, however. We all have our weaknesses, and failures, and occasions when we seem to succeed but succeed less well than we might have with greater care. Everyone is prideful. Everyone can be self-indulgent. Everyone loses patience. Everyone draws boundaries around what they will and won't endure from others. All have sinned and fall short of the glory of God.

Many of the disorders identified in compilations like the DSM are matters that would have been considered moral issues in an earlier day; not really "disorders" because they are matters common to the human condition, matters over which we have control in the exercise of God-given agency. The answer to moral issues is not psychological therapy, but rather appeal to moral absolutes; to confession; to forgiveness; to spiritual renewal.

Such moral appeal, to be effective, necessarily means also so-

---

12 This was a key theme of *The Mountain and the River*.
13 Bauman, Zygmunt, *Liquid Modernity*, (Malden, MA: Polity, 2000).

cial approval and disapproval. As we shift from the moral to the therapeutic worldview, approbation or opprobrium on moral grounds dissipates, and replacement grounds of self-care are substituted. You can hear it in the reflexive therapeutic vocabulary now common. Approval or disapproval attach based on how thoroughly we embrace the therapeutic conception of self. Guilt and shame become disorders themselves, rather than a natural consequence of violating the conscience.

What makes one trait normal and another a sign of mental illness? Social norms define this to a far greater extent than we tend to realize. But social norms in the postmodern world are fluid and evolving, the very definition of relativism. Very little of what makes a human being is regarded as innate, or God-directed, or objectively true. The "right" answer is what society has normalized, not necessarily what is objectively true.

Social norms have been facts of life for societies down through the ages. But these have been limited in that they bent to hard facts of external, unchanging sources of value and truth. That's less true now, because socially-derived norms have so much pushed out other sources of understanding. There's a reason people never conceived of changing their sex until five minutes ago. People in societies less moved by malleable social norms were not more stupid nor less sophisticated than we are today. They just didn't look to social prescription for guidance on every question about who and what they were. Instead they looked to eternal unchanging values, which society's norms often reinforced.

The push to participate in therapy has mounted in recent years, with suggestions (by financially interested parties) that failing to participate in therapy, or at least being open to it, is itself a disorder.[14] Progressively less burdensome difficulties are to be the subject of therapy. In time we're all just talking to others who set themselves

---

14 Freya India writes compellingly on this point in "No, Not Everyone Needs Therapy," *Girls* (Substack), November 7, 2023.

up as authorities on the inner id, submitting to "analysis" whatever little stressor or bump in the road we encounter. We can spend so much energy talking about our lives that we don't get around to living them.

Think what all this means about mental health in general. It means one's mental health is profoundly affected by the surrounding society. And that means mental health can be a matter of social contagion.[15] This has become increasingly obvious in the age of social media. Gender dysphoria, for example, is suddenly epidemic. The word "gender" was re-purposed to mean the sex of the discovered inner self, which, according to gender ideologues, may be at variance with the sex of the body. It is significant that such an idea is new in the history of the world. Even occult and Gnostic idealizations of androgyny did not go so far.

The therapeutic mindset does not improve mental health. In fact, the evidence is that it degrades mental health.[16] The very fact of continuous rumination on one's interior well-being or mental health can deteriorate that mental health. The hyper-focus can turn us into hypochondriacs (or sufferers of "illness anxiety disorder") about our own mental state.

The therapeutic is bad thinking, however; not sick thinking. It illustrates that whole societies can become not sick, but ideologically captured. We can live a lie and then spread the lie. So social contagion is real enough, but again, it's ideological, a failure of critical thinking, a product of ignorance and immoral selfishness. It proves out Dietrich Bonhoeffer's theory that (translated): "stupidity is a

---

15 Watters, Ethan, *Crazy Like Us: The Globalization of the American Psyche*, (New York: Free Press, 2010).

16 At this point the social indicators are overwhelming, but efforts to document this rather than merely argue it are contained in Abigail Schrier's *Bad Therapy*, (Chicago: Sentinel, 2024) and the efforts of Jean Twenge, including *iGen*, 2017, and *The Narcissism Epidemic*, 2009.

more dangerous enemy of the good than wickedness"[17] because it propagates wickedness far and wide, unthinkingly. By "stupidity," Bonhoeffer did not mean an absence of innate intelligence. "There are people who are intellectually agile who are stupid, while intellectually inept people may be anything but stupid." So, by "stupidity" he meant refusal to engage critical thinking, mulishly going along with whatever the crowd presents. In his day, the crowd's Nazism. In ours, acquiescence to Machine dogma that we listen exclusively to our feelings. Bonhoeffer:

> The Bible states that the fear of God is the beginning of wisdom. Thus, the inner liberation of man begins by living responsibly before God. Only then may stupidity be overcome.

It cannot be emphasized enough that the therapeutic means a failure of critical thinking, and the failure of critical thinking has dire consequences, for individuals and for society. Our entire tradition of freedom of thought depends on it. The dominant methodology of psychological therapy today is cognitive behavioral therapy, sometimes shortened to "CBT." CBT is supposed to encourage critical thinking: a dispassionate and rational reconsideration of self-defeating beliefs. Critical thinking is a crucial skill in everyone. It is what we do when we test ideas according to universal principle rather than emotive reaction; when we evaluate in good faith rather than deconstruct and dismantle solely to advance our own power-driven ideology. When critical thinking is weak or lacking, CBT is intended to correct it.

The principle behind CBT is that psychological maladies result from distorted beliefs about the world, but what makes a belief distorted? As we might expect, what constitutes a "distorted" belief is

---

17 "Letters and Papers from Prison," written before his death in 1945; discussed by Alexandra Hudson at *Civic Renaissance* (Substack) November 2023. See also John Leake, "On Stupidity," *Courageous Discourse* (Substack) August 24, 2023.

in the eye of the beholder; i.e., the therapist. So while the idea behind CBT might be valid, it rests on the variable of the therapist's buy-in to the therapeutic worldview him- or herself. And this is not merely theoretical. Therapy itself reinforces the therapeutic worldview in the minds of both therapist and client. The therapeutic worldview is likely what drove the client to seek therapy in the first place, and the therapist to seek the profession in the first place. Once inside the worldview, it's hard to see outside of it—that's what "worldview" means. If the therapist has rejected moral realism and has embraced the emotivist ethos, then the blind is truly leading the blind. The necessary toxicity of the therapy will overwhelm rather than cure.

The "distorted" beliefs that ought to be the subject matter of CBT are things like "catastrophizing" thinking, unfounded fearfulness, and the like. But it also is supposed to encompass emotional reasoning, which is essentially what the therapeutic worldview consists in. The entire premise of the DSM and the professional organizations that sponsor or promote it is that distorted beliefs disorder the individual's interior psychology; moral considerations enter into it only insofar as antiquated feelings of guilt or remorse may be the client's problem.

For these reasons there is increasingly an observed phenomenon given the name "reverse CBT."[18] It means certain kinds of influences inculcate, rather than eliminate, distorted beliefs, manifesting in more disorder. It is a reversal of critical thinking, in that distorted cognitions are implanted or enhanced, rather than eliminated. Most relevant here, emotional reasoning can be embraced rather than confronted, reinforcing a distorted belief that one should be protected from any upsetting circumstance. The world must conform to that which is subjectively believed needful for psychological equanimity, even if it means shutting down free speech

---

18 See, e.g., Greg Lukianoff and Jonathan Haidt, *The Coddling of the American Mind*, (New York: Penguin, 2018).

and open debate and engagement with conflicting ideas in the world. But that's exactly the wrong way to go. "It's only by connecting to objective reference points *outside* the self that we can correct the distorted perceptions *within* the self."[19]

The therapeutic worldview drives out religious faith. It is reflected in social norms, as noted, but also in law and in cultural movements toward nurture and care and protection of the inner being, which houses the new god Identity. This deference to ultimate subjectivity is untethered not just from God but from any remaining sense of transcendence or objectivity or universality or moral realism. Among those of us old enough to have seen the rise of the therapeutic worldview (as opposed to having been born into it), the felt loss of meaning and purpose to life is palpable. This goes beyond the disenchantment of the world Max Weber wrote about,[20] or Matthew Arnold's lament about the "melancholy, long, withdrawing roar" of the Sea of Faith.[21] It is not merely the diminished attraction to the aesthetic and mysterious that inheres in the religious impulse. It is something worse; something darker. It is the re-shaping of mankind, from the moral creatures we're meant to be, to something more animalistic, yet without the internal resilience even of an animal. We're reduced to safety-seeking comfort. Freud's concept of mankind as principally governed by pleasure-seeking and pain-avoiding was not true, but is becoming true, as a self-fulfilling prophecy. Genuine private religious belief is not enough, on its own, to preserve us from this dismal tide, because we're social creatures. Morality must be restored so our dignity will be restored, else future generations will grow so encultured by the therapeutic that they cannot find their way back because they don't see the need to. They won't know what they're missing, and will look back on the

---

19 Gaskovsi, Ruth, "Horses in the Heart: Passions, Distortions, and Ultimate Hope," *School of the Unconformed* (Substack), March 14, 2024.

20 Weber, Max, *The Protestant Ethic and the Spirit of Capitalism*, (Pantianos Classics, 1930), first published 1904.

21 *Dover Beach* by Matthew Arnold, 1867

pre-modern and modern worlds with genuine puzzlement. Perhaps some, however, will experience a glimmer of recognition, a felt sense of loss of something they almost but not quite had for themselves, and respond with desire to confront honestly the inescapable tragic sense, grasping the greater scope of reality that includes an assurance of things hoped for, the conviction of things unseen—a renewed desire to take God seriously.

13
IDENTITY

Magical Identity

We can make great headway in understanding post-modernism simply by taking special care with word definitions. Through sleight of hand, words in common usage become re-adapted with a slightly different meaning. While we're assuming the innocuous original meaning, the post-modernist is engaging in deft elision to a meaning much more sinister. The new meaning is inseparable from the ideology of which it is part. This isn't the result of carelessness. It is intentionally disingenuous.

"Identity" is such a word. It is now a magical word, to psychological man. But what did it mean before, in the context of one's self-conception? Before postmodern erosions of objectivity and universality, a person would hardly have occasion to speak of his or her "identity." It would not be regarded as a matter under internal construction, nor hidden within, to be sought out and discovered. "Character" of course would be relevant and a matter for attention. But character has to do with virtues, or the lack thereof—it is part of the vocabulary of morality, rather than of psychology.

If we thought about our identity at all, it would be phrased in terms of objective realities: My parents reared me according to a describable set of values and influences; I have acquired an identifiable set of political and religious views; perhaps my accomplishments and failures might be cited for their contribution to my "identity." Identity, in other words, was socially negotiated. It was the sum of innumerable social interactions that contribute to the unique me. Something like this would be one's identity—again, were there occasion to speak of identity at all.

So how did "identity" acquire the special significance it has now? Various strands of popularized postmodern philosophy contribute to a new tribalism wherein we embrace certain groups within society with which to "identify," especially if those groups can claim some sort of aggrieved or oppressed status, enabling it to reflexively adopt a stance of transgression and negation, the signifier of the privileged sect of victimhood. Group identification is preceded by victim identification. Victim identification underwrites victim-group identities.

A problem with this way of thinking of "identity" is that it's not merely some describable feature of one's personality, but is understood instead as what he is at the authentic core of his being. If a person "identifies" as gay, for example, he doesn't *do* the sin, he *is* the sin. Any suggestion that perhaps homosexual acts are morally wrong is therefore taken as a personal attack. Injection of the "identity" paradigm onto same-sex attraction requires jettisoning moral critique. It thus becomes impossible to reckon with the morality of homosexuality. The question is evaded, not answered.

It seems normal, now, to self-identify according to the combination of *psychological* influences on us. We evaluate our past influences according to how we imagine they have affected our inner psyches. I might come around to the view that I am *nothing but* that combination of psychological influences. While psychological man for the most part is passive in reception of this identity-formation, he may nonetheless subtly steer the sense of identity in a way congenial to socially approved values. Psychological man participates in his own identity formation in this limited way, by sniffing the air for social approval, emphasizing some elements of his existence and not others.

There is a levelling effect from the process of social negotiation so that the discovered self is not so unique after all, but formed according to social norms that will not bruise the tentative swaying reed of the interior. We participate in formation of the buffer between self and other. Society must be regulated so as not to damage the psyche with noxious ideas. At the same time the inner being is formed so that it is not too far out of sync with that negotiated exterior. It is easy to see, in this environment, why some sets of ideas are so screamingly unacceptable to psychological man, and how those who hold them can only be regarded as sub-human. They must be canceled. We recognize this way of encountering the world in someone who says "I identify as" one thing or another. It's not a statement of preference, however, as for a consumer item or a sports team affiliation. The word "identify" signals a belief that the choice springs unbidden from the inner being, rather than as the product of personal agency.

The inner, discovered self is what is meant by "identity," in the parlance of the therapeutic. The rightness or wrongness of how one conducts himself is weighed according to its effect on that identity. This obviously profoundly contrasts with foundational tenets of all religions, and especially the monotheisms, in which God authors a hierarchy of moral order that is fixed in the cosmos and in the human heart.

Discovered Identity

In *The Rise and Triumph of the Modern Self*,[1] Carl Trueman effectively re-started the public conversation on the rise of the therapeu-

---

1 Trueman, Carl, *The Rise and Triumph of the Modern Self/Cultural Amnesia, Expressive Individualism, and the Road to Sexual Revolution*, (Wheaton, IL: Crossway, 2020).

tic worldview. Its subtitle is *Cultural Amnesia, Expressive Individualism, and the Road to Sexual Revolution.* As pointed out earlier, the phrase "expressive individualism" is not really about individualism as compared to collectivism. Trueman's intent becomes clearer upon reading one of his shorter essays, titled "The Rise of the 'Psychological Man.'"[2]

How did people form their sense of self before we all became "psychological man?" Once upon a time the sense of self was formed from relations outside oneself. People grew up forming their sense of identity on the basis of love relationships: son, brother, friend, citizen, child of God. A person's sense of his own "self" would be formed from beliefs concerning the nature of reality that he acquires from his environment and from reason. That sense rested on an understanding that there is a common human nature, containing the conscience and basic principles like the givenness of moral categories.

We might refer to that former agentic sense of self as the "negotiated" self, rather than the "discovered" self, as discussed in chapter 3. These terms suggest a key difference: the presence versus the absence of agency. The "negotiated" self is agentic in its own formation, meaning that the personality emerges and makes conscious decisions of good and evil, and the sum accretes over time to make the person. The person is an active, decision-making agent in the process. We are what we are in large part because we make ourselves that way.

Not alone, of course. The making of a person entails innumerable collisions; contests between this idea and that, in the exercise of reason; between this person and that, in the clash of wills; between this material choice and that, in the struggle for sustenance in a world of scarce resources; and between one's own desires and empathic desire founded in love for others. These collisions are the result of the dichotomous nature of reality—binary opposition all

---

2 *Public Discourse*, November 9 and 10, 2020 (www.thepublicdiscourse.com).

the way down. In the beginning God created the heavens and the earth, and all of our reality cascades out before us in innumerable overlapping differentiations of this-not-that. Each differentiation is its own contest, its own thesis and antithesis, and the individual participates in this, pushing idea against idea and so on. It is in this sense that the resulting identity is "negotiated." Purposeful participation in the moral universe produces the self.

The "discovered" self, by contrast, is passive. It is not something one implicitly develops in the course of negotiating the exterior world. It is Identity, found within. This passive stumbling upon Identity has to occur on a conception of amorality because moral responsibility is an agentic undertaking, and this discovered conception of identity is passive. Evaluation of others will still operate on a moral perspective, however, because it may affect psychological man's own well-being. To say it slightly differently, psychological man does not govern his own conduct according to standards he understands to be "moral." It is in that sense that his view is amoral. But he does evaluate others' conduct according to moral standards, because it affects his own emotional and psychological well-being. Alisdair MacIntyre expressed the phenomenon as follows (understanding "modern radical" to mean psychological man):

> The modern radical is as confident in his moral expression of his stances and consequently in the assertive uses of the rhetoric of morality as any conservative has ever been. Whatever else he denounces in our culture he is certain that it still possesses the moral resources which he requires in order to denounce it. Everything else may be, in his eyes, in disorder, but the language of morality is in order, just as it is.[3]

Sex is central to identity formation, regardless whether one is infected with the therapeutic worldview or not. If the inner, "true"

---

3 *After Virtue*, p. 4.

self is the source of identity, however, then even one's sex can be discerned by looking within, and this can be imagined to trump the obvious external bodily indicator of sex category. This helps explain the intractability of trans identity activism. From the trans activist perspective, how dare you not accept whatever I say I am? From the objective truth perspective, how is it compassionate to affirm delusion? The tension is acute when we're talking about children. Is "gender affirmation" genuine kindness? Or is it indifference tricked out as virtuous tolerance—cruelty originating in moral cowardice?

The sexual attraction one feels can also be a source of identity. A male attracted to males, for example, may not think of himself as a person who is tempted to the sin of same-sex sexual experiences. He may instead conceive himself as a distinct category of human: a gay man. That's his "identity," a sub-category of human being to which he consigns himself in eternal conflict with other sub-categories, and by which he signs on to the overarching normie/transgressor paradigm that underlies identity politics.

With the turn from faith to psychological self-formation, the concept of sin is discarded. The truth is that an inclination to sin is present in every heart; we're to actively resist it to be the best person we can be. We live our lives swimming around at the mouth of a whirlpool. We can fight it by swimming away from it, to the weaker outer edges of the vortex, staying always athwart the current. Or we can relax, deny the existence of the vortex, and be sucked into it. Children don't know any better, if we don't teach them, so that's what they will do.

With the thinking of Jean Jacques Rousseau and many another after him, a shift began away from the Christian understanding of mankind's inclination to sin, toward an understanding that we are essentially good except as corrupted by society. Evil does not exist in my own heart, in other words. It invades me from the outside. We come to think of our moral task as repulsing the corrupting evil outside ourselves, rather than suppressing the evil in our own heart.

The line between good and evil no longer runs through each individual heart, on this understanding.

In the last two or three generations or so, the evil in the heart is increasingly denied and is thereby given rein because that's what we do: we fall into destructive patterns of thought haphazardly if we are not conscious of sin and our own frailty in dealing with it. Part of the problem is that we've collectively become allergic even to the *word* "sin." The demons laugh their heads off when we recoil at mention of sin. We must be willing to accept that it's here in the heart, not just vaguely out there somewhere. It's a little monster inside each of us that becomes as big as we allow.

If evil is external, it follows that the uncorrupted discovered self is an expression of moral purity. The necessary corollary to the discovered self as basically good is that any attempt to abridge the discovered inner identity must be evil. That attempt is bigotry, the new original sin, words and attitudes that would deny the pure discovered identity. Denial of the discovered identity is not just to be fought as evil corruption, it is to be fought as an existential threat, quite literally. A person's identity is their very self; denying that identity means denying their selfhood; denying their very existence.

A person immersed in the therapeutic conception of self sees evil only in what he calls bigotry. He may not conceive of a dark side to his own being, so focused is he on how good he is. How open-minded. How accepting of other people. How unwilling to call evil "evil." You do you. Indifference is transmuted alchemically to moral uprightness.

The paradigm of discovered identity has profound implications for relationship to authority. Absent belief in God and the reality such belief discloses, we come to consider internal predilections, feelings, emotions, and desires as being authoritative. External sources of authority are suspect. Even, or perhaps especially, the authority of fathers, but certainly all human sources of authority for which the father is archetype.

Some time ago in child psychology circles there arose a new concept called "oppositional defiant disorder." It's a phrase to describe children who oppose authority and are defiant toward it. But that's true of every child, to some degree or another, why is it elevated to a mental health "disorder?" It's a therapy-language response to the observation that so many children and teenagers in this day reflexively oppose authority in the abstract, and, being children, oppose it particularly as it is embodied in parents, and especially the father. External authority is a threat to the internal authority of one's discovered identity, which must be protected in its emergence from the subconscious inner being.

It's quite difficult, in this environment, to turn to religion to understand reality. We can easily ignore its factual narrative supporting hard principles, and substitute vague "spirituality." This is why moral therapeutic deism has replaced Christianity in too many ostensibly Christian churches. It is a capitulation of the church itself to the paradigm of psychological man.

A consequence is that we are incapacitated from grasping that our default state is to turn to evil. Evil is not the difficult thing to explain about humanity; good is. The cultured, educated, disciplined state we try to bring about in our children must include an understanding of how to renounce evil so we don't "lean on our own understanding."[4] Instilling that self-discipline and that truth about selfhood is what it means to rear a child, rather than just keeping him and feeding him like a pet. Left to his own devices he will feed the monster within, the self in a state of nature, the discovered self.

The psychological turn has coincided with the loss of a sense that there is a common and stable human nature, with the result that, in Trueman's words, "all that remains of human purpose is the attaining of personal psychological happiness in whatever form

4 Proverbs 3:5.

happens to work for the individual concerned."[5] This is utter relativism and utter narcissism. Our identity emerges from the raw material of inner being, like mushrooms from nightsoil, without reference to its impact on others. It appears from the outside like self-absorption producing false contrived identity, with violence-tinged indignation aimed at the supposed onslaughts, peremptory to imagined identity-denying "violence."

People who have not gone 'round the bend on psychological self-formation are often puzzled at regularly being called bigots, or homophobes, or transphobes, or something similar. It's puzzling because they see a clear distinction between the evil ideology, on the one hand, and the person who adopts it, on the other. Communism is evil, but that doesn't mean a billion Chinese people are. Likewise, a trans person is the confused victim of transgender activism and the triumph of the therapeutic, not a personification of evil himself. The idea that one can love the sinner but hate the sin is entirely lost on those who discover identity in the inner id, because for them there is no distinction. Ideology and self are ineluctable. Disagreements about ideas—especially ideas about what a human being is— are taken as disagreements about another's right to exist.

Words are the instrumentality by which we affirm or deny the discovered, internally-derived identity. Denial is thought to be injury, conceptualized in psychological terms. "Misgendering" a trans person by using the "wrong" pronoun, for example, or "deadnaming" them, is deemed equivalent to a physical assault. Speech conformity is imposed to alleviate this "violence." For another example, an objection to homosexual practices may be taken as denial of the selfhood of another, an act of political violence. You can say you believe marriage to be between a man and a woman, and that sex belongs only inside that marriage, but a person who identifies himself as "gay" is not going to hear this as disagreement about appli-

---

5 "The Rise of Psychological Man," *Public Discourse*, November 9, 2020, (www.thepublicdiscourse.com).

cation of universal moral principles. He's going to hear it as a denial of his very existence.

We don't just use words to disagree about things. We disagree about the purpose of words. It's the age-old problem of the serpent in the garden, the misuse of language that distorts objective meaning, a source of man's universal morally compromised state. The serpent employs deceptive language rendering us, if we are not vigilant, unable to assign objective and transcendent meaning to *anything*.

One needn't be a theologian to be greatly concerned with how secular philosophies degrade our conception of reality as informed by religion. We can't engage the world without understanding its garbled notions of what a person even is. Trueman:

> The needs of this hour are not so much that of explaining the church to the world. First, we need to explain the world to the church.[6]

Sex and Identity

In the therapeutic worldview, one's identity is built to a significant degree around one's conceptions about sex. A person may willingly "identify" according to invented subcategories of human. We should reconsider these new subcategories, rather than taking them as given. In any public discussion, the genesis of these new subcategories is leapt lightly over, as if it were self-evident. But why do we think "gay" is a subcategory of human? Or feminist, lesbian, trans, or any of the other proliferating categories of sex "identification?" Or race, for that matter? There is no reason. It's not as though science or even philosophy is settled on why there are now multiple categories of human, based on sex or sex attraction or sex advocacy or race. It's all theory, for political ends. It's made up to serve the

6 "The Impact of Psychological Man - and How to Respond," *Public Discourse,* November 10, 2020.

new god Identity.

"Identity" is thought to have the force of unalterable givenness that was formerly applied to biological sex and opposite-sex attraction, precisely because sex-related elements are so fundamental to one's psychological self-conception. If a boy says he "identifies" as a girl, that's to be taken as a statement that his inner being differs from his biological sex. "Identification" means one's emergent inner being, which may be a boy or a girl; straight or gay; polyamorous or asexual. To refer to one's "identity" or to "identify as" signals the therapeutic paradigm.

But what if the poor boy is just a boy not poisoned by ideology? We only ever look for clues that he identifies *against* his natural body; never that he identifies as what his body says he is. Basic consistency would mean that if a boy "identifies" as a boy, it's because he obeys the voice of his emergent inner being, but that inner being's sex just happens to coincide with his bodily sex. But it's never presented that way. The sex of the body is definitive, but even those who serve the god Identity accord it a presumption. A boy who feels he's a boy is just *being* a boy, there's no need for the "identity" rhetorical device to signal a whole new process of self-identification. The boy's boyness is just given, and no one queries why it ought to be presumptive. There's an ideological tell, here: the "identity" language is only invoked when necessary to signal ideological departure from nature.

The word "identify" refers to the discovered self created from the raw material of the primal id. But that creation is not the product of conscious decision-making whereby one rationally weighs the alternatives and chooses. Instead the choosing itself is the chooser. The process is the substance. The choosing is a happening inside me; an agency not mine, that is acting in and through me. There is no being, only becoming, and the becoming is the chooser, the gradient of time as a personal telos that trumps the conscious, individual, exercise of agency. Individual agency dissipates into the liquid flow that psychological man gives himself over to.

Thus, a boy deciding he's a girl isn't making a rational, conscious decision that, all things considered, he prefers for himself the other side of the male/female divide. Rather, he's so imbued with the psychological self-conception that he believes there to be a dynamism at work within him that produces "identity." He passively accepts the seeming mandate generated in the well of formless void that is his inner being, over which his conscious agency is pacified to serve only as guardian.

The boy "identifying" as a girl acknowledges and validates the fixed, categorical opposition of biological male and female, by virtue of transitioning from one to the other. Yet he denies the categories are ontological: existence precedes essence. Nonsensical denial of fixed categories is the whole point, for psychological man. The gradient of time rules reality; nature does not, and certainly reality is not dictated nor superintended by a putative "God."

Transitioning from category to category doesn't feel like a conscious choice because of the psychological self-conception. A male doesn't feel that he's choosing to be a female. He's convinced of the need to protect the authentic self that emerges from the depths of his mysterious charged being. A boy doesn't so much choose to be a girl as he chooses to obey this inner voice. And he chooses to obey because that inner being is authoritative, replacing God, and nature, and a morality fixed in the cosmos. He's not a child of God with moral agency. He imagines himself created from the formless void within, though he is actually responding to society's privileging of "brave" neo-Gnosticism concerning sex.

Such a person (and, God help us, a child) welcomes the voice within as a god-like co-creator. The voice takes the form of serious dysphoria, the sense of discomfort and even disgust with his/her body. In the case of gender dysphoria, discomfort or disgust specifically with the sex of that body. The dysphoria means the voice within owns him or her, he/she doesn't own it. It's demonic. There is no scientific or even logical basis for the conclusion that "gender" (even in the word's new usage) can deviate from sex. It is a raw assertion utterly belied by material fact: biological reality in every cell of the body.

We should be particularly focused on the implications of the re-defined word "identity," in understanding psychological man. When a male experiences gender dysphoria, a turbulence in his psychological state, he may decide the turbulence is quelled if he can transition to his "true" self, a female. But what makes female the "true" self? There is no answer, even if one is to rely entirely on the subjective feeling. And yet the operating assumption is that we can just know; we just kind of feel it. Gnosis, esoterically sourced. But what if the feeling is wrong? What if we misinterpret the "voice" of our inner id? What if we mistake its authoritativeness? What if it's demonic, even? The word "demonic" means, after all, etymologically, a scattering of that which is formed and structured as the accurate product of rational thought process. Even discounting supernatural influence, why would we suppose the sub-rational inner id authoritative, accepting uncritically the product of a mysterious stew from which our real self emerges?

None of this usually gets explained in such raw terms. Rather it is expressed as a felt reality, a truth more true than the biology that nature cruelly set at odds with the inner being. To repress one's identity is thought the deepest of transgressions psychological man can make. Manifesting that identity is what it means to be a self at all. Instead of acting on God-given agency to decide one's direction according to universal principle, the subject acts on self-imposed duty to protect the inner being.

Broken Relationship

In light of all we've covered about the therapeutic worldview, it's no wonder statistics on marriage are so disheartening. Marriage requires reaching out into the world beyond our heads, to embrace the fundamental other of sexual difference. If the psychological self is the only point of reference for normalcy or values, how can the otherness of a mate be accommodated?

Added to that, if my identity is ever under construction, and so is that of a potential mate, who are the people getting married? In the past marriage was an important part of identity-formation. Each would form part of his/her self-identity from relationship with the other. They grow together, in that sense, becoming "as one" in their self-identity. But as we've seen, "identity" has a new meaning, with the advent of psychological man. Identity is formed in the inner being, unguided by the exercise of independent agency directed toward objective and universal virtues. This is a radical new variable. Really, who am I, on my wedding day? And who will I be tomorrow? And my spouse, who is she? Who will she be tomorrow? How can a lifelong union even be conceived, in this dynamic flow?

This reality about marriage applies to social interactions more generally, if less vividly than in the marriage example. It is ever more difficult to form close attachments to others, and certainly more difficult for those attachments to endure. People in the therapeutic culture are ever more siloed, insulated from others who might pose a threat to one's ongoing project of self-care.

In families, intergenerational conflict is qualitatively different than in generations past, through all of history. There have always been disagreements, of course, between parents and adult children. Usually about politics or principles of child-rearing or other elements of how one goes about the business of life. Such disagreements would typically be rooted in mutual concern for the other, however. Love was the substrate for the disagreement; the reason for having the conversation in the first place. A father might critique a son's life decisions, for example, because of the father's natural concern for the well-being of the son, with an expectation that the son will duly consider the critique because of that love. The son might consider and decide to go his own way, or even roll the eyes at his fuddy-duddy father. But this would not necessitate outright rejection, by which every other person in the world has a claim to the son's affection superior to that of his father.

Or so it has been in the past. Longstanding rifts in family relationships now develop to an extent and degree that is unprecedented, not just because the disagreements are more profound, but because the persons having the disagreement are so different. If the son in our example is given over to the therapeutic, but not the father, the critique is received as an attack, and not help. The critique may have as its object virtues or objective value, or a hierarchy of being to which the son is presumed to aspire. But if the son is concerned with protection of the inner being before all else, and finds values in horizontal process rather than vertical ideal, and is aligned with a social reality ahead of the family relationship, then how is the critique to land, other than as an attack on the son's very personhood? This is no mere disagreement. It is an entirely different way of looking at the world. There is no value shared; no common ground on which to even commence a debate; nor is "debate" a meaningful concept, given therapeutic precepts for interacting with the world. The interaction doesn't just result in inability to make oneself understood. It can only be understood as a personal expression of animosity that drives out love.

As in families, so in society more generally. The therapeutic worldview cannot coexist with the logos worldview. For psychological man, the very fact that one must look outside himself to find truth invalidates the truth claim. It must come from inside, to be valid. Accordingly, he is not bound to the unchanging, eternal, and objective standard of capital-T truth held by a religious person, or one who has the logos worldview of transcendence even if not otherwise religious. So there is no common ground on which to engage in disagreement. No mutual deference to objective values.

As the culture changes, psychological man changes with it, but religious man adheres to an unchanging hierarchy of values, so evolution of culture can go only so far except by the turn of generations. Current Western culture increasingly re-affirms the therapeutic worldview and disaffirms with hostility the logos worldview of transcendence. To psychological man, the logos worldview surrounds and suffocates. It amounts to a threat, not a disagreement. An attempt to conquer, overcome, and suppress. Hence the "snowflake" sensitivity to other points of view. Hence the hysterical revulsion against the tormenting old guards who insist on the chastity belt of religion.

To logos man, every expression of emotivist thinking is, first, a puzzling irrelevance. And then, a rejection of any coherent category of meaning; and more than that, of love. It is a rejection of the very categories of human relation that enable love, and special affection, and loyalty, and of the anchoring of self in the world of individualized other humans.

The therapeutic is a distinct paradigm altogether from the transcendent, as we have thus far emphasized. If there is common ground, for psychological man, it is only with those who share the therapeutic way of thinking: that emotional self-care is one's purpose in life. Of course one might argue that self-care is served by deference to objective value, but that's not how psychological man sees it. There's not a fixed standard to which he aspires. The feeling of well-being is itself the only standard. Whatever serves that feeling is "right," or "true," and that shifts as society does.

The hierarchy of value is scrapped, for the therapeutic, but its vocabulary remains. That is the significance of Alisdair MacIntyre's observation (seconded by Carl Trueman) that emotivism is not a theory of meaning, but of *use*. To say something is true or right is only to express subjective preference. James Nolan, Jr. addressed the point this way:

> To fail to express is to be in denial or to be dishonest. In this sense, the very notion of honesty is redefined, because the basis for honesty becomes one's willingness to be in touch with and express one's feelings. It is not honesty in the sense of truthfulness to an objectively measured empirical reality or to an external worldview that enjoins the individual to hold certain things as true and adjust his or her behavior accordingly; nor is it the honesty of intellectual deference to reason or even, in some instances, to conventional protocols. It is honesty defined by the open

communication of one's feelings.[7]

So honesty is defined simply as that which is sincerely felt, not what is objectively true. If you speak what is objectively true to psychological man, but without the conviction of feeling, psychological man is dismissive. What this looks like from the worldview of moral realism, however, is straightforward immoral dishonesty. And that from a position of utter self-absorption, inflated ego, a sense of entitlement, and ingratitude. A bafflingly impenetrable narcissism.

Despite all this, it cannot be said that the therapeutic mentality is devoid of moral direction. Human beings are steeped in considerations of morality, all day every day, though this fact may be clouded by language. "Morality," the word, is not popular, now, because it has baggage. It is associated with an unwavering and just God, frowning down upon us. But the concept is certainly in play. In fact, given the ebb and flow in what is considered right and wrong, it is more important than ever, in the popular imagination. Precisely because it is thought changing and temporal, rather than unchanging and eternal, considerations of right and wrong command a great deal of attention in contemporary society. They are invoked, in fact, to control others; to hector and coerce and bully them into compliance with therapeutic imperatives, to eliminate the heterodox threat to postmodern therapeutic orthodoxy.

What are the highest standards of right and wrong in society now? Not honesty, selflessness, humility, service, or gratitude, the opposites of psychological man's character traits. Those would be moral aspirations of an individual aspiring, alone within the conscience, to objective virtue. Those are not aspirations of psychological man. The therapeutic mentality means emotional well-being is the highest goal, and what serves that goal is acceptance socially, above all else. All must be brought into mutual social acceptance. This is a ground-clearing exercise for the advent of totalitarian ide-

---

7 *The Therapeutic State*, (New York: New York University Press, 1998), p. 6.

ology, because it means fluid social mores replace unchanging universal values. Authority shifts from sacred order to the zeitgeist. This portends a re-shaping of political constitutions that were developed over millennia to minimize abuses of power. The subjective sense of comfortable fellow-feeling is purchased at the cost of freedom.

14
THE TRAJECTORY

The advance of the therapeutic worldview has had a profound effect on societies formerly defined as liberal Western democracies. In this section we examine the effect of the shift from morality to psychology on tendencies to socialism in those societies.

Iron Cage

In the postmodern era there has been increasing concern with the drift to automation of human beings, and the societies in which they live. We have seen how this is exacerbated by the rise of the therapeutic. We placed the beginning of the postmodern era at the turn of the twentieth century, more or less, and that coincides not only with Freud's emerging influence, but with an early expression of this concern for automation, Max Weber's "iron cage," to which he referred in his *The Protestant Ethic and the Spirit of Capitalism.*[1] Weber's purpose was to describe the "spirit" of capitalism and trace its origins in Protestant theology. He considered the spirit of capitalism to be the ethic of seeking economic gain for its own sake, and he argued for its origins in Reformation theology.

---

1 1905, first published in English, 1930.

Weber famously described capitalism's systematizing effect on people and their societies, comparing the result of this tendency to an "iron cage." The imperative of economic efficiency to maximize financial gain meant hierarchical public and private organizations with increasing specialization; a bureaucratization that, combined with stability of markets and traditional social norms, had a stabilizing but automating effect on individuals and society.

As compared with pre-capitalist (and pre-Reformation) societies, people live out their lives inside relatively confined social and economic structures; the "iron cage" to which Weber referred. Individuals, too, developed a hard shell of rigidity in interactions with others and their society, as better suggested by the German phrase *stahlhartes Gehäuse* translated to "iron cage." This added to the ever-confining course of capitalist social development, fueled also by the hyper-rational focus and attention of the post-Enlightenment era, the left-brain grasping and controlling part of our natures, we might now say, using Iain McGilchrist's terms.[2] This tendency was abetted in the twentieth century with the vogue of psychometrics; an attempt to reduce personality to a combination of traits, serving to further instrumentalize human beings.[3] It manifests now also in recreational self-tests of personality like the Enneagram and the Myers & Briggs personality tests, gateway drugs to occultic identity-formation.

We can understand the effect of the iron cage if we take notice of the extent to which our lives are governed algorithmically. "Algorithm," the word, is associated with computers. It is the series of actions governed by gates: If a then c, but if b, then d. They are more complicated in quantum computing and advanced computing confusingly called "artificial intelligence," but the same principle applies. Algorithm just means a logic sequence, it is not limited to

2 Iain McGilchrist, "The Matter with Things," *Perspectiva*, 2021, and *The Master and His Emissary*, 2009.
3 Yates, Christopher, "The Cult of Personality," *The Hedgehog Review*, Spring, 2024.

computers. When you're told to cook the hamburger for 42 seconds and then scoop it up and put it on bread, you're following an algorithm. We can't help but notice, if we're paying attention, that human actions are increasingly encompassed by algorithms, in the same way our machines always have been.

There is a building aspect to this. The following of algorithms is itself algorithmic. We now reflexively reduce tasks to algorithm, and thus ourselves to algorithm.[4] The practice of laying down algorithms for ourselves or others leads to further algorithms, all in the name of iron cage efficiency:

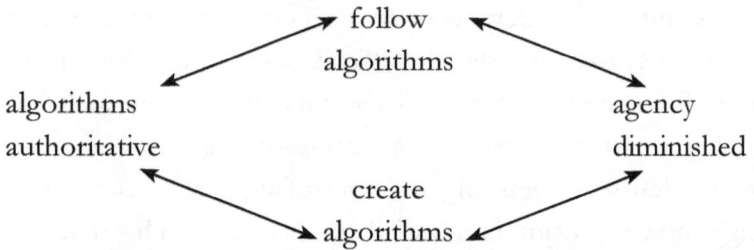

We can readily envision this as a wheel that can turn in either direction, and it doesn't stop there. There are wheels within wheels; a succession of these cycles reverberating out through society in every direction, all the time. The result is a feeling that the course of so much of our lives is already laid out for us in fairly restrictive terms, with the aesthetic, creative, and meaning-seeking aspects of our being pushed aside to inconsequential margins. The austere rationality and stratification on the basis of expertise, and the overweening bureaucratic structure, create a machine-like feel to our existence.

This is the opposite of freedom. It is a kind of slavery without masters. Some would blame our iron cage on capitalism, as a machine exciting a pitiless exploitation of the relatively powerless, who

---

4 See Christian, Brian and Tom Griffiths, *Algorithms to Live By/The Computer Science of Human Decisions*, (New York: Henry Holt and Company, 2016).

become a form of capital themselves, slaves not of a particular master, but of the system capitalism creates, and so capitalism is itself
the grand machine in which lesser machines operate. An anti-capitalist pitch on moral terms might be that individual morality is swal-
lowed up in the machine, because the machine enables off-loading
of personal responsibility, and as a result, the machine of capitalism
deprives us of our humanity. People with this view we might regard
as being on the left, who would tweak capitalism in a socialist direction, or else dismantle it at its foundation. The imperative to scaling
or systematizing or automating of commercial processes reinforces
and revitalizes the iron cage.

But the Marxist alternative lacks a plausible replacement which
would reduce unfreedom. In fact, there are no clearly articulated
socialist alternatives, only an insistent march toward ever-more-thor-
oughgoing collectivism, which is a machine by purposive design
more obviously than capitalism is said to have by default. Capital
itself is inert, having no motivation of its own, but human beings
are motivated in various ways, some good and some bad, to deploy
capital in ways that result in machine unfreedom. So some would
blame our iron cage on human misuses of capital, exploiting it for
further personal gain without sufficient regard for higher moral values. This means the problem arises not in "capitalism," but in the
moral decisions of individuals, including individuals in position to
drive the ethos of commercial and other institutions. These are people who we might say are on the right, who would keep the freedom
of capitalism but would also recognize the need for mitigation of its
machine effects by reinvigorating timeless virtues and ongoing reconsideration of what humanity is about other than rationalistic Enlightenment grabbiness.

Thus, the iron cage effect is enhanced both by the (left's) secular democratic socialism in prosperous Western countries, and by
the (right's) limited-government vision unaccompanied by the external authority of sacred order. Because the therapeutic worldview

shifts us from a moral to a psychological vision of humanity, it exacerbates the creeping automation of the iron cage either way. Our problem is not properly understood in left/right terms or even socialist/capitalist terms. It's properly understood in terms of sacred/secular; love/power; sin/syndrome; subjective/objective; vertical/horizontal; psychological/moral. Instead of a linear spectrum with two endpoints, one could devise a multi-dimensional architecture with many points.[5] One point would be the position that capitalism is a "system" and is fatally corrupt because it self-propagates systematically, so it must be burnt to the ground. This is presumably the position of the Antifa's of the world, and our newly-minted pro-terrorist antisemites. Another point would be that capitalism is not a "system" at all, but the absence of a system, merely the name we give to the totality of innumerable individual decisions. Another point would be held by those who unthinkingly push for ever-greater technological capture, heedless of the consequences so long as they are personally remunerated by it; who see no concern with techno-oligopoly and the global village instrumentalizing the non-elite, because this would feel like a more "open" society. All of these points are spin-offs of what we already have, however, and all of them are materialist, proceeding on a presumption of amorality. We'll all be better off if we follow their prescriptions, the materialist elites declare, and that's the end of that.

There are other categories, but probably not properly called "political" categories, in this age in which the public overruns its banks onto the adjacent private and we all stand in the swirling muddy waters of Narrative formed in culture, religion, "democracy," government, privileged and politically activist NGO's, taxation-as-social-control, and the over-arching and interconnected machine of which these are all a part. These, combined, comprise the bureaucratic state in Weber's "iron cage" vision. The sum of the

---

5 N.S. Lyons did this, partially tongue-in-cheek, in "A Better Model of Political Categories," *The Upheaval* (Substack), February 28, 2024.

differing kind-of-right, kind-of-left viewpoints all end up more alike than different: continuing growth of the public/private bureaucratic state, indifferent to human automation and the dispiriting loss of meaning to life.

The automation does not expand into new, untrammeled territory. It expands into formerly private territory. As the bureaucratic state expands, the private non-automated self contracts. The inner self is ever more precious but also ever more precariously situated, so that it must be protected in its emotional purity. If we understand that good and evil run through every heart, the battle is brought to the evil within. But if my Identity is good and under threat from the evil of the external world, I must take the battle to the world. This means ever-growing ideological antagonism added to all the ever-growing petty trespasses of industrial automation and the pent-up feeling imposed by iron cage bureaucracy. It's no wonder we increasingly feel helplessly bound by the Machine.

Conformity

Concern about growth of the Machine did not end with Weber. In the course of the twentieth century it was not expressed entirely as overt anti-capitalism, but rather as anti-conformism. A movie, *The Man in the Gray Flannel Suit* typified the many artistic expressions of post-war concern over conformist pressures of the prosperous new world. Explicitly anti-capitalist neo-Marxists prescribed socialist cures to the anti-humanist aspects of iron cage automation, but with some restraint in light of the excesses of Stalinism and the Cold War Soviet Union.

And so reaction took a more nuanced and psychological form. Neo-Freudian liberationists like Herbert Marcuse and other architects of the sexual revolution were seeking liberation from the depersonalizing bureaucratic state that they vaguely put down to "capitalism." Marcuse decried "one-dimensional man" as self-satisfied machine part, fed scraps of entertainment and prosperity but denied his soul, an example of the Marxist version of alienation accelerated through increasing automation.[6] His premise was that one-dimensional man was no longer oppressed in the old-school Marxist sense. Instead he was thoroughly co-opted into the machine which deprived him of the ability to think critically. Satiety dulled the sharp edge of critical thinking, as we became repressed by the urgency of manufactured needs, controlled by a desire-producing machine so that we identified with our consumer choices rather than some more authentic formation of self. In this way, Marcuse suggested, we become subject to ideological capture.

Marcuse correctly observed a growing machine capable of ideological capture, but drew disastrous conclusions about how to address it. He observed early symptoms of ideological capture but misdiagnosed its cause as uncontrolled capitalism rather than rejection of God. There was indeed a growing form of ideological capture, within capitalism, but it was enabled by the very materialistic conception of mankind that Marcuse and most intellectuals of the century championed.

Marcuse attributed social conformity within prosperous capitalism to "introjection," re-formation of the inner man from the outside to complete his ideological capture by the Machine:

> [I]ntrojection implies the existence of an inner dimension
> distinguished from and even antagonistic to the external
> exigencies—and individual consciousness and an individ-
> ual unconscious apart from public opinion and behavior."[7]

Reinvigorating this "inner dimension" was to be our salvation, the source of resistance to the Machine of automated conformity. Marcuse was a chief architect of the rise of Freud-infused neo-Marx-

---

6 Especially as set forth in *One-Dimensional Man*, 2nd ed., (Boston: Beacon Press, 1992), originally published 1964.

7 Ibid., p. 10.

ism, beginning after the Second World War and accelerating through the beat years, a high point being publication of his *Eros and Civilization*[8] in 1955. The ensuing Dionysian frenzy of the sixties and seventies was an attempted working-out of his solution (and that of other Freudian evangelists of Marxist "critique") to the problem of one-dimensional conformity. The whole project rested on a hubris like that of the Enlightenment lumiéres,[9] alone prophetically able to perceive the comfortable servitude of their fellows, this time in the self-perpetuating machine of capitalism.

Ideological capture was caused, not cured, by Freudian neo-Marxist prescriptions. It took some time to vanquish religion's continued hold on the culture. A stew of angry cultural Marxist and Freudian materialism produced or facilitated the rise of the therapeutic culture. It's not that the therapeutic culture itself is the capturing ideology. It's that the therapeutic mentality disarms the individual from resisting. The resistance advocated by Marcuse to "introjection" to break the mold of one-dimensional man involved reinvigoration of the "inner dimension," which hastened the formation of therapeutic man, no longer a critically thinking potential combatant, but rather a passive receptor of neo-Marxist ideology.

The search for meaning within was thus in large part a reaction to unease with the state of automated man. Neo-Marxist cultural criticism was until its recent ascendancy more a posture of dissent than a competing program unto itself. It was largely a buzz of psychological dissonance borne within, stirring the interior of the heavily "buffered self"[10] in reaction to the dehumanizing exterior. It di-

8 Boston: Beacon Press, 1955.

9 "Lights," late eighteenth-century religious skeptics who saw themselves as lighting the way out of religious superstition and obscurantism. Some of the New Atheists of the early 'oughts of this century adopted a version of the self-designation, "Brights," in the course of their failed attempt to finally put down religion altogether.

10 Charles Taylor's phrase, from *A Secular Age*, to describe a sealing off of the self from the religious enchantment of spirits or cosmic forces with which we formerly felt we interacted in "porous selves;" also the buffer between self and other resulting from the atomizing effect of religious disenchantment.

minishes the "porous self"[11] of the enchanted world, prompting a turn inward to locate the missing sense of deep meaning. We now attempt to find it in the mysteries of the subconscious Freud bequeathed us, rather than the charism that religion did. Psychology substitutes for religion, one-to-one.

The Machine

Alana Newhouse:

> A new and decadent power center has been built, made up of the federal government and a constellation of corporations and nonprofits that operate as connected wings of the same sprawling complex. The people who control the key platforms and networks are aggregating power to themselves at the expense of everyone else. These people and the institutions they dominate are not interested in social justice, or any other kind of justice, except to the extent that they can be used as shields. They festoon their corporate headquarters with slogans about women's rights, Black rights, and trans rights while hoovering up millions of jobs and billions of dollars that once belonged to small- and medium-sized American businesses and shipping it all to China. Through their networks of foundations and NGOs, they have emptied out America's free press and turned most of it into a quasi-governmental political propaganda apparatus that is remarkably empty of meaningful information about how power works in America and why the quality of so many people's lives keeps getting worse.

> Different people have different words for this new monolithic reality, but everyone who isn't either naïve or craven knows that it exists. I envision it as a pyramid—one that contains the sum total of every slogan and brand name and source of prestige, acting and speaking in unison. To

---

11 Again, Charles Taylor's formulation, to describe the outlook of pre-modern man, whose stance of looking out on the enchanted world was not that of an isolated "buffered" observer, but of one integrated with it.

live in its shadow, to take one's moral or political or social cues from the pyramid's overseers, is not simply an act of idol worship; it's a form of servitude.[12]

Among the different words used by other writers for this new monolithic reality, besides "the Pyramid:" the Machine, the Technium, the Cathedral, the Swarm, the Iron Cage. "The Monolith" would serve. As would Babylon, or Babel.[13] These are ways to describe the force behind the cloying sense that we're being herded into a Brave New World of ideological conformity, like cattle into the slaughterhouse chute.

Perhaps there has always been concern over the possible rise of a Machine overlordship. At the heart of (classical) liberalism is caution against its rise, but our emotivist inward turn puts us to sleep at the ramparts. The liberal West overcame Machine creations in World War II, thank God, at the expense of much blood. But the Machine is a hydra-headed monster, it resurfaces in new form. Normally the Machine creeps up subtly and furtively and incrementally, unseen because we don't want to see, but at times it thrashes its dragon-tail in unavoidably visible ways. This happened in the pandemic, when the climate of false emergency made the Machine's stirring visible.

One positive result has been a renewed watchfulness among those with eyes to see.[14] Aside from general unease over our seemingly limitless desire for psychological quiescence, there has been a reexamination of the potential for totalitarian abuse and dehumanization at the hands of the Machine.[15] We can see it developing. It's in material we can open and read, about Davos and the World Economic Forum and other multicultural globalist theory and manipu-

12 "The Jews Who Didn't Leave Egypt," *Tablet Magazine,* April 14, 2022.
13 Genesis, chapter 11.
14 The Brownstone Institute, brownstone.org, is a useful resource in this regard. Likewise Naomi Wolf, *Facing the Beast,* (Vermont: Chelsea Green, 2023).
15 An excellent reading list was compiled in early 2024 by Ruth Gaskovski and Peco, at their Substack, *School of the Unconformed*, "Unmachined Words: A Reading List to Keep You Human," February 29, 2024.

lative Covid lying and the effects of the new gods Narrative, Automation, Materialism, and the meretricious "diversity, equity, and inclusion" movement, consolidating elements of the collectivist Machine that absorbs our God-given agency. In the years of covid and resurgent neo-Marxism we saw open contempt among our lordly overseers exasperated that we question Narrative. We're supposed to just revel in our supposed joyous "freedom," not question it. And all the while the word "fascism" was worn out with overuse, and with no sense of irony. The totalitarian tendency of the Machine collective gained significant ground. A significant movement toward *real* fascism, just as Mussolini meant by the word.

With a proper perspective on time, we can come to understand how quickly things can change, motivating us to look more closely at what's really going on. We can avoid being gulled into thinking all's well if there's no war on. World War II didn't just happen one day. It was part of a longer story: the world-wide effect of dismissing the Author of Love and substituting Power, the man-made god, in His place. We're still living inside this story.

Something new and even more ominous than old-school fascism is upon us. What is being installed is a form of socialism that blinds us to creeping totalitarianism—not the clunky classical Marxist communism, but something more sinister. It's not felt as oppressive because we're softened by the culture's therapeutic shift. Emotivism prevails over objectivity, enabling Leviathan to establish evolving and relativist values through a narrative of care. The new form of communism is presented as a return to the womb in infantile "oceanic feeling:" the State as Mother, feminized and globalized, but otherwise well-mapped onto Mussolini's fascist vision.

The danger is overlooked, by psychological man, because this vision so much accords with his interior emotional state. The sexual revolution, nicely nested in the premises of psychological self-care, has overtaken sexual mores dating to the dawn of mankind. Sexual disenchantment has been the result, producing a whole generation, now in adulthood, lacking in self-confidence, heir to a world that, in Matthew Arnold's words, "Hath really neither joy, nor love, nor light/Nor certitude, nor peace, nor help for pain."

The casualties lie all around us, manifesting in, among other things, Cluster B disorders on a massive scale,[16] "gender" confusion, sexual and general licentiousness, addiction, loneliness, emotional insecurity. This isn't confined to the margins of society. Too many people are genuinely suffering. What we call tolerance for you-do-you identities and lifestyles is just dressed up indifference, what you'd expect when love is leached out of the world and replaced with that "rough beast"[17] Power.

The Managerial State

In his 1951 *The Forest Passage*, Ernst Jünger presciently set out his concern with the gathering cloud of identity-conforming Machine technocracy, the tendency to what he called "automatism."[18] James Burnham warned of the consequences of the rise of a managerial class in his 1941 *The Managerial Revolution*.[19] Dwight Eisenhower famously cited consequences of the "military/industrial complex" in a speech in 1961. N.S. Lyons recently wrote that democracy "has long since been redefined to mean the uninterrupted rule of the managerial elite and the undiluted supremacy of their ideological values."[20]

Automatism means we internalize the effects of systematizing technology and this changes our subjectively-felt relationship to the

---

16 Rufo, Christopher, "The Cluster B Society," *City Journal*, September 24, 2023.

17 From "The Second Coming," poem by William Butler Yeats, 1920.

18 Telos Press, 2013 (first published 1951).

19 Lume Books, 2021 (first published 1941).

20 "Poland and the Demon in Democracy," *The Upheaval* (Substack), January 29, 2024. Even more recently, see also Lyons' articles of October 16 and 23, 2024 at his substack *The Upheaval*, and Nathan Pinkoski's November, 2024, *First Things* article, "Actually Existing Postliberalism."

increasingly powerful collective, society understood as a social "system." This makes us ever more vulnerable to instrumental usage by the collective. We are trained to think and act like machines in order to be used as such. Technology makes us more open to machine-like manipulation, willing cogs in the operation of the managerial state.

The phrase "managerial elitism" captures the idea of centralized and collectivized management, ever more presumptively a function of elite "experts" in this field or that, running the world "scientifically." The concern is with power concentration in the increasingly amorphous, borderless collective. The movement is toward globalization of technically all-powerful and manipulative power centers including the state, but also ostensibly private state allies and the unaccountable administrative state, all taking us to an ideology of hyper-rationalized and hyper-organized automation. The instrumentalist attitude toward self and others is abetted by disintegration of support institutions like family and church. Instead of political leadership of otherwise free individuals, we have the hive collective, and the chief function of the collective is to coerce ideology. The question now is how to hold on to one's individual humanity as against this tide, to retain our "primal relationship to freedom," in Jünger's words.

The expertise of elites in and out of government is management to unthinking automatism, the inexhaustible mechanization in all things, including human beings. Elite managerialism is both cause and effect of automatism. Automatism is the unquestioned driver of the relentless "progressive" unreality of postmodernism. In this socialist postmodern democratic age, the personal is political, and so everything is presumed within the remit of the collective, and so the range of "issues" deemed appropriate for collectivist treatment is infinite. Very little is left to the purely private.

Political parties together advance the interests of the Machine, the "scientific," centralized, top-down management of all of life, saving only those inconsequential details left to individuals, tokens left to aid us in our self-delusion of individuality and autonomy. You can identify with brand x instead of y because you're unique. But you can't prefer your homeland or your people because that would be bigotry. You can deviate somewhat from political talking points of platforms on offer, because you're unique. But you can't advocate for the ability to opt out of the Machine altogether. You can quibble over lesser points of Machine ideology, because you're unique. But you can't throw over the Machine altogether, because that means hiding alone, naked, and hungry in the wilderness. We have choices about little things but not big things.

The American promise has been inverted. We have what the state gives us, rather than the state having what we give it.

Management elites support what amounts to a uniparty within ostensibly democratic societies because it secures their elite status. This isn't just craven careerism, however. Elite expertise means sound management. Sound management means elite expertise. They're trying to improve society, who could argue with that? Automatism is not expressed in creeds, it is expressed as a sum of positive attributes like efficiency, improvement, expertise, and prosperity, but without counting the human cost, nor the constricted philosophical premises.

The managerial elites take precepts of automatism as a given; as being self-evidently right. They don't have to be persuaded to it as a totalizing system like classical Marxism or religion. It is an über-ideology, one that inhabits and empowers political movements but is not recognized as a movement unto itself. It can equally empower democratic socialism or Bolshevik totalitarianism or fascism, because these, like the Machine, are about Control. It is an enemy, however, of freedom. Automatism and the Machine it produces preclude consideration of that most important of all political questions, now and in all times and all places: *Who decides?*

The benefits of automatism personally to management elites is not recognized as a motivating factor in embracing it. They don't just produce automation, they are products of it. The underlying assumptions have been drivers their whole life, wherein you "succeed," whatever that means, incrementally and through striving, competition, and "getting ahead," not to put others down but to personally excel and thereby benefit the world with your striving. Who could argue with that? So automation self-reinforces. Management elites are unconcerned with its erosion of individual agency, because it's felt less by the automatizers, and more by the non-elites caught in its machinery.

We must understand that everything important to us and about us is not given to us by Machine elites. They take it from us. They formulate an entire web of collectivist interactions which "serve" us but also ensnare us, a spider's web we don't recognize until it's too late. They take from us and collectivize safety, security, prosperity, and "freedom" of the limited brand-choosing sort. But these originate with us. The collective through its elite engineers takes it from us and returns it in denatured form. In this way we come to believe the collective is the source of our potency. Without it we are defenseless, we feel.

But it's all backwards. Take the inviolability of the home, which the collective promises to provide. Jünger, in *The Forest Passage*:

> In reality, it is grounded in the family father, who, sons at his side, fills the doorway with an axe in his hand.[21]

That is the source of all power, ultimately, if not blanched from our bones in the collective's iron cage management of us. That fortitude, that resilience, that immovability is what is taken from us. It is dissolved by the therapeutic collective at great resource-draining cost and returned, if at all, in time of need in diluted form, exercised in an impersonal way that yet keeps the collective's interests foremost. Try filling the doorway with your sons instead of calling

---

21 p. 73.

the state to protect you. See where that gets you.

These are matters of moral courage, and courage is the guarantor of all other virtues. Where is the church in all this? It is distracted and literally de-moralized, chasing after rhinestone baubles dangled by the culture, on little strands of feel-good sentiment that seem to vaguely resemble something the church said, long ago, when revelation was fresh. We worship our safe little baby in the manger and forget God the Father filling the doorway, axe in hand. The church is handmaiden to the state, and the state is prostrate to the elite ideology shared out and enforced among the power centers of Big: big tech, big media, big academia, big NGO's, all in ideological lockstep.

Relinquished Agency

The Machine is formed by and exists to further ideology. "Ideology" means a set of ideals that include mechanisms for suppression of dissent. Ideology is antihuman, because it is commitment to the bloodless abstraction of amoral materialism over the reality of lived human experience. Though it conflicts with reality, it has the capacity to override reality in our minds, changing it to conform—for a dismal season—to its substituted abstractions. This institutes totalitarianism, the purposed ends of Machine manipulation of human beings.[22]

Ideologies develop from oversimplified principles expanded to all-encompassing vision. They're presented as benefiting humanity, able to solve its more intractable problems, so suppression of dissent seems justified. Dissent would include resistance on the grounds that the ideological premises are not as simple nor as consonant with natural reality as its evangelists insist. The ideological program is presented with revolutionary zeal, so interruption of the unanim-

---

22 These are among the themes of Hannah Arendt's *The Origins of Totalitarianism*, 1951.

ity of that zeal means not mere disagreement, but hate rightly suppressed and its fomenters scapegoated.

Ideological totalitarian movements feed on individual agency. That is, agentic initiatives of individuals in the exercise of their own responses to moral authority are re-directed to the Machine, and the Machine exercises that ceded agency collectively to advance the ideology's imperatives. This is why the rise of the therapeutic is both cause and effect of the Machine's totalitarian tendency.

We have noted already that psychological man retreats from the exercise of his own moral agency in that he is motivated by, and sees reality through the lens of, his interior psychological well-being. This is the opposite of exercising one's agency to strive for moral virtue. It is reactive and passive. The emotions are allowed to drive thought and conduct, and the emotions are uniquely susceptible to simplistic distortions of reality toward hoped-for utopian ideals. This translates to all-in deference to the Machine's distortions of reality to achieve social harmony on a grand scale, to put to rest at last the petty conflicts that bedevil mankind.

The therapeutic is therefore a cause of Machine totalitarianism. But it is an effect, too. The therapeutic industrial complex is a machine within the Machine, a systematization and institutionalization of therapeutic imperatives across society. Dissent is unacceptable. To reject the ethos of self-care is to reject the ethos of other-care as well, according to the ideology, so you're a hater if you disagree. Embrace of objectivity and universality of virtues and of meritocracy is "privilege," a haughty rejection of earthy "lived experience" and of the immanent frame of postmodern new paganism. Just as society produces "truth" in Narrative through dialectic, so we're to individually produce Narrative-conforming Identity through the inner dialectic of Becoming. And that inner process wells up within, emerging as Identity to be worshipped. It is not something we create in humble imitation of our Creator.

This is what is meant by "ideology:" the reduction of the complexities of human experience to a manageable system. It is about acquiring control; about listening to the serpent in the Garden to make ourselves gods. Through ideology we give in to our desire for instrumentalizing usage of the world and others in it. Our desire is for a comprehensive system that we control in our illusion of sovereignty over all things. Automation follows, replacing God.

The opposite of Machine automation may seem like fearsome chaotic void. Even drab total-system political theories may seem preferable to the dark of the unknown; of mystery, chaos, confusion, and fear. People in thrall to Machine ideology become isolated, lonely, and full of trepidation for a future in which they no longer have a sense of control, having ceded their agency to the collective. They are pushed and pulled in different directions by would-be masters, causing them to opt for further incremental Machine automation. It will be understood as less than ideal, but then the ideal seems unattainable.

Managerial socialism seems an acceptable compromise, in this climate of fear. The inhuman Machine is a dictator, but it has benefits. We all have food, so long as we take it from the "hand" of the Machine. We all have business to attend to, meaningless in a large sense, perhaps, but then the Machine trains us not to think in a large sense. Rather, our busy-ness is a focus on trifles and on this makework, this commute, this corporate passivity, this personal estrangement, this tasteless food, this infantile TV program. We wake up daily to do it all over again, and though from a high angle it is indistinguishable from the activity of a gerbil on a treadmill, it engages in the moment. In this way our life-blood drips out of us a bit at a time, until we are too old and feeble to second-guess how it was spent. This is the gray life the Machine delivers us. Everything is wonderful all the time.

Isn't it?

Democracy

Can this happen in a democracy, though? There is almost ritualistic invocation of "democracy" as if by totemically saying the word we avoid the march to totalitarianism. Into the bargain, we can continuously congratulate ourselves on how enlightened we are; how safe from the Hitlers and Stalins of the world because democracy protects us from their depredations. Democracy is sacred. It is hallowed. Democracy is the god that protects us from ideological tyranny.

Alas, it is not so. We should ask ourselves: really, what is democracy, as applied and not merely in theory? And what is it to others? Because it turns out there are different views, and a very prevalent view makes "democracy" not just a set of political procedures the *hoi polloi* get to participate in, but a set of social norms that take us inevitably to totalitarianism. Democracy and totalitarianism are not mutually exclusive. Totalitarianism is the installation of an ideology that absorbs the agency of the individual. The therapeutic mentality enables this willing dissipation of individual freedom. "Democracy" can be the engine of the collective's absorption of individual freedom, rather than a preventative.

There's this word "freedom," that we associate with "democracy." The word "freedom"—just like the word "democracy"—is meaningless, by itself. In a "democracy" you have a vote for one among a slate of candidates for a given office. That is the extent of your "freedom:" choosing Tweedledee over Tweedledum to lord it over you with all the power of the unelected administrative state at his back, allied with similarly unaccountable and ostensibly private powerful organized ideological interests. We tend to think of democracy as representative government, and it's nominally that. But it doesn't insulate you from corrosive ideology. Differences in ideology are not meaningfully in play, as among the candidates. They represent slight tweaks this way or that, to particular issues, but they

The Trajectory ∾ 267

do not step outside the narrow parameters of the postmodern zeit-geist, including its therapeutic, psychological aspect.

The vote seems to be a personal choice of one set of princi-ples over another, but it also constitutes approbation of the entire ideological system of the managerial state. It thus signals approval of corrupted democracy, the ever-expanding totalitarian Machine of managerial elitism that has wormed its way into our political struc-ture and deposed the quaint notion of authority vested in "we the people." The candidate's "policy" stance is a weak statement of sen-timent as against the monolith of which he is a part. Increasingly, we vote for vibe, and fail to see the monster ideology unchangeable by individual candidates. This is not true consent of the governed, but manipulated appearance of consent. It is a vote in favor of the illu-sion of freedom rather than an exercise of genuine freedom.

Voting in such a system devolves to kabuki for lending legiti-macy to the Machine. Elections are between the party platforms or, worse, individual personalities. Because they are not between free-dom-lovers and the managerial elite, they are merely emotion-laden dust-ups within the parameters of the Machine, diverting our atten-tion away from the movements of the uniparty Machine in its total-ity.

The democratic collective absorbs individual agency in a range of human activity that is expanded obscenely beyond any reason-able boundary. But on top of that, elected components of the Ma-chine cede away much of the responsibility reposed in them to pow-er centers unaccountable to the vote: the administrative state, incestuous public/private partnerships, NGO's, foundations, inter-national agencies, and even other countries. How is that "democrat-ic?" The managerial elite infests all of these, not just those we pull the lever for. We don't get a vote on the movements of the admin-istrative state nor the state's ideologically aligned, partnered power centers. If democracy means we the people have a say in govern-ment, then all of the collective's ceding away of the agency we repose in it is, definitionally, anti-democratic.

We're trained to believe democracy gives us freedom to control our destiny, but only a massive pruning of the reach of the collective would do that. The modern democratic process by which the Machine keeps us docile will not. The managerial elite employs the forms of democracy to legitimize its ideological progression. We're not asked to approve the Machine or its ideology, just the "democracy" the Machine has corrupted to enable it. The vote cannot register dissent against Machine technocratic control because its ideology is bigger than any combination of elected officials we might vote in. Freedom-lovers bail water from the Titanic with a teaspoon.

Democracy requires competing candidates or parties, but the parties participate in a process and an ideology that perpetuates automatism and elite control. The resulting uniparty in effect exploits disagreement over inconsequential things to camouflage growth of the "scientific" management of people as if they were cattle. Fomenting hate aids the project of control because by vilifying other groups (like the other half of the uniparty, or groups out of favor such as Christians or straight white men) the vilifiers invoke the ideology of the Machine, further signifying commitment to the managerial state's ideological control.

Imagine you're one of the candidates for a particular office. How do you get elected? Certainly not by casting an entirely new vision for what government should and shouldn't do. You work within a carefully circumscribed range of possibilities, and it is necessary to pander and invoke the shibboleths of the day. You can't get all the votes, but you need to appeal to a large number. Strategically, that means reaching into the pool of swing voters to extricate as many as you can from your opponent. This means an inexorable pull to the ideological mainstream, which means you can't vote in or out a deconstruction of the Machine.

The administrative state and allied private power centers need be only minimally responsive to elected representatives; they are even more intractable than politicians to political change, except of course for their own incremental consolidation of power. This state of affairs means the zeitgeist Narrative[23] is more important by far than any combination of elected officials. The ideological mood of the entrenched administrative state controls "democracy."

Perhaps it should be that way? A democracy can in this way exclude extremes. But on the other hand, it means democracy preserves the ideological drift of society and reinforces it. So if society is on an ideological path that leads to totalitarianism, democracy does not effect a correction. To the contrary, democratic process reinforces the decline. It can properly reflect the will of the *demos*, but the will of the *demos* may be given over to ideological capture. In that event democracy merely superintends society's destruction.

To understand this, let's first re-visit what "ideology" means. It's conventionally defined as a collection of ideals systematized according to some underlying values. But it is also used pejoratively, to mean a set of ideals that contain within them the seeds for squelching dissent. So for a pertinent example, Western liberalism ostensibly prioritizes the free exchange of ideas, "free speech," to maximize intellectual freedom to enable sound voting decisions among the *demos*. But there has arisen a corruption of the free speech ideal, in the vast and undemocratic "misinformation" and "disinformation" complex which imposes control on ideas. This comes about through subtle measures—deliberately made subtle so the ordinary voter who remembers the principle of free speech doesn't notice its theft. Here are a few ways this happens.

One, by ignoring dissenting views as inconsequentially peripheral, so that ideas presented by the dominant ideology are simply presumed correct, and so given exclusive airing in public discourse. Ryszard Legutko describes the phenomenon this way (his reference

---

23 And note we seldom pause to consider that "pushing the Narrative," or "shifting the Overton window" is simply lying with selective facts, because cosmic Truth, we believe, no longer exists.

to "liberal" having the American meaning opposing "conservative;" he actually means *illiberal* in the classical sense):

> [L]iberals always assume a dominant position, claiming they know how to dismantle freedom in the optimal proportions and, therefore, deserve to be the ultimate and irrevocable referee. This is an outrageous claim. . . . The final aim of the liberal agenda is, therefore, not to have a free and open society but to have a society in which everything is subservient to liberal dogmas.[24]

Illiberal ideologues set themselves up as the accrediting tribunal before which we're to seek legitimacy, but it does not legitimize itself. This is the methodology of political progressives, but also that of entities we might have looked to for neutrality in a simpler day, like the mainstream press, which is now given over to dishonest ideological shaping of public opinion.

This is how Narrative is created. The purpose of Narrative is to shape complicated arrays of fact to choose selectively among them to create an ideologically-friendly story. Narrative is naively thought to serve the centering of ideology so that "extremist" positions can be identified as such. But Machine ideologues do not compose Narrative as a fair regression analysis of available facts. It is composed to advance the ideology. This is why there has been, in recent decades in the West, a significant shift in how news is disseminated. There are no longer reliable neutrals to whom non-elites can turn. Consequently free speech is now more important than ever, and this is why the Misinformation Industrial Complex is hard at work to shut it down.

"Democracy" has in this way come to mean a living ideological story to which we are all expected to subscribe, bracketed tightly against views peremptorily labelled "extreme" by elites who arrogate to themselves control over the direction "democracy" must

---

24 Legutko's interview with N.S. Lyons, *The Upheaval* (Substack), March 13, 2024.

take.[25] Narrative reinforces "democracy" as the dominant story-line within the boundaries of a fought-over Overton window. Freedom only means voting in government officials beholden to the elite-maintained Narrative, ever-farther removed from accountability.

Two (and remember, we're talking about free speech now subject to ideological capture), by direct government censorship, as with government programs or government-funded or government-partnered private programs, to control internet dissemination of some media sources and not others,[26] or the now well-publicized efforts of the United States government to squelch dissent concerning the efficacy or long-term effects of the covid vaccines, through pressure on privately-held social media companies. A Narrative is gaining traction that "something must be done" about "misinformation" and "disinformation," but this is inimical to the principle of free speech. The principle is that false speech can be overcome with true speech, but there should be no compulsion for or against either. The opposite of free speech is Machine gatekeepers arrogating to themselves authority to sift true from false. Again, as always the ultimate political question is *who decides?*

Three, by simply expanding government to the point that much of it falls within democratically-unaccountable "administrative" bodies that do not merely administer, but set innumerable substantive regulatory constructs on otherwise private initiatives, and, worse, work in "partnership" with private industries in a non-adversarial climate of advancing some ideals and not others to advance ideology. Or by participation in globalist initiatives which outsource broad-brush policy movements away from the governed *demos*. Re-

---

25 As with the suggestion of John Rawls that we bracket public discourse away from comprehensive doctrines and confine it to those elements we can "reasonably" agree upon for political purposes, which means exclusion of any metaphysical, or ultimate, conception of justice.

26 See for example an exposé at unherd.com of April 16, 2024: "Inside the 'Disinformation' Industry."

moval of government decision-making from the reach of the vote is undemocratic, obviously. It nullifies the benefits of free speech to accountable democracy.

The effect—and remember we're only looking at free speech by way of example—is to disable the accountability element that makes democracy democracy. Not only does the structure of representative government dictate a continuity of ideology, but ideology favored by elites is actively advanced by government with the vote so attenuated from its proceedings. Elite opinion favors a version of "democracy" that is by no means limited to representative government. The work of philosophers on the cutting edge of social consensus, like John Rawls and Richard Rorty, along with the horizontal workings of other postmodern process philosophies,[27] shape a conception of democracy as a way not of reconciling differing opinions, but of shaping opinions into a coerced "consensus" so they fall in line with the prevailing ideology. Here for example is Richard Rorty:

> There is no way in which the religious person can claim a right to believe as part of an overall right to privacy. For believing is inherently a public project: all us language-users are in it together. We all have a responsibility to each other not to believe anything which cannot be justified to the rest of us. To be rational is to submit one's beliefs—all one's beliefs—to the judgment of one's peers.[28]

So to be clear, we have crossed over a major division in how we conceive democracy. Formerly, traditionally, democracy meant majority rule with certain procedural protections to prevent tyranny against the minority. This was combined with a relatively smaller scope of government activity, in deference to individual and private initiative. It depended on a source of values that procedural democ-

---

27 See *The Mountain and the River*, chapter 22.

28 Rorty, Richard, *Pragmatism as Anti-Authoritarianism*, (Cambridge, MA: Belknap, Harvard University Press, 2021), p. 21.

racy could not itself provide. It was possible, in other words, because of Christianity, though perhaps another source of cohering sacred order might have sufficed politically.

Now, Christianity has faded into the corners and no external source of values takes its place. The scope of government has expanded so that no part of citizens' lives can be untouched by it. The underlying ethos is no longer tolerance of dissent, but elimination of it, to bring about shared vision at all costs; to coerce a contrived "consensus" concerning where we, collectively as a society, are headed. "Democracy," so-called, thus becomes an engine of totalitarian tyranny[29] indistinguishable, in any way that matters, from those called communism and fascism in simpler times. Western liberalism defeated those demons in the twentieth century, but they've returned, stronger and better disguised. They're now masked as liberalism itself.

With that background on a major postmodern challenge to Western liberalism, we can turn again to the therapeutic worldview, and what it means to our ongoing loss of political, as well as individual, agency. Psychological man is uniquely vulnerable to the totalitarian slide. People are basically good, for psychological man, and people collectively produce good environments for the individual. We're all well-meaning. The idea that there will be corruption no matter how many safeguards we build in is foreign to a person governed by the therapeutic. As previously emphasized, the rise of the therapeutic corresponds to the collapse of critical thinking. Everything seems fixable with more and more rules for how we do things, and there's no danger in outsourcing to unaccountable agencies. We're all in this together.

And besides, feelings are the driver, not principle. Insistence on political principle can be seen as made-up reasons to engage in conflict for the sake of conflict. Therapeutic man does not want to

---

29 See, e.g., Finley, Emily, *The Ideology of Democratism*, (Oxford University Press, 2022).

engage in a rough-and-tumble with political adversaries. What he wants is to have no political adversaries, because that serves his desire for psychological equanimity above all things. There is one important exception, however, and that is the inevitable political enmity with those hold-outs who insist on the constraints and structures of a morality-based logos; who would interfere with the unconstrained flow of relativist values and emergence of the inner discoverable self. Those people—those religious nuts—are enemies. They are literally existential threats, because for psychological man existence precedes essence, and "those people"—the Deplorables,[30] the Trash[31]—question the dogma of inner-formed essence. So, a political structure that excludes them but promotes unanimity among the "reasonable" must be supported.

Well, not just "supported." We're in an age of Western neo-Maoism, wherein the elite in and out of government control the progress of Marxist ideology by the divisive technique of culture-wide struggle sessions, wherein those engaged in wrongthink are vilified, and those on board are encouraged to join in the vilification. You're a good person or a bad one, there is no in-between. A bad person is one who dissents from the machine of the therapeutic industrial complex; who insists on a world outside our heads with which we engage through individual agency, forming a rationally negotiated sense of self. A good person is one who passively absorbs social dictates, just as he passively discovers his emerging inner Identity. The therapeutic blinds one to the inevitability of totalitarianism on this path.

In *Charisma*, Philip Rieff noted that in ancient Israel the creedal forms contained within themselves an openness to possibility, rather than the rigid left/right way we approach things now. The terror of God, the terror of open-ended possibility, results in denying Him and in joining the construction of man-made systems of

---

30 Hillary Clinton's succinct description of half the population of America.
31 Joe Biden's succinct description of half the population of America.

constraint and control to supplant religious interdicts.

> Released from the constraints of charismatic authority, Western culture can engage freely in its own destruction. . . . All hope dies of a democracy that is not a dictatorship of the empty by the phony.

Why? Because in a society imbued with the charisma,

> [t]he highest authority is subjective knowledge of God.

But:

> [t]he highest knowledge under the authority of the thera-peutic is the objective knowledge that there is no God.[32]

If there is no sacred order, there will in time be only fascist order, or no order at all.

---

32 *Charisma*, p. 39.

15
TOWARD HOPE

Are The Kids Ok?

A result of the tectonic cultural shift away from faith and toward psychology is that we tend to pathologize everything; indeed, this tendency is inevitable in the therapeutic age. Bad thinking can even drive real disease. Internal psychological turmoil kills hope, and that is a mental dis-ease that drives physical disease. Fear, agitation, alienation, distrust, and hopelessness combine in a self-reinforcing cycle of despair. They fuel a felt need for self-preservation. We shore up the defenses, build the walls higher, and over-react to minor trespasses.

Poet Christian Wiman writes:

> It requires no great prophetic power to recognize that we as a species, as a communal *soul*, have withered, and that as a direct consequence, the world around us is dying. The despair is too much to turn one's attention to, so most of us turn away.[1]

This is the state of psychological man. So many people, and especially young people, are not doing well at all. So many articles with titles like "The Kids Are Not OK."

---

1 "The Burning World," *American Scholar,* October 26, 2023.

There is a pervasive feeling of being trapped in a world not of our own making and over which we have no control. Absence of control means loss of agency. The psychological worldview makes one the passive receptor of socially-dictated attitudes and ideology. Suppose the ideology is an oversimplified vision of "equality," as a central driving political given. The problem is that we also observe actual inequality and may then conclude that a person's fortunes and misfortunes are not their own doing. People are puppets of their environments; their problems the fault of sociological movements. One's distress is then ascribed to physical or mental health issues, an explanation that relieves them of personal responsibility for it. It's not your fault you were violent. You were provoked. It's not your fault you lack energy, initiative, and drive. You're oppressed. It's not your fault you're uncomfortable with your body and the pressures of adult sexuality. You have gender dysphoria.

People are different in how they assess their own degree of agency. People with an internal locus of control tend to see themselves as more in charge of their own destiny. Those who conceive of a more external locus of control, on the other hand, have higher rates of anxiety and depression and are more likely to abuse drugs and neglect their health. "When you believe you have no control, you don't," writes Gurwinder Bhogal.[2]

But this idea of internal vs. external "locus of control" is more descriptive than explanatory. *Why* does a person's sense of locus of control shift from internal to external, in the age of the therapeutic? Why the erosion of individual agency? Why, suddenly, do so many feel they're only the sum of external influences on the timorous inner "identity?" Why the default to temporal flow, in conception of the self, rather than self as *a being*: more than a meat machine, and more than a time-bound pinball batted about by uncontrollable external forces?

The answer has to be in relationship. How do you perceive

2 "The Pathologization Pandemic," *The Prism* (Substack), July 6, 2023.

yourself in relation to that which is outside yourself? Is there any source of unchanging eternal value? Is anything in the universe fixed and perceivable as such? Or is all value formed and reformed in an oozing lava flow that never hardens? Is all in the universe chaotic and meaningless, so that your inner identity crouches continually in fear?

Perhaps belief in psychological vulnerability makes you psychologically vulnerable. Self as victim, a bundle of Freudian impulses, righteously lashes out at whatever throws those impulses into disharmony, provoking emotional responses that are instantly self-justified as the defense mechanism for the tender and precious "identity." The inner being, "identity," is vulnerable and victimized by what we would have called, in better times, the ordinary pressures of living in a society with other people. Because the world around us is a threat to the child-like innocence of the emergent inner being, our lives consist in self-care.

Contrast the alternative formerly prevalent. It was the idea that the self is a thing to be tamed, rather than nurtured. It was the idea that we are "prone to wander," as the old hymn has it, so we must look outside ourselves for guidance on how to be. That meant a look up to universal principles external to ourselves, to actively shape character, with discipline. The self is not ushered into the world only to hunker in a constant state of alarm. You're here to live out loud. And then die, of course, when it's your time, but that's within God's remit, not yours, and so not something for you to even worry about. The fact of death feeds the tragic sense, of course, but that tragic sense is the prodding you feel to seek God.

The inner self is unreliable. Instead of yielding discovery of right and wrong, it yields whatever self-preserves in the social environment. Right and wrong are then thought of as situational and relative. Society tells us what is true and right. But as social norms change and religious doctrine is ignored or tacitly amended, then the interdicts of the conscience may be disregarded and social norms substituted as authoritative. As with former social interdicts against sex outside of marriage, now modified socially and often overriding the conscience. It's not made right because everyone says it is. Instead of being guided by the conscience as the natural law receptor of objective principle, we accept collective adjudication of principle. If a person becomes habituated to entire reliance on social norms concerning what is right and wrong, this will effectively silence the "still small voice" of the conscience.

In deference to the psychological paradigm, society is telling us the gravest sin is to victimize another by interfering with their self-created and -developed inner being; their "Identity." We valorize victimhood because we believe identity is our true essence, always under threat. The threat to inner identity makes us a victim, and victim status is a prized possession. Repudiation of personal responsibility means repudiation of agency in favor of the collective, and victimhood is the necessary result. Victimhood is therefore the sign, symbol, and seal of the therapeutic worldview. It stands in for moral innocence. To the extent one is not a victim, he is morally responsible for his acts and omissions and thoughts. To the extent he is a victim, he is morally blameless.

Thinking that departs from objective reality is a fair beginning point for defining mental illness. This can and does happen across whole societies, it's not necessarily an individual one-off. We now witness the inescapable fact of social contagion of mental illness. We've seen the phenomenon of trans identification going off-the-charts in just a few years. Within living memory of any adult, there was no chart at all. The new identity paradigm and its attendant victim valorization is just such a social contagion. We should want people cured of delusion, not affirmed in it.

In thinking through the phenomenon of social contagion, consider the strange and rare mental condition called Munchausen's syndrome. It's a mental illness in which a person self-inflicts physical or mental injury or illness. This makes them a victim, and as a victim therefore worthy of our attention. In its most obvious manifestations, a person takes a poison or injures herself without disclosing the source of the injury, in order to draw attention to herself as victim (females are more likely so afflicted). Munchausen's is a mental illness, and is more readily understandable when the underlying self-inflicted or exaggerated illness is physical. But the underlying self-inflicted or exaggerated illness could be mental. It's not hard to imagine a person becoming convinced that, through no fault of his/her own, he's schizophrenic or bipolar or untreatably addicted or born in the wrong body or unalterably grossly overweight, all with the effect of putting himself or herself in the position of attention-deserving victim, relieved of personal responsibility. So why isn't victim pathology a form of Munchausen's? An indicator of mental illness?

We can continue to understand the victimology of psychological man through examples less obvious than feminism, trans ideology, and homosexuality. Race identification is a major source of rancor and division in our society. It's another instance of misguided identity formation. Some people preface their thoughts with "as a black woman," or "as a white man," a linguistic or mental tic that dictates whatever comes after. We fold such formulations into the scope of reality as we apprehend it, and in this way normalize identification by race, finding it to be a significant element of the inner-formed identity. And, importantly, assuming it to be an element of everyone else's inner-formed identity, too. In this way racial animosity is entrenched and becomes ineradicable. Tribalism by race ensues, rather than a withering-away of bogus racial classifications.

If a person's sense of self is derived from within, and not so much in relations to ideas and people outside the self, he's going to chafe at any kind of limitation on personal freedom. Limits to freedom sounds bad, but what are we really talking about? Don't we routinely place limits on self and others in ordinary affairs of life? Certainly we limit our children's freedom. In a loving environment we construct guardrails on their development, including punishment for misbehavior. We don't leave them in animal stasis. This is normal rearing of children: limitations on them that are building in love. Of course there's a benign power behind it, but it's the power of love.

This understanding is not limited to the rearing of children. We live with guardrails on our conduct all through life, in the exercise of mutual consideration for each other's interests and humanity. This is an outworking of the Golden Rule, whereby intersubjectivity causes us to see the world through others' eyes, so that we constrain our own conduct to avoid trespasses against them. There is no ultimate individual freedom, without a breakdown society-wide which would mean all-against-all, and ultimately less freedom individually because of it. The consequence of abandoning love in favor of power is less of both, and retreat to an inner safe zone where the vulnerable and afraid inner being crouches in fear.

This phenomenon of thinking in terms of psychology rather than faith creates an aura of antagonism, a buzz of angst making us all a bit more frayed and volatile. In fact, this identity problem, more so than tectonic political shifts, better explains the heightened feelings of isolation, loneliness, purposelessness, and anomie we all now experience. Those feelings feed further mental pathology. Mental illness accelerates, snowballing into social contagion. And, incidentally, hollowing us out to make us more vulnerable to political control. Perhaps that's the point.

The Re-Discovered Self

As was pointed out early on, what makes a way of thinking a "worldview" is its comprehensive way of encountering reality, and that comprehensiveness can obscure our ability to see beyond it, to understand another point of view altogether. The therapeutic worldview and the logos worldview are quite distinct paradigms. A person inside one will understandably have a hard time imagining the alternative. It's possible to do, however, with a little work. This book is an effort to overcome that limitation. It's important to try, if we have an interest in living in truth; in living well; and in compassionate understanding of our fellow human beings.

If the arguments here make rational sense and you agree, or you disagree but can calmly articulate the reasons for the disagreement, you're likely living in the full sunlight of the logos. But if your first reaction is inarticulable anger, you may be the psychological person being described.

There's a way of interacting with the world in which you rationally assess a situation or an argument or an emotion. This doesn't mean a robotic machine-like reaction. Obviously people have emotional responses, sometimes strongly felt, and they arise first before the gears of rationality can engage. But for those living in the sunlight of rationality the abiding first principle is that we should use our brains, in everything, rather than immediately unleash limbic reactions, rationally assessing only later. A key virtue is self-control. Emotions are the subject matter of that control. Emotions are not "right" or "wrong" as such. Self-control doesn't mean eliminating them, it means understanding them and properly channeling them. Uncontrolled emotion can do a lot of damage, to self and others. Our emotional responses may not align with virtue. Not all indignation is righteous.

Of course the foregoing is expressed in the language of logos, which, admittedly, is like saying "in the words of words," but words themselves supply rational telos. Everyone communicates in words, even psychological man. And the words of someone steeped in the therapeutic are not all babbling and incoherent. They may express ideas, however ill-formed or inchoate or scattered. But the ideas are a front for guarding emotional evaluation, and so cannot be trusted from a logos perspective. The words used by psychological man express convictions produced subjectively; not truth observed objectively. Consequently, they are expressions of desire translated to truth-language. This is an emotivist response.

If your reaction to these thoughts, or to anyone with whom you disagree, begins with a kind of intense inner frustration before the words in response come tumbling out, that is the dissonance of emotion being transmuted into language of rationality. The objections may come fast and furious from the therapeutic mentality, if accompanied by high intelligence. And they may even contain a kind of internal logic because psychological man, living in the twilight of the logos world, has acquired skill at decoding. But ultimately he uses words as an elaborate screen for expression of emotional desire, a way to siphon off the oppressiveness of having to live in the two worlds of warm feeling and cold logic. It can be exhausting trying to live inside one's own head but speak in the language of the world beyond one's head, the world of ultimate order and of an ultimate order Giver.

Brief mention was made of Charles Taylor's concept of "the buffered self," to describe our self-conception now in contrast to that of the person of faith living before the era of disenchantment.[3] The buffered self contrasts to "the porous self." There was a time when the self was "porous" because open to interaction with the order of the cosmos and the hierarchies evident in the world, and of the spirit world understood to be real and not hypothetical. The person with porous self lived entirely in the world beyond his head; the self was integrated, unselfconsciously formed in relationship with others and with nature, and with the Unseen of spirit.[4] The porous self did not reflexively assess each relationship on the basis of its otherness to self. He lived and moved and had his being in the world and cosmos and spirit out there.

Through a process of cultural evolution in modern times, however, the self became ever more "buffered" from the world out

3 *A Secular Age*, 2006.
4 Hebrews 11:1.

there by an inward turn to conscious self-awareness. Cartesian mind-body dualism contributed to this self-consciousness, as did new challenges of modernity that contributed to a me-they way of thinking. Philosophers influenced by the French Revolution and precursors of it like Rousseau redirected a Romantic focus on the "I" of self, with the unintended effect of emphasizing me/they difference. A broadened social awareness brought with it a habit of suspicion of social systems[5] that might be devised apart from the natural order of things. And most importantly, the Unseen world faded in the imagination, as religious skepticism increased.

Taylor also referred to this "buffered" self as the "bounded" self, in opposition to "porous," to signify a sense of being individually sealed off from the world outside. And that increasing sense of boundedness contributed to the interior turn for authority. The self is the one true thing, *cogito ergo sum,*[6] the only reliable anchor in a changing and hostile world. All of this progression to self-as-fortress enhanced the inward turn to subjectivity.

Taylor's observations were well-founded. But we perhaps need to build on them, to understand what's going on now. Certainly the shell of the individual hardened, as religious belief dissipated. But we're not all now living entirely inside turtle-shells of bounded isolation. The therapeutic mentality certainly makes us look inward to discover the self, but what forms that inchoate inner self? Gnostic esotericism has been suggested, except that unlike with the Gnostics of yore, the source of knowledge is not spiritual, it is social. It is an emotional distillation of ecstatic desire: the ecstatic—*ex stasis*—meaning the feeling of standing outside oneself and in harmonious community, which in turn is felt to require absorption of the com-

---

5 This would include Paul Ricoeur's "hermeneutics of suspicion," a habit of negation of existing forms and structure of ideas, a baseline approach for thinkers like Marx, Freud, Nietzsche, and Marcuse. See, Paul Ricoeur, in his *Freud and Philosophy/An Essay on Interpretation*, (Yale University Press, 1970).

6 Some commentators cite the thought of René Descartes (1596-1650) as among the first indicators of the inward turn.

munity's shared consensus.

The desire for *ex stasis* belonging, in harmony, is reconciled to turtle-like withdrawal through calming the outside world rather than toughening the inside self. The world beyond one's head must be re-formed to prepare for the self's timid emergence. The self concentrates on the self formed esoterically in the interior being, but a purely introverted existence is impossible, lacking outlet for the intersubjectivity of human beings, the need we all have for community. The inward turn must be overcome by a countervailing outward-seeking posture, but that is problematic, for psychological man, in a world so pluralistic as to support entirely distinct worldviews like the religious or logos conception of objective realism in morals and truth.

In consequence, therapeutic vulnerability makes one unable or unwilling to turn outward to face the gales of competing comprehensive belief systems. The outside world must be tamed. Psychological man wants *ex stasis* experience, but in a comfortable atmosphere congenial to his psychological needs. The way forward is to force the outside world to conform to those needs, rather than the reverse: making his psychology resilient to withstand the conflicts of the outside world. This becomes a collective undertaking, as more are given over to the therapeutic worldview. The insular nature of the therapeutic defies many-voice pluralism, casting into outer darkness dissenters who pursue glimmers of spiritual enchantment in the world. The therapeutic worldview brings a hardening of tribal intolerance.

Psychological man walks a fine line between the buffeting of the hostile world, on one side, and the frustrated desire for openness in community, on the other. Rage against the heterodox external world is psychological man's response, when not sheltering behind diagnoses. The rage is against that which is; it typically takes the outward form of political conviction, always in the leftist direction of suspicion, critique, and negation; of rebellion, tendentiousness, and Nietzschean "ressentiment." And yet it is not primarily the product of frustrated political conviction. Rather, it is the internalized desire for an end to all conflict; an end to division and strife and struggle; for a world in which debate and compromise are not necessary, because we all will be as one.

Religion is a non-starter for psychological man because Christ does not bring peace, but a sword,[7] ongoing this-not-that differentiation of moral good and evil, and it's all too wearying; all too demanding. For one steeped in psychology instead of moral ordering of vice and virtue, the first step in fixing the world is to eject God from it. The problem is that God does not cooperate. The self to be discovered is not within, but is here in the dynamic cambium of the integrated self's agentic interaction with the world. The psychologically stable self is formed there. The way to be at peace with the world and happy with your place in it is not to "self-actualize," but to strive for virtue. Those virtues, being universal, comprise the "how" of interacting with the world in terms of peace—not by politically-coerced false "consensus," but by mutual deference to ultimate values even as we disagree, in mutual tolerance, with opposing points of view about this issue or that.

How does this work? You and I might disagree profoundly about some series of political issues, but if we agree on what a person is, and on the moral structure that everyone—*everyone*—is formed in and bound by, then our disagreements can be on those abstract principles, and how they apply in a given situation. And this rather than ideology internalized so that any disagreement is rejection of the very selfhood of the other. We can disagree in peace and mutual tolerance only if the foundation of our disagreement is universal principle.

The virtues are hierarchical. Courage enables them all. Kindness and empathy and tolerance are among the virtues, if not transmuted to indifference and coldness and coercion. The hierarchy by

---

7 Matthew 10:34.

itself suggests a pinnacle which holds it up, and God rests at that pinnacle. He is out there and up there. He cares what you do. Your identity is formed among people around you, and theirs, like yours, is formed in an unseen architecture of moral value, the latticework of invisible structure more real than the stones and soil of the ground you walk on. God superintends all this. Ultimately, your identity is in Him.

Maybe you're not at peace with God. Maybe you never plan to be. But the principle here of vertical values is true and right and valid, regardless. It includes the realness of truth and morality. It includes their objective and unchanging nature. And it includes their universality; their equal application to all though we are manifestly unequal in our individuality.

The therapeutic mentality is a false apprehension of the world and of our identity within it. It is a malformed identity birthed in ideology and the darkness of excessive rumination. It is not real. But the illusion can have the effect of entombing us in a prison of self, no longer fully alive nor sensitive to the reality of moral structure requisite to human dignity. If you find yourself in that tomb, look up and climb out like Lazarus. Return to the enchanted world.

BIBLIOGRAPHY

Arendt, Hannah, *The Origins of Totalitarianism*, 1950.

Bakan, David, *The Duality of Human Experience*, Boston: Beacon 1966.

Bauman, Zygmunt, *Liquid Modernity*, Malden, MA: Polity 2000.

Chalmers, David, *The Conscious Mind/In Search of a Fundamental Theory*, Oxford: Oxford University Press 1996.

____. *Reality+/Virtual Worlds and the Problems of Philosophy*, New York: W.W. Norton 2022.

Clarke, Jonathan, "What's Left of Psychoanalysis?" *City Journal*, Autumn 2023; https://www.city-journal.org/article/whats-left-of-psychoanalysis; accessed January 22, 2025.

Crawford, Matthew B., *The World Beyond Your Head*, New York: Farrar, Strauss, and Giroux 2016.

____. *The Workings of the Party-State*, three parts, Archedelia (Substack) August, 2023.

Dalrymple, Theodore, *Admirable Evasions/How Psychology Undermines Morality*, New York: Encounter Books 2015

____. *Life At the Bottom: The Worldview That Makes the Underclass*, Chicago: Ivan R. Dee, 2003.

Davidson, Bruce W., "The Fall of Critical Thinking," *Brownstone Journal*, March 24, 2024; https://brownstone.org/articles/the-fall-of-critical-thinking/; accessed January 22, 2025.

Davidson, John Daniel, *Pagan America: The Decline of Christianity and the Dark Age to Come*, Regnery 2024.

Durkheim, Emile, *The Elementary Forms of the Religious Life*. New York: Macmillan 1915.

Esolen, Anthony. *Sex and the Unreal City/The Demolition of the Western Mind*. San Francisco: Ignatius 2020.
____. *No Apologies/Why Civilization Depends on the Strength of Men*. Washington, DC: Regnery Gateway 2022.

Favale, Abigail. *The Genesis of Gender/A Christian Theory*. San Francisco: Ignatius 2022.

Federici, Michael P., *Eric Voegelin/The Restoration of Order*, ISI Books 2002.

Foster, Charles, *Being A Human*, New York: Metropolitan 2021.

Frazer, James George. *The Golden Bough*. NY: McMillan 1922.

Freud, Sigmund, *An Autobiographical Study*, New York: W.W. Norton 1952 (first published 1935).
____. *Civilization and Its Discontents*, New York: W.W. Norton 2010 (first published 1930).

____. *The Future of an Illusion*, Mansfield Centre, CT: Martino 2010 (first published 1928).

Fukuyama, Francis, *The Therapeutic Society*, The Public Interest, Summer 1998.

Gelernter, David, *Tides of Mind/Uncovering the Spectrum of Consciousness*, New York: Liveright 2016.

Giddens, Anthony, *Modernity and Self-Identity/Self and Society in the Late Modern Age*, Stanford, CA: Stanford University Press 1991.

Girard, René. *I See Satan Fall Like Lightning*. Maryknoll, NY: Orbis 2001.

Guénon, René, *The Reign of Quantity & the Signs of the Times*, transl. Lord Northbourne, Hillsdale, NY: Sophia Perennis 2001, first published 1945.

Harrington, Mary, "Blasphemy is Dead, Long Live Blasphemy/ The 'marketplace of ideas' was nice while it lasted," *Mary Harrington* (Substack), October 26, 2022; accessed January 22, 2025.
___. "Normophobia," *First Things*, April 1, 2024; https://firstthings.com/normophobia/; accessed January 22, 2025.

James, William. *Psychology/The Briefer Course*. Mineola, NY; Dover 2001 (first published 1892).

Laing, J.D., *The Divided Self*, Penguin Books 1990 (first published 1959).

Lasch, Christopher, *The Minimal Self*, New York: W.W. Norton 1984.
___. *The Culture of Narcissism*, New York: W.W. Norton 1979.

Lasch-Quinn, Elisabeth, *Ars Vitae*, University of Notre Dame Press 2020.

Lears, T.J. Jackson, *No Place for Grace*, New York: Pantheon 1981.

Legutko, Ryszard, *The Demon in Democracy: Totalitarian Temptations in Free Societies*, New York: Encounter Books 2016.

Lewis, C.S. *The Abolition of Man.* New York: MacMillan 1947.

___. Space Trilogy (*Out of the Silent Planet, Perelandra, and That Hideous Strength*) New York: Simon & Schuster 1996 (first published 1943).

Ley, David, "Forget Me Not: The Persistent Myth of Repressed Memories," *Psychology Today*, October 6, 2019.

Lukianoff, Greg, and Jonathan Haidt, *The Coddling of the American Mind*, New York: Penguin 2018.

Lyons, N.S., "A Prophecy of Evil: Tolkien, Lewis, and Technocratic Nihilism," *The Upheaval* (Substack), November 15, 2022; https://theupheaval.substack.com/p/a-prophecy-of-evil-tolkien-lewis; accessed January 22, 2025.

MacIntyre, Alasdair, *After Virtue*, 2d ed., University of Notre Dame Press 1984 (1st ed. 1981).

MacIntyre, Auron, *Total State*, Regnery 2024.

MacLeod, Adam, *Essences or Intersectionality: Understanding Why We Can't Understand Each Other.* Witherspoon Institute March 1, 2020.

Marcuse, Herbert, *Eros and Civilization/A Philosophical Inquiry into Freud*, Boston: Beacon Press 1955.

___. *One-Dimensional Man*, 2d ed., Boston: Beacon Press 1992 (originally published 1964).

McAlister, Ted, *Revolt Against Modernity/ Leo Strauss, Eric Voegelin, & the Search for a Postliberal Order*, University Press of Kansas, 1995.

McGilchrist, Iain, *The Matter With Things*, London: Perspectiva 2021.

___. *Resist the Machine Apocalypse*, First Things, March 2024.

Milosz, Czeslaw. *The Captive Mind.* New York: Vintage International 1990 (first published 1951).

Minogue, Kenneth, *The Servile Mind/How Democracy Erodes the Moral Life.* New York: Encounter Books 2010.

Mussolini, Benito, *The Fundamentals of Fascism,* 1935.

Nichol, Armand M. Jr., *The Question of God,* New York: Free Press 2001.

Nietzsche, Friedrich, *On the Genealogy of Morals,* translated by Walter Kaufmann and RJ Hollingdale. New York: Vintage Books 1989 (first published 1887).

____. *Twilight of the Idols.* Oxford: Oxford University Press, 1998 (first published 1889).

____. *The Gay Science, 1882.*

Nolan, James L. Jr., *The Therapeutic State/Justifying Government at Century's End,* New York: New York University Press, 1998.

____. *The Therapeutic State,* New York: New York University Press 1998.

Norton, Albert, *Dangerous God: A Defense of Transcendent Truth.* Nashville: New English Review Press 2021.

____. *Intuition of Significance/Evidence Against Materialism and for God.* Eugene, OR: Resource Publications 2020.

____. *The Mountain and the River/Genesis, Postmodernism, and the Machine,* Nashville: New English Review Press 2021.

Perry, Louise, *The Case Against the Sexual Revolution/A New Guide to Sex in the 21ˢᵗ Century*, Medford, MA: Polity 2022.

___. "We Are Repaganizing," *First Things,* October 1, 2023; https://firstthings.com/we-are-repaganizing/; accessed January 22, 2025.

Plantinga, Alvin. *Knowledge and Christian Belief.* Grand Rapids, MI: Eerdman's 2015.

Polanyi, Michael, *Personal Knowledge/Towards a Post-Critical Philosophy*, University of Chicago Press 1958.

___. *The Tacit Dimension*, University of Chicago Press 1966.

Reich, Wilhelm. *The Mass Psychology of Fascism.* New York: Farrar, Straus and Giroux 1970.

___. *The Sexual Revolution.* New York: Farrar, Straus and Giroux 1986 (first published in English 1945).

Rieff, Philip, *Charisma*, New York: Vintage 2008.

___. *My Life Among the Deathworks/Illustrations of the Aesthetics of Authority*, Charlottesville, VA: University of Virginia Press 2006.

___. *Freud: The Mind of the Moralist*, Chicago: University of Chicago Press 1979 (3ʳᵈ ed.) (first published 1959).

___. *The Triumph of the Therapeutic/Uses of Faith After Freud*, ISI Books 2007 2d ed., (first published 1966).

Riley, Alexander, "What's Wrong With the Intellectuals?" *Chronicles,* February, 2024; https://chroniclesmagazine.org/view/whats-wrong-with-the-intellectuals/; accessed January 22, 2025.

Rorty, Richard, *Pragmatism As Anti-authoritarianism.* Cambridge, MA: Belknap, Harvard University Press 2021.

Rosner, Brian, *How to Find Yourself: Why Looking Inward is Not the Answer*, Wheaton, IL: Crossway 2022.

Rousseau, Jean-Jacques, *On the Social Contract*, translated by G.D.H. Cole. Mineola, NY: 2003 (first published 1762).

Rufo, Christopher F., "The Cluster B Society," *City Journal*, September 24, 2023; https://www.city-journal.org/article/the-cluster-b-society; accessed January 22, 2025.

Schiffman, Mark, "The Victimological Imagination; 'What is Ideology,' *Archedelia* (Substack) March 15, 2024; https://mcrawford.substack.com/p/the-victimological-imagination; accessed January 22, 2025.

___. *What is Ideology*, Wiseblood Books 2023.

Schrier, Abigail, *Bad Therapy*, Chicago: Sentinel 2024.

Schwab, Klauss and Thierry Malleret, *Covid-19: The Great Reset*, Geneva: Forum 2020.

Siedentop, Larry, *Inventing the Individual*, Cambridge, MA: Harvard University Press (2017).

Sommers, Christina Hoff and Sally Satel, *One Nation Under Therapy/How the Helping Culture is Eroding Self-Reliance*, New York: St. Martin's 2005.

Taylor, Charles, *A Secular Age*. Cambridge, MA: Belknap 2007.

Torrey, E. Fuller, *Freudian Fraud*, Harper/Collins Publishers 1992.

Trueman, Carl, *The Rise and Triumph of the Modern Self/Cultural Amnesia, Expressive Individualism, and the Road to Sexual Revolution*. Wheaton, IL: Crossway 2020.

___. "The Rise of the Psychological Man," *Public Discourse*, November 9, 2020; https://www.thepublicdiscourse.com/2020/11/72156/; accessed January 22, 2025.

Twenge, Jean, *iGen*, New York: Atria 2017.

___. *The Narcissism Epidemic*, New York: Atria 2009.

de Unamuno, Miguel, *Tragic Sense of Life*, transl. by J.E. Crawford Flitch, SophiaOmni Press 2014 (first published 1912).

Voegelin, Eric, *The New Science of Politics: An Introduction*, University of Chicago Press 1952.

___. *Science, Politics & Gnosticism*, Regnery 1968 (first published in German 1959).

Watters, Ethan, *Crazy Like Us: The Globalization of the American Psyche*, New York: Free Press 2010.

___.*The Forgotten Lessons of the Recovered Memory Movement*, New York Times, September 7, 2023.

Weber, Max, *The Protestant Ethic and the Spirit of Capitalism*, Pantianos Classics 1930 (first published 1904).

___. *The Sociology of Religion.* Boston, MA: 1922 (2nd ed.).

Williams, Thaddeus, *Don't Follow Your Heart*, Grand Rapids, MI: Zondervan 2023.

INDEX

91, 187, 222, 254-255, 258
Newhouse, Alana 256
Nietzsche, Friedrich/Nietzschean 68, 92, 112, 286
Nolan, James L. Jr. 18, 196, 245
Normophobia 98

O

Oceanic feeling 14, 47, 64, 72, 117, 163, 169, 201, 203, 206, 258
Ontological insecurity 53-55
Ontology/ontological 9, 23, 50, 53-55, 61, 96, 115, 119, 169-170, 174, 189, 200, 241
Otto, Rudolf 117, 206

P

Plantinga, Alvin 110, 117, 202
Polanyi, Michael 49, 128-130
Positivist/positivism 24, 67, 69-70, 74, 178, 181-182, 185
Presentism 26, 28-29
pre-social conscience 104
Process philosophy 13, 114, 180
Progressive/progressivist/progressiv-ism 90, 92, 97, 99, 177-178, 182-183, 186-187, 216, 222, 260

R

Reformation 139, 248-249
Religious impulse 14, 73, 77-80, 94-95, 97, 108, 115-116, 118, 146, 164, 171, 176, 201, 208-209, 228
Remission/remissive 37, 71-72, 95, 101, 122, 131, 148, 153, 156, 170, 175
Renunciation/renunciatory 71, 89, 95-96, 131, 148, 156-157, 170, 175
Reverse CBT 227
Ricoeur, Paul 102, 284

Rieff, Philip 14, 37, 67, 71, 78, 94-95, 100-101, 107-108, 131-132, 148, 151, 157, 173, 185-186, 198-200, 274
Rorty, Richard 272
Rosner, Brian 17-18
Rousseau, Jean-Jacques/rousseauean 18, 140-141, 144, 157-158, 182, 235, 284

S

Schiffman, Mark 63, 176
Schiller, Friedrich 71, 140
Schizoid/schizophrenia 53-55, 146
Schrier, Abigail 196, 211, 216-217, 225
Simon, Marilyn 46, 192, 214
Social Emotional Learning 214
Socialist/socialism 29, 31-32, 59-60, 64, 70, 73, 90-91, 105, 122, 142, 177-179, 202, 205, 248, 251-253, 258, 260-261, 265
Surrealist 150

T

Tacit knowledge 49, 128-130
Taylor, Charles 14, 43, 58, 255-256, 283-284
Totalitarian/totalitarianism 28-29, 32, 68, 70-71, 74-75, 83, 99, 103, 105, 112, 135, 204, 246, 257-258, 261, 263-264, 266-267, 269, 273-274
Trueman, Carl 14, 22, 58, 232-233, 237, 239, 245

U

Universal/universality/universalism 10, 35, 60, 62, 81, 83, 90, 96, 109, 134, 136, 163, 223, 228, 230, 264, 287

www.ingramcontent.com/pod-product-compliance
Lightning Source LLC
Chambersburg PA
CBHW020526270326
41927CB00006B/462